CW00763768
EX LIBRIS
ENDURE FORT

THE LINDSAYS OF BALCARRES

A Century of an Ancient Scottish Family in Photographs

Ludovic Lindsay

THE LINDSAYS
OF BALCARRES

A Century of an Ancient Scottish Family
in Photographs

Pimpernel Press

Pimpernel
Press ltd
www.pimpernelpress.com

A catalogue record for this book is available
from the British Library.

Designed by Robert Dalrymple
Set in Jeremy Tankard's Kingfisher type

ISBN 978-1-910258-57-6

Printed and bound in China by C&C Offset
Printing Company Limited

9 8 7 6 5 4 3 2 1

Front jacket: James Ludovic Lindsay, 26th Earl of Crawford & 9th Earl of Balcarres, Hereditary Standard Bearer, Great Steward and Premier Earl of Scotland before the coronation of King George V, 1911.

Front endpaper: a bookplate incorporating the Lindsay coat of arms and crests, originally designed for the Revd Hon. Edward Lindsay by his aunt Lady Jane Lindsay, *c.* 1935.

Frontispiece: a portrait session. The Lindsay family gathers on the Haigh Hall terrace as a professional photographer prepares his equipment (1907).

Back jacket: 'Rory won't jump', on the beach at Elie, Fife (1892, see pages 120–21).

Contents

Foreword

It gives me great pleasure to write a short foreword to this interesting and informative book by my nephew Ludovic.

Ludovic has assembled a remarkable collection of photographs, which chronicle an important century in the history of our family. They are accompanied by excellent biographies and annotations, the product of his meticulous research. They give a fascinating insight into the lives of our forebears and illuminate several aspects of social history. Many of the images are enjoyable in their own right. They also illustrate the development of photography from its earliest beginnings.

I am absolutely delighted that Ludovic has undertaken this work. He should be congratulated on his great achievement. He has given us a work that will be of lasting interest to both the scholar and the general reader – and one that will also give great pleasure.

ROBIN CRAWFORD
Robert Alexander Lindsay,
29th Earl of Crawford & 12th Earl of Balcarres,
KT, GCVO, PC, DL

Balcarres, 16 October 2020

Preface

A collection of leather albums hidden in a marquetry cabinet at Balcarres, Fife, remained almost completely forgotten for seventy years. A wet afternoon often allowed time to explore, and on such an occasion I found myself taking my first look into the most personal of records. These books, filled with images from another age, had gone unnoticed by the many who had walked past and had rarely seen the light of day. Yet here were the faces of the people who had been so instrumental in forming the Lindsays' more recent history – part of a timeline that can be traced back centuries, to before the Norman conquest.

As I investigated further, it became clear that within these volumes there was a wealth of annotated portraits that over time would allow me to finally identify these more recent ancestors – beginning with James, 'Lord Bal', 7th Earl of Balcarres, who appears in the earliest daguerreotypes of about 1840. I found often remarkable pictures that revealed other aspects of their lives – from the people who worked for them to travels to what were then exotic lands pursuing scientific discoveries. Windows into industries that would for a time reverse a family's declining fortunes were all captured. This did not appear to be the typical aristocratic family in search of simple pleasures, quarry or bohemia. This unique record had all the makings of an important piece of social history.

In order to give the project some boundaries, I needed a structure on which to hang the images, so I focused on just those descendants of the Lindsays who had lived, for part of their lives at least, at the main family homes of Balcarres, Haigh Hall (Wigan) and Dunecht (Aberdeenshire). This meant that it includes all those who had descended from James, 5th Earl of Balcarres (1691–1768). A few cousins were able to unearth similarly long-forgotten albums. So much has already been written elsewhere on the family's great art collections and libraries that I have avoided focusing on those areas. Similarly, their roles in politics, even though often played out at pivotal times in our history, neither fit in to the photographic theme nor dovetail successfully into the narrative. I have tried to concentrate on their private lives, reflecting the nature of the albums.

With the help of so many, I have, by choosing a selection from some 3,500 black and white photographs, endeavoured to illustrate the changing world of a family over the hundred years from the birth of photography, for today's and future generations.

Dunecht
Aberdeen
Edzell
Balcarres
Edinburgh
Ridley Hall
Muncaster Castle
Holker Hall
Wyedale Hall
Haigh Hall
Wigan
Lathom Hall
Hoar Cross Hall
Belvoir Castle
Wimpole
Hedingham Castle
Eynsham Hall
Westonbirt
Burcote House
Lockinge
London
Welford Park
Deer Park
Stepleton
Hambrook

Introduction

It is perhaps no coincidence that the golden age of photography neatly coincided with the revival in fortunes of the Lindsays. Generations of the family had been closely aligned to affairs of state, but siding with the doomed Stuarts during the civil war and the Jacobite cause brought on a period when they lost much of their status. Fortunately, marrying into the Bradshaigh family in the late eighteenth century, whose lands lay over some of the country's most productive mineral seams, meant that they now found themselves at the potentially extraordinarily profitable coalface of the industrial revolution. This allowed them to embrace new opportunities and rebuild their estates while profiting from the new technologies.

It was the pioneering Louis Daguerre who publicly announced the first viable photographic process in 1839. News of these miraculous images spread wide, even though the 'daguerreotypes' could not be replicated, were expensive (each image required its own silvered sheet of copper) and could take up to thirty minutes of exposure time. It was not long before licences for Daguerre's process were in heavy demand around the world. In around 1840, James Lindsay, 7th Earl of Balcarres and something of a technologist himself, became curious and commissioned portraits of his family and staff at Haigh Hall. He had already enthusiastically adopted a host of other new technologies and in time became a keen photographer.

There was now a race to create the most viable form of photography and the leader in the United Kingdom was William Henry Fox Talbot. He had already produced small, one-inch square 'negatives' on glass, the same essential principle on which all photography relied until the digital camera arrived. His first 'photogenic drawing' was made in 1835 so he was understandably disappointed when Louis Daguerre presented his results. But in 1841 Fox Talbot's new 'calotypy' process was patented and slowly became the standard. For the first time countless images could be enlarged from one negative and distributed. While they lacked some of the crispness of the daguerreotype, the advantages were obvious.

The British aristocracy were the first to indulge in this new technology. The examples of both equipment and images at the Great Exhibition of 1851 had a galvanizing effect and within twelve years of Daguerre's great claim – 'I have seized the light! I have arrested its flight!' – photography became hugely fashionable. It did not remain an exclusively male pastime for long. Lady Lucy Bridgeman, Lady Jocelyn and Viscountess Hawarden became celebrated exponents of wet-plate photography. These women mastered the difficulties of handling often highly poisonous chemicals and showed considerable talent. Indeed, had they been more commercial, they might have become as well known as Sir Coutts Lindsay's friend Julia Margaret Cameron, some of whose works appear here.

The country house was the perfect environment for photography to blossom. There was always available space to create a studio, which the enthusiast could fill with equipment from outfitters such as Horne, Thornthwaite & Wood or George Houghton & Son. They could supply cameras, all the chemicals, glass plates, tents, tripods and papers. Photographic studios could be found at Hardwick Hall, Osborne Lodge (Princess Beatrice was a keen photographer) and Windsor. Coutts Lindsay would build his own studio at Balcarres, his Scottish home.

The subject matter became as diverse then as it remains today. Photographs of family and staff, buildings or interiors may seem unimaginative to us, but they chronicle the lives of our nineteenth-century antecedents better than any other medium. It is understandable that the succeeding generations of the Lindsay family would be less interested in looking at those earlier pictures and inevitably the albums, boxes of daguerreotypes and slides slowly disappeared from sight. It has been said that someone's spirit only dies when their name is mentioned for the last time. Similarly, something of the figure in the photograph comes alive once again when seen afresh. They can continue to give us a tangible and even emotional connection to someone long gone.

Acknowledgements

I was particularly keen that my father's elder brother, Robin, the Earl of Crawford & Balcarres, might approve of this book. I wanted it to be an acceptable addition to the many, far weightier and more thorough histories that already fill a large section of the Balcarres library. For him to contribute such a foreword has made me feel that it has all been worthwhile. His daughter, Lady Iona Mackworth-Young, was both supportive and instrumental in making sure this happened. I am hugely grateful to him and his wife, Ruth, as well as his son and daughter-in-law, Lord and Lady Balniel, for their time and hospitality, and for giving me complete access to the images and archives, without which none of this would have been possible.

No one can expect to be an expert in all the biographical accounts of nine generations, so I owe a great deal of gratitude to the historians whose research and writings have explored them so thoroughly. I knew I was entering a crowded market of exceptional works. Lord Lindsay wrote the three-volume *Lives of the Lindsays* that exhaustively details the family's history like no other. My great-uncle, James Lindsay, drew on this with his own research to produce an eminently more readable *More Lives of the Lindsays*, while his nephew, Christopher Arnander, expanded on it in his *A Lindsay Family Story*, one that does much to place the characters in a more understandable context. Christopher also edited *Private Lord Crawford's Great War Diaries*, written by his grandfather, the 27th Earl of Crawford, which has added so much more to our archive. He was always available for advice, knowledge and support, despite knowing that our books could have conflicted. In 1977, Nicolas Barker published the definitive *Bibliotheca Lindesiana,* the seminal survey of the lives and collections of the 25th and 26th Earls of Crawford, which he and my grandfather presented to the Roxburghe Club, the oldest society of bibliophiles in the world. Without his colossal undertaking, my book would be a pale shadow of its current form.

Jason and Demetra Lindsay of Hedingham Castle have the keenest interest in our gene pool's lineage and, as knowledgeable custodians of a rich repository, provided some excellent photographic material. Jason's mother, Ginnie Lindsay, was also able to fill in gaps of our own parents' generation. Christopher's half-sister, and my godmother, Francesca Wall, had many stories of a childhood caught up in the escape from the Nazis in Rome and of then finding themselves as refugees in Britain. Her photograph albums are worthy of a book in themselves. My second cousin, Christopher Lindsay, turned out to have a large collection of photographs that had come down from my great-great-uncle Lionel.

Tom Loyd, who now owns the Lockinge estate where Robert and Harriet Loyd-Lindsay lived, gave me full access to their own exceptional archive in their beautifully curated museum, whose head archivist, Christine Wardingley, not only provided me with a wealth of information but also made some vital corrections to my earlier drafts. Annie Lindsay went to great efforts to ensure I received a previously unknown collection of stereoscopic slides, one of which happily shows the family at Haigh Hall being photographed. Meeting Elizabeth Gilroy, my great-aunt Barbara's daughter, was special in itself, as well as for her input. Anne Parsons, daughter of Lady Mary Manningham-Buller (née Lindsay), also brought me photograph albums that were full of useful cuttings and interesting images. Lucy Cavendish kindly allowed me to copy photographs from the Holker Hall collection. The Hon. Charles Pearson lent a rare image and had useful information on Dunecht, about which the archives are frustratingly light. Cecilia, Lady Goodlad, allowed me to use her albums, which added greatly to the information I had on her mother, Barbara, and others in the family.

Photographing the very earliest daguerrotypes was problematic due to their reflective nature. My first cousin, Alexander Lindsay, a renowned photographer, had the skills to capture them perfectly. John Davis and Karen Moran enlightened me further on the 26th Earl's involvement in astronomy when I visited them in Edinburgh at the Royal Scottish Observatory with its great Crawford Library of scientific books and manuscripts. Kenneth Dunn also made time to introduce me to the vast family archives at the National Library of Scotland.

Robert Dalrymple designed the layout in a way that has made me proud. Serendipitously, he and all the Lindsays in the book are descended from his namesake and our mutual ancestor, Sir Robert. Editing was undertaken by the highly recommended George Miller, who probably underestimated the task he was set. Gay Harris, Sarah Clark and Nat Rothschild all helped by reading the last drafts and made important corrections. Others who took their time to read sections and give me feedback included Marcus de Ferranti, Sophie Ziegler and my brother James. Mary Killen and John Hatt gave me invaluable recommendations on publishing routes and cleverly chose Pimpernel Press, who patiently took on and guided this endeavour. My mother, Amabel, gave unswerving support and material. Finally, I'll be forever grateful to my sons, Merlin and Cosmo, who have endured over a considerable period of time my indulging in this project and have listened to endless newly discovered stories of their ancestors' lives. Yet they have always shown unequivocal support – but now ask: 'What next?'

NOTE ON CURRENCY

The National Archives Currency Converter has been used throughout this book to provide a rough guide to today's values.

Family Tree: The Lindsays of Balcarres

The numbers shown in RED correspond to the chapter numbers in this book

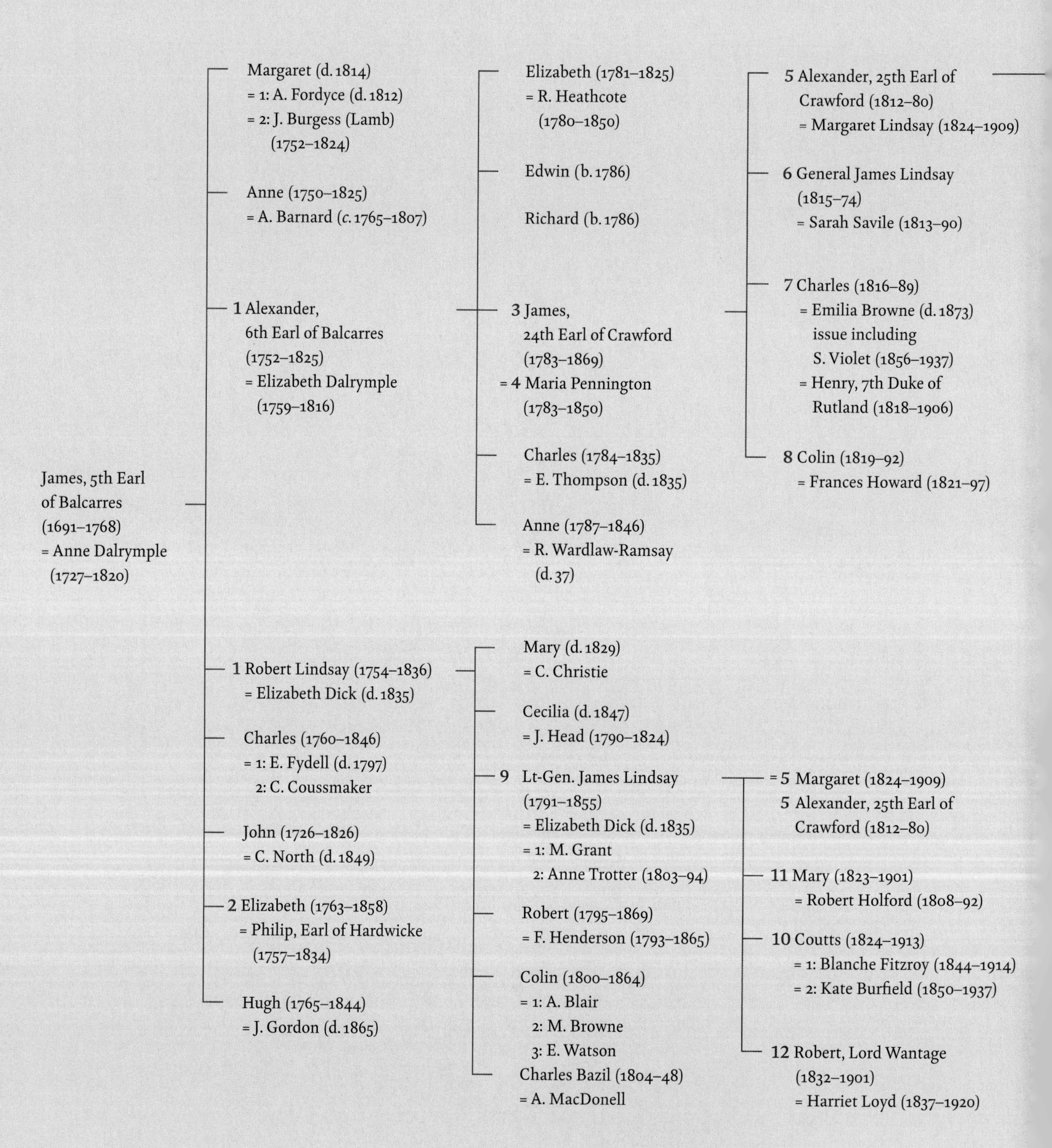

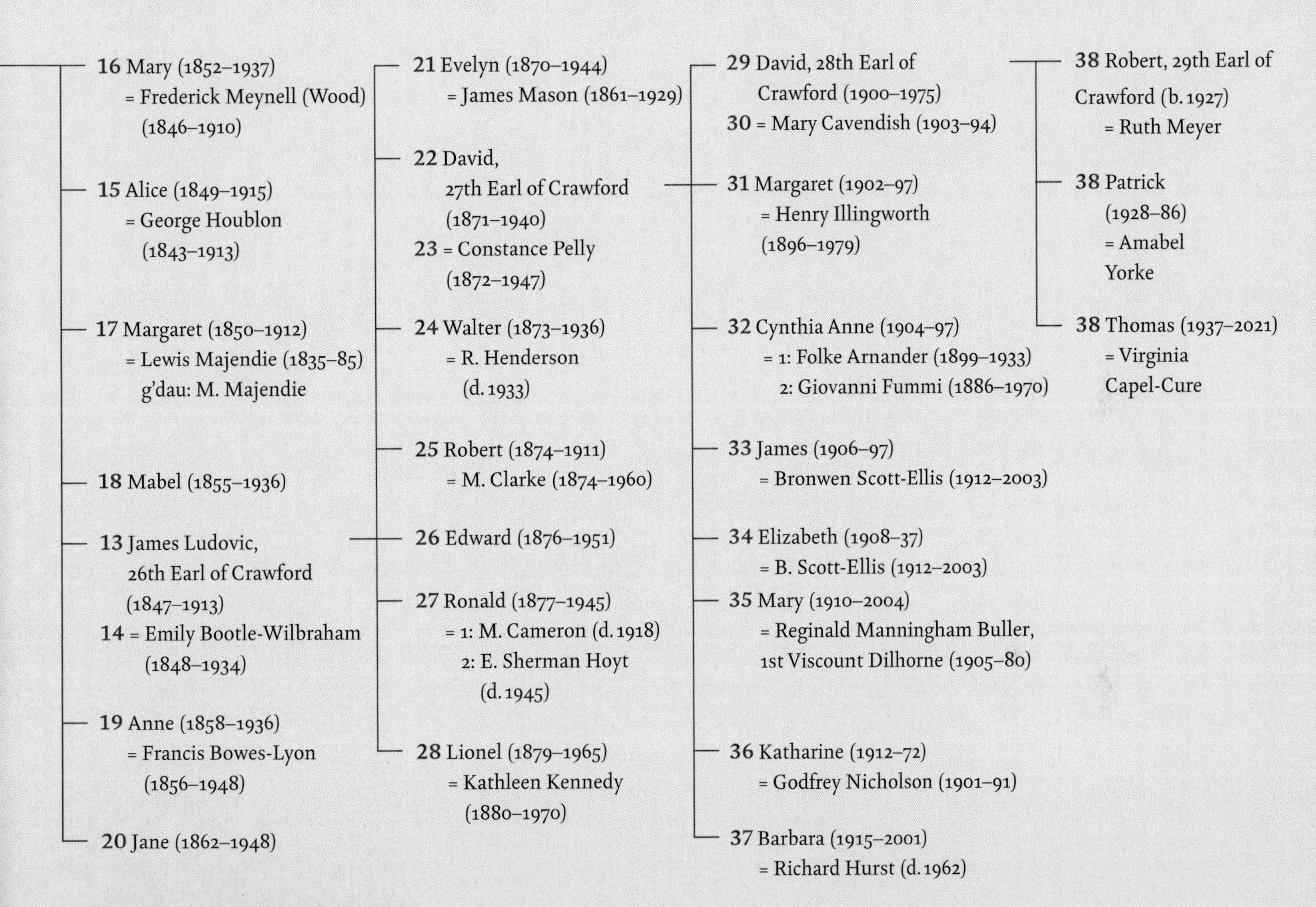

The Lindsay armorial bearings, issuing from an earl's coronet, *or*, the head, neck and wings of a swan, *proper*. Over Quarterly, 1st and 4th, *gules* a fess chequy, *argent* and *azure* (for Lindsay); 2nd and 3rd, *or*, a lion rampant *gules*, surmounted by a ribbon, *sable* (for Abernethy). On either side a lion guardant *gules*. Beneath, the heraldic slogan, or motto 'Endure Fort' (Keep courage).

1

'The Grand Project'

General Alexander Lindsay, 6th Earl of Balcarres, 1752–1825, and Elizabeth, Countess of Balcarres (née Dalrymple) 1759–1816, and the Hon. Robert, 1754–1836, and Elizabeth Lindsay (née Dick), d. 1835

The characters found in these images are best understood through some account of their immediate forebears. James, the 5th Earl of Balcarres, had distinguished himself in both the navy and army. Unfortunately, supporting the Stuarts in 1715 meant that he remained a disappointed and increasingly impoverished officer. He had retreated to Balcarres in Fife when he fell in love with Anne, the daughter of Sir Robert Dalrymple, who was thirty-six years his junior – 'an old young woman and I am a young old man'. They went on to have eleven children, but we shall only follow the two eldest sons, Alexander and Robert, who were both to make Balcarres their home.

Alexander had served in Canada at the beginning of the War of Independence, where he commanded the Light Infantry, a *corps d'élite*, and fought honourably before being injured and captured. On release he returned home, where he developed a 'solid liking'[1] for his cousin Elizabeth 'Bessie' Bradshaigh Dalrymple. Their union in 1780 was pivotal to the family's fortunes over the next two hundred years. The last of the male line of the Bradshaigh family, the 4th Baronet, Sir Roger, had died in 1770. His widow, Dorothy, who died fifteen years later, with no issue, had been left free to do as she pleased with the estates and so, with no other heirs, bequeathed her Lancashire estate, Haigh, to Elizabeth, Roger's sister's granddaughter. Dorothy had 'so great an affection for [Elizabeth] that I almost look upon her as a sort of child given to me.'[2] Nonetheless, she felt no obligation to be overly generous in her will. She had expressed deep concern on hearing that Alexander had once lost £1,000 while playing cards, something he could ill afford. But she was encouraged to leniency by Elizabeth's father, who wrote passionately in defence of the young earl. Dorothy was swayed – though her legacy would come with a price. The house, estate and collieries had all been allowed to deteriorate and required substantial investment.

Another opportunity to add to Alexander's reinvestment funds arose in 1790, when his brother, Robert, agreed to buy Balcarres. Augmented by a loan of £4,000 (approximately £307,000 today) from Philip, the 3rd Earl of Hardwicke, who was married to their sister Elizabeth, Alexander could now throw himself into the development of the Haigh estate, although much of this effort would have to be accomplished while he was serving abroad. He would follow his three principles of agriculture: 'Residence, Perseverance in drainage and Detestation of the Plough'.[3]

Robert had left home at the age of fourteen for Spain and India, where he remained in the Bengal Civil Service for eighteen years. His time is still regarded with respect in Sylhet, now north-eastern Bangladesh, once one of India's poorest regions and which, during his time, became one of its richest. He helped steer the local economy away from

1 Balcarres from the south-east in 1790, when it was sold to the Hon. Robert Lindsay to further brother Alexander's 'Aggrandising Fund'.

the cowrie to the rupee, introduced mulberry trees for silk production, transformed the lime industry (needed for paper production, cement, fisheries and tanneries) and developed a flourishing trade in Asia's workhorse, the elephant. Having bought Balcarres two years after his return home in 1788, he set about improving the estates with eager energy: 'It is as you know my favourite amusement and it gives bread to a great many people who are at present ill off.' Nonetheless, he magnanimously declared: 'never shall I permit myself to become attached to it till I have given my elder brother the power of resuming it should fortune enable him to do so.'

Robert had known Elizabeth Dick since childhood and, shortly after his return from India, they married. She was the daughter of Sir Alexander Dick, Scotland's most eminent doctor, who became the President of the College of Physicians of Edinburgh. A social figure, he enjoyed entertaining such luminaries as Samuel Johnson and James Boswell.[4]

Meanwhile, the French Revolutionary War had interrupted Alexander's plans. In 1794, after an appointment as governor of Jersey, he took on the same position in Jamaica for eight turbulent years, at a time when it was a more important colony to Britain economically than India. This gave him a much-needed financial lifeline. However, his tenure resulted in a controversy over a course of events that is disputed to this day, his word against an aggrieved general and the descendants of those who believed that Alexander had, by not honouring an earlier agreement, ensnared a number of Maroons and had

2 Lord Bal's watercolour of Haigh Hall before he started to rebuild the 'much dilapidated' home in 1828.

them sent to Nova Scotia. While he was respected for his governorship by many of his colleagues, the loss of trust still persisted: one event he was instrumental in is remembered as 'the Treacherous Feast'.

Whether he was a particularly sophisticated individual may be judged by one description by Lady Nugent, who was nauseated by his habits at table: 'I wish ... [he] would wash his hands, and use a nail-brush, for the black edges of his nails really make me sick. He has, besides, an extraordinary propensity to dip his fingers into every dish.'[5] Tales of the 'profligate and disgusting scene' which marked his 'domestic conduct' convinced her that he was 'more than half mad'.

The coal mines under Haigh had been developed in the sixteenth century by the Bradshaighs, though they were now had fallen into in a 'state of Dilapidation and Ruin'. The fortuitous combination of the next generations of Lindsays' intelligent application and the industrial revolution meant that this abundant source, along with other minerals, including iron ore, would benefit the family for the next two hundred years. It also became one of the most significant industrial entities in the country.[6]

Alexander impressed on his son that coal was now the 'root, basis and stamina of the family and must ever remain the foundation of our prosperity.'[7] Subsequently, James inherited an estate with a neglected house, but also with finances that were in the strongest state they had been for over two centuries.

2

A Vicereine of Ireland

Elizabeth Yorke, Countess of Hardwicke (née Lindsay), 1763–1858

3 The only photograph of Lord Bal's aunt, Elizabeth, Countess of Hardwicke (*c.*1850). It was her husband's loan that enabled the family to start rebuilding its fortune.

Lady Elizabeth Scot Lindsay was born seventy-six years before the invention of photography, so the sole extant image of the ageing Countess of Hardwicke creates a unique connection to a time further back than any others taken of the family. She was able to tell the story of King Charles II giving away the bride at her grandparents' wedding.[1]

Her father, James, 5th Earl of Balcarres, died when she was only five, leaving her mother to bring up ten children on only £350 a year, but everything changed for her and her family with her marriage to Philip Yorke, 3rd Earl of Hardwicke.[2] His was a distinguished line: his grandfather and father had both been Lord Chancellors, while his uncle and father were the centre of the 'Hardwicke Circle', which controlled the affairs of the Royal Society.

In 1801 Philip was appointed Lieutenant-General and General Governor of Ireland.'[3] In effect, the couple were Viceroy and Vicereine for five years. While the country continued to experience anti-unionist dissent, it remained relatively quiet during his tenure due to his approach of doing little, along with his support of Catholic relief and patronage. Robert Emmet's failed rebellion in 1803 tested his conciliatory approach, but he remained in favour of Catholic emancipation.[4] Elizabeth made it her mission to embrace all classes, which meant Dublin Castle became the centre of society, attracting both talent and the leading wits of the day.[5] Eventually, disagreements with Pitt came to a head and Hardwicke was recalled, a change much regretted by Dublin society.

Philip was made Knight of the Garter, a trustee of the British Museum and appointed High Steward of Cambridge University, which was conveniently close to Wimpole, their magnificent home – a position he held until his death. Like so many of the age, the couple suffered their fair share of sadness with the loss of four of their sons. The youngest was only seven months old, while two others died aged four. The eldest, Philip, aged twenty-four, was tragically washed off board his ship during a tremendous storm at night off Lübeck while returning from an extensive eighteen-month journey through Scandinavia, Russia and the Crimea.[6] However, their four daughters survived long into adulthood, supported by Elizabeth, who lived to the ripe age of ninety-four.

3

'Colliers we are and colliers we must ever remain'

James Lindsay, 24th Earl of Crawford & 7th Earl of Balcarres, 'Lord Bal', 1783–1869

The earliest images we have of any member of the Lindsay family include James, 24th Earl of Crawford, known as 'Lord Bal', and his wife Maria. These fine and unusually large daguerreotypes were made around 1840, which makes them some of the earliest photographic portraits in the country.[1] Photography at this time was both new and expensive, so the inclusion of some of their staff indicates how much James appreciated the extent to which their lives were intertwined.

4 Lord Bal embraced technology, including commissioning daguerreotypes of his staff and family in front of his newly built Haigh Hall. From the series of the earliest known three photographs of the Lindsays (*c.* 1840).

Lord Bal's father had secured his son's entry to the army at the age of eleven, and later, when fourteen, he obtained a company in the 20th Dragoons. In 1801 he was made an extraordinary aide-de-camp to his aunt Elizabeth's husband, the 3rd Earl of Hardwicke, Viceroy of Ireland. But he left the army in 1804 to concentrate on opportunities at home.

Lord Bal was described as a character 'of manly appearance with powdered hair, who can ride well, fence well, dance well, and has been well drilled by the great Sergeant Gould.'[2] It was said of him that 'every mortal high and low entirely adores him, although every mortal could slay him a hundred times a day for his provoking teasing ways.'[3] His grandmother described him as a 'charming boy full of fire and thoughts, taking nothing implicitly from anyone … with a divine temper and the greatest humanity.' His wife Maria, daughter of Lord Muncaster, was 'in appearance very well but no beauty', but was to play an important role in the welfare of the workers both on the estate and in the family's industrial interests.

Maria's father, Sir John Pennington, 1st Baron Muncaster, was not without misgivings over the extent to which the Lindsay wealth was dependent on 'commercial speculation', when in 1811 his only daughter married Lord Bal. There may have been other reservations relating to his father's role in Jamaica, as her father was a great friend of William Wilberforce and was deeply involved in the movement for the abolition of slavery. Maria was brought up in this environment and brought a strong moral and religiously held approach to her work and influences on her family. Nonetheless, James

5 *below* Lord Bal was no romantic, but saw the importance of reclaiming the earldom of Crawford, created in 1398, enabling the family to celebrate its quincentenary in 1898.

6 *opposite* 'Lord Bal knew how to build solid masonry ... a mansion house, which tho' far from beautiful is a monument of honesty and strength' – David, 27th Earl of Crawford.

inherited his father's legacy of shares in slaves. The Slave Compensation Act of 1837 allowed him, and approximately 45,000 other applicants, to successfully claim over £14,474[4] (almost £875,000 today) which, although bringing no succour to the victims of the appalling trade, benefitted the family, allowing them to build on their inheritance and invest in local industries.

While they were living at Muncaster with their four children, Haigh Hall was decaying as his father was concentrating his energies on the collieries. Alexander was delighted when the young family finally moved to join him at the Hall: 'Your residence here will be delightful to yourself and the pleasing reflection that we have extricated ourselves from the mire of corroding poverty and acquired independence in fortune, without which all is dark and dismal.'

Lord Bal was no romantic. After his father's death in 1825, he used his considerable engineering skills to become his own architect, builder and contractor for the house. He deplored the sort of intense interest his eldest child, Alexander, was developing in pictures and books. This brought him into a lifelong struggle over his son's academic and cultural leanings: 'Take pictures, as an example – there is no doubt they are most beautiful and ornamental pieces of furniture, proper to adorn the dwellings of the wealthy and being among the highest order of the mechanic art and combined with a great deal of mental association they are pleasing, but with regard to the nice distinction of names it matters very little whether the picture is painted by Vandervelde or Vanderbert: the name of a painting ought not to give additional value to it.'[5] His attitude to the classics, literature and collecting books was no less harsh: 'If indulged in as an amusement would not be objectionable, but as a business, as an occupation of time and the thoughts of more than half your waking hours – it is as absurd as it is disadvantageous.'

His unsentimental approach included abandoning his attachment to Scotland. He wrote that they were

now an 'English family'.[6] But he did not completely renounce his lineage. The earldom of Crawford had filtered down a separate line, causing the title to fall into abeyance after the 22nd Earl died with no immediate heir. Lord Lindsay, as Alexander came to be known, felt it necessary to go to the great effort, and expense, of claiming back the title, which they believed was still extant. After a ten-year investigation, they were able to prove the existence of the line of every male descendant going back to Sir David Lindsay of Edzell, who had inherited the title in 1542. On 18 July 1848 Lord Bal thus became the 24th Earl of Crawford, while his late father then became de jure 23rd Earl. The importance of this claim was that the ancient title was the premier earldom of Scotland recorded on the Union Roll. In 1898 the family were able to celebrate the 500th anniversary of the earldom's creation.

Less successfully and at vast cost, they went about claiming back the dukedom of Montrose, resulting in a 720-page report to the Court of Lord Lyons outlining the arguments before the claim was finally declined. In 1488 James III had granted the dukedom to David, 5th Earl of Crawford, but James VI, by the Act of Rescissory, made it void by granting it for the term of his life only. It was the King's decision to later alter the initial granting of the dukedom *retrospectively* that had given rise to the claim.

Fortunately, the family's industrial concerns were going from strength to strength, but it seems Lord Bal may have been the only member of his family who enjoyed living at Haigh. His son wrote: 'The country is getting more and more covered with smoke and chimneys – they spring up in every direction, and the population multiplies every hour. I don't believe it will be possible for a gentleman to live there 30 years hence, if this goes on.' But Lord Bal had invested much of his time and efforts in rebuilding the new home and estate since his boyhood. His interest in Haigh went beyond mere proprietorship, earning him lifelong respect, loyalty and trust from his workforce, even in the face of what he saw as the tyranny of the growing power of unions and societies. Fortuitously, at least for

7 Dunecht, the 'get-riddable property', gave the Lindsays a foothold once more in the land of their forefathers (*c.* 1890).

his descendants a century later, he had considered how long personal businesses last compared to a landed estate.

The left side of Lord Bal's brain was clearly the dominant one as he took great pleasure in devising technological solutions to every problem. He was one of the first to invest in the new railways as his father had done in building canals. Sadly, he did not photograph his smoke abatement box, his patent machines for cutting stone and mixing mortar into cement, the coal-weighing machine, or his organ. His self-winding water clock must have been a fabulous contraption. As well as the time of day, it showed sidereal time (the rotation of the earth with respect to the stars), the rising and setting of the sun and moon, the date and, of course, the age of the moon. Using a bucket of water that would empty and reset itself, it ran for three years without being touched. There was also the automatic safety valve for the Haigh boilers; the adjustment for the organ stops; and in 1834 a 'coffee steam apparatus', whose 'liquor was pronounced excellent', anticipating the espresso machine.

As owner of his pits and ironworks, Lord Bal was both fully engaged and popular. Fortunately, he had developed a good rapport with his employees, who defended their pits and the Hall when they came under threat from aggrieved Chartists frustrated at the slow pace of electoral reform. On one occasion, five hundred of his colliers armed with pickaxes saw off a riotous mob who surrounded and threatened the house itself. But when legislation was introduced to help the workers' conditions, it was not always universally appreciated – his support for the efforts to ban women and children from working down the pits, which he thought morally wrong, strained relations with colliers who relied on the higher income they received when women and children worked in the mines rather than around the pit heads. But there were many who did agree and in time such legislation was carried.

The family did what it could to relieve the distress caused by a series of economic crises by handing out extra food and offering work on the estate. Many were caught up in the textile depression that was brought about in the aftermath of the Napoleonic Wars. Exports were being increasingly stifled by new international competition that had hitherto been constrained by the conflict. After the passing of the Reform Act (1832) there was great disappointment among those who believed it would put an end to their troubles. As the town's population was increasing and the strain on facilities intensified, the family attempted to help out. 'Schools like these my father is building', wrote James's son Colin, 'are battering rams against the towers of Dissent of which so many have been raised while we slumbered.' An adult school was also created, which attracted three hundred enthusiastic mature students.[7]

By 1840 the collieries had become extremely profitable and it was deemed sensible to invest in more land. Cousin James recommended Scotland and initially they looked at Forfar as it was the home of the original 'country' of the Lindsays. They decided on Dunecht in Aberdeenshire for the simple reason that is was a 'get riddable property'.[8] As Lord Bal gave it to his son, Alexander, he felt some sadness for he had hoped his heir would come and live with him or nearby at Haigh. But the young Lord Lindsay now had a place of his own, where he could augment the ever-growing library, away from the soot and polluted air of Wigan and Haigh. When Lord Bal first travelled up there by train, he remained in his brougham anchored to an open carriage throughout the journey. In time, as befitting a locomotive and rolling goods manufacturer, he had his own railway saloon built that could be joined to the back of the train.[9]

Lord Bal's granddaughter, Lady Jane Lindsay, remembered the ageing and now rather stooped earl fondly, though she was only seven when he died.

8 Passionate technocrat aristocrats, Lord Bal and his grandson, Ludovic (*c.*1860).

9 Lord Bal, a widower for nineteen years, spent an increasing amount of time with his family at the palatial London home they had built at No. 10 Grosvenor Square (*c.*1865).

She recalled how he would be 'dressed in black cloth with buttoned tailcoat and white, I suppose, muslin round his neck ... the slim figure in the long blue cape lined with scarlet.' Despite what appeared to be a strict demeanour, 'we were ... taken every night to say goodnight to him by Nanna, when a diminutive slab of chocolate was inserted into my mouth and we joined him in the regular routine of singing. The crescendo had to be deafening, he shouting and waving an imaginary baton ... I can feel myself clinging to Nanna's ample coloured twill skirt when the amused grandfather (or shall I say amusing) pulled his high collared black coat over his head and hunching up his shoulders advanced growling "Bones and all".'

In 1828 Lord Bal had had an accident while supervising works on the house, which caused fainting fits and became a greater concern in later years. He became a widower in 1850, which brought steadily closer to his daughter-in-law, Min.[10] The photograph taken in 1863 with his grandson, Ludovic (later the 26th Earl of Crawford), shows a slightly hunched figure, probably suffering from this earlier injury. He would stay with the young family in their vast new London house in Grosvenor Square, where they gave him his own rooms on the ground floor. From there he would take long daily drives out into the nearby countryside in the brougham with its pair of fast-trotting bay horses.[11]

Father and son had a difficult but not embittered relationship. 'Hot-tempered, sweet natured, blustery and yet affectionate he was devoted to his sons – but his sympathies were with an active rather than a studious career, and although he never for a moment quarrelled with his eldest son, Alexander, he neither understood nor liked his tastes.'[12] His life was devoted to the collieries and so he ploughed much of the profits back in to strengthen the businesses as they became more rationalized. When he died at Dunecht, he left 'a vast and complex concern, commercial, agricultural and financial, collieries in Lancashire and Wales, five estates in England, one in Wales and one in Scotland.' He was undoubtedly a titan of his age.

4

'In appearance very well but no beauty'

The Hon. Maria Margaret Lindsay, Countess of Crawford & Balcarres (née Pennington), 1783–1850

Maria was to inject a particularly strong and long-lasting ethical element into the family. She was brought up at Muncaster Castle. Built on foundations dating from the Roman era, it had remained in the same family since possibly before the Norman conquest, always passing down through an unbroken male line. As an only child, Maria came under the influence of her father, Sir John Pennington, 4th Bt. He was a progressively minded figure in parliament, who in 1783 became the first Baron Muncaster. He took this title so he could further his one goal, the passing of the Abolition of the Slave Trade Act.

10 Lord and Lady Bal, possibly with their grandchildren, in one of the earliest daguerreotypes (*c.*1840). Her work in abolition and cotton famine relief, guided by strict Christian principles, had a lasting influence on her family.

This led him to a close association with William Wilberforce, who wrote: 'You and I are true in the same key as the musicians speak – we strike in unison.'[1] The two would be frequent guests of each other in their Lake District houses and became firm friends. The result of this friendship was Muncaster's 1792 publication, *Historical Sketches of the Slave Trade and of its Effects in Africa.*

Maria was enlisted to help in his affairs and his work with the evangelical movement, transcribing material for books and pamphlets in their campaign. She took this sense of duty with her to Haigh, after her marriage to James, 'Lord Bal'. She threw herself into whatever she could do for the relief of the growing hardship in the area, particularly during the Lancashire Cotton Famine: 'I have begun in earnest my district visiting. I am much pleased with all that has occurred: the people are glad to see me and we talk pleasantly and I hope profitably together. There is so much misery around us among the poor weavers but as a body they behave admirably, bearing their sorrows patiently.'

Stoicism was a key tenet for many of that time, not least Lady Bal. She believed that to use a drug to avoid pain was an evasion of the Christian virtue of fortitude. At one time, her son, Lord Lindsay, was looking after his nephew, Hugh, who needed some painful dental work. Worried about her stance, he felt it necessary to write: 'I hope you will not be vexed when you hear that after consultation with James and Anne I have decided to use chloroform, if sanctioned by the surgeon. You have no idea how severe the operation will be – four teeth to extract. And as

for being afraid James says that any man might dread it, so do not think the worse for this.'[2]

If Lady Bal appears to have been limited by her strict adherence to such principles, it did not prevent her from a warm attachment to her children: 'All my dear sons, though their characters are very different from each other, have in common the endearing qualities of making themselves always acceptable at home. This maternal opinion does not seem confined to the Old Lady for they all seem to please wherever they go.'

But her religion was never far from her thoughts, not least when she travelled: 'There is a Railroad mania at present and the Velocity with which people are to travel on it, viz. *30 miles an hour*, is enough to turn one's head.'[3] Her faith succoured her: 'I have no dislike of this flying method of travelling but am thankful when I am out of the train. The tunnels are awful – the long ones especially – the darkness is so very black it is felt, but I was devoid of fear as one seemed to be more thrown on the kind protection of God in such a situation than in any other I have ever been placed in.'

Much of what Lady Bal achieved can be gleaned from the reactions after her death. She died in 1850 aged sixty-six, predeceasing her husband by nineteen years. She had made the welfare of the people of Haigh and Wigan of paramount importance to her. Her actions were not vain gestures to make herself feel good but came from profoundly held spiritual views on duty and care. At a time when the country had seen great social unrest, such a prominent family could have been singled out for retribution. But the Lindsays set great store by their morals and did as much as they could to be fair and decent landlords and proprietors. The family's wish for a small private funeral was overturned by Wigan's mayor. A mass of colliers, cottagers and workpeople turned out, including those from the almshouses she had so keenly supported.

Her son, Lord Lindsay wrote:

On leaving the park lodge, the Mayor, Corporation, clergymen and gentlemen of Wigan placed themselves at the head of the cortège – the tenants on horseback and the colliers to the number of about a thousand in companies of about twenty under their leaders joined on behind our carriage as part of the family and they were followed by the carriages sent by private persons. The streets were lined the whole way but there was not the slightest levity shown – all were grave and respectful. The shops were shut and the blinds of private houses drawn down, with scarcely an exception. It was striking to see so much sympathy, respect and sorrow shown by the poorer classes ... It was supposed there were fifty thousand persons present. The ironworks and all the mills in the neighbourhood had stopped working.

Soon after the funeral I met one sad old reprobate who had been here, he and his fathers, for three hundred years and has been a friend and associate of my brothers in rat killing and such like pastimes since their boyhood – he is a trusty and most loyal fellow too and would die in our cause ... I called and spoke to him and the poor fellow faced right about with his back towards us and burst into tears.[4]

Haigh Hall

'Far from beautiful is a monument of honesty and strength'

Among a group of early daguerreotypes, made around 1840, is one that portrays James, 'Lord Bal', 24th Earl of Crawford, with his family, standing beside his newly completed Haigh Hall, the latest incarnation of a house built on this site. By 1947, the house had been in the same family for over 754 years, passing by marriage from the Norreys, who had been there since 1193, to the Bradshaighs in 1295 and finally to the Lindsays in 1785.

Local historian Thomas Whitehouse described the Hall's setting in 1820:

On an eminence two miles from Wigan stands Haigh Hall ... an ancient edifice built at several times and inhabited through a long succession of ages of Saxon origin ... The Hall stands beautifully and is considered one of the best situations in Lancashire. From a large mount and summer house, in the park area are seen on a clear day, thirteen counties of England and Wales, together with the Isle of Man, and yet so well are the gardens and grounds sheltered that vegetation here puts on her richest and most luxuriant garb. From here ... the town of Wigan is seen below, as standing upon a hill in the midst of a fine valley.

This view was about to change forever with the rapid encroachment of industry. In came the mines' gallows-like winding towers, mills and factories, blast furnaces and iron foundries, with their chimneys coughing up smoke that turned snow black within hours. Threading through the valley below, between the newly built workers' terraces, were the Lancaster Canal, roads and rail lines that replaced those fields, woods and old tracks.[1]

When Alexander and Elizabeth inherited Haigh from her great-aunt Dorothy in 1785, they found themselves with a large empty house and an estate that was steadily beginning to deteriorate. With the mines in a poor state, this was far from a marriage of convenience bringing new wealth to the strapped Lindsay family. This new legacy was going to require a great deal of investment. However, by selling their Scottish home, Balcarres, to his brother Robert, borrowing from his brother-in-law, Philip, Earl of Hardwicke, and income from his roles as governor and commander in chief to Jersey and Jamaica, the couple were able to build up his 'Aggrandising Fund' and sink much of it into restoring the farms and developing the industries.

Further funding came from James's claim for reparations after the abolition of slavery.[2] Eventually, he moved in to Haigh Hall in 1823 and his widowed father moved into nearby Haigh Cottage. Within two years, Alexander died and James immediately started on a complete rebuild. In 1828 a foundation stone was laid on the hard bed of cannel coal rock that had now been cleared, dug and deepened by his miners.

Lord Bal, as James became better known, felt that he had learnt enough to become its architect after gleaning engineering skills from the mines, helping his father repair the house and from his research of the works of Inigo Jones and William Kent. Subsidence caused by mining meant far stronger building materials were needed, so he developed the first steam-powered mechanical saws to cut the ingeniously designed interlocking blocks of bright, coarse gritstone from the nearby Parbold Hill quarries. He also invented a machine to tear horsehair into shorter pieces needed for the mortar.

The main structure of the finely proportioned house, completed in about 1840, was certainly well built and resisted subsidence. His approach as an engineer meant that he stuck to a more classical style, though he may have missed an opportunity to deliver a house of architectural note. But he was a realist rather than a romantic. It was with some regret that his great-grandson, the 27th Earl,[3] wrote:

One of my forebears allowed the wonderful Haigh Hall to be dismantled. It was certainly in a very dilapidated condition and badly shaken by mining subsidence, but it seems to have been condemned without one pang of regret. There was no serious effort to preserve its fine historic features. A handsome facade by Inigo Jones, the chapel with its fifteenth-century glass and dated armorial timber and the still earlier oak staircase.

Nevertheless,

Lord Bal knew how to build solid masonry – in fact the quality and craftsmanship of everything he did is superb

11 Haigh Hall from the north-east, looking over Lady Mabel's Wood towards Wigan (*c.* 1900).

12 *right* Haigh Hall's main entrance, the Plantation Gates, built *c.* 1840. The gatekeepers slept in the small lodge on one side while their kitchen and sitting room was on the other (*c.* 1910).

13 *opposite, near right* The drawing room (*c.* 1935).

14 *opposite, far right* The altarpiece in the hall was made up of two separate artists' panels, including Bicci di Lorenzo's *Virgin and Child Enthroned with Saints* (now in Westminster Abbey) and his *Annunciation*, forming the pinnacles on either side of Ugolino di Nerio's *Crucifixion* (*c.* 1890).

... Anyhow we have good reason to be grateful to Lord Bal for having erected a mansion house, which tho' far from beautiful is a monument of honesty and strength. [4]

Paris was the source for much of the plasterwork and parquet floors and Pringle in London supplied most of the oak bookcases and doors, though local craftsmen and materials were used where possible.

With a ready supply of cannel from their nearby mines, the highest quality of coal that burnt hot and clean, the household was able to enjoy one of the few air central heating systems in the country (hot water central heating did not become common until the late nineteenth century). Initially, the house was lit with a combination of candles (to a design by Lord Bal that prevented flickering), lamps burning naptha, a coal gas, and oil lamps that used spermaceti from the sperm whale or colza (from cole seed) for the less important areas. The lamp room in the basement had large oil tanks where each day a member of staff would trim wicks, clean, polish and refuel the lamps. Gas was only used for cooking. Water was now piped through bored-out six-foot-long elm logs, pumped up from a reservoir in Wigan.

Lord Bal's grandson Ludovic[5] was a pioneer in electricity, so it is curious that there was no generator at Haigh until 1898. When the system was eventually installed, it had 124 storage batteries that supplied 371 lights and 452 plugs. The house's system was immediately greater than that of the whole of the Wigan Corporation.[6] When his yacht, the *Valhalla,* had her engines renewed, one of the old ones was brought to Haigh to be used as a generator.

These innovations were seen as practical and eminently sensible, not vulgar, pretentious or indulgent. But it must have been an exciting house to visit as it had all the latest mod cons, some of which were designed there. Lord Bal's granddaughter, Lady Mary Meynell, noted that 'the house was full of my grandfather's inventions – windows which shut so that no draughts were possible, doors which opened and shut in a special unforeseen way, cisterns which filled with water by stepping on the floor, clocks which went by water etc.'[7] It even had one of the first water closets. Security was taken care of by doors and windows that could not be opened from the outside. There was even a lift – no doubt using mine technology.

Such houses demanded a large company of staff to ensure efficient operation. The children were looked after by their nannies and normally a French governess as well as their own footmen. Downstairs, the staff were headed by the butler, who, like the groom of the chamber, was distinguished by his black attire. The former's bedroom adjoined the strong room to guard against burglars. 'The comely flock of women servants ... captained by Mrs Joyce, our beloved Nana who became housekeeper'[8]

(whose rank was equal to the butler), was often complemented by those accompanying their visiting employers – all were treated in order of precedence of their mistress's rank. For many occasions, including when they were brought up to London when the family was entertaining, the under-butler and porter along with four footmen and the night-watchman would wear the Lindsay livery of blue coats (with polished brass buttons embossed with the jousting tent and ostrich crests beneath a five-balled coronet), scarlet knee breeches, pink stockings, all accentuated with blue, red and gold woven in braids. Long into the nineteenth century the latter staff were still expected to wear powder, though the custom of powdering hair or wigs had started losing its popularity at the end of the eighteenth century with Pitt's powder tax. The head coachman with his under-coachmen and sometimes the grooms were similarly dressed, though distinguished by their frockcoats.

Separate from the usual household accounts were those for the librarians – sometimes as many as nine were employed by both the 25th and 26th earls. In 1822 there were about thirteen staff tending to the family. By 1920 this had more than doubled.

James Higson, the gatekeeper from 1866 to 1891, at the estate's main entrance, known as the Plantation Gates, was a celebrated figure in his own right. He had fought in India from 1843 until being sent to the Cape, where he took part in the Xhosa wars in 1851. Then, he fought and was decorated for his role in the Second Opium War. He was discharged after his twenty-one-year service in the army. He had married Elizabeth Andrews in his early soldiering days and she remained by his side throughout his campaigns. They returned to the area and he was appointed night-watchman before being made keeper of the Lodge. They remained here for thirty-four years and witnessed 'four generations of

15 *below* An early daguerreotype of some of the staff at Haigh Hall (*c.* 1840).

16 *bottom, left* Lewis, Haigh Hall's butler (*c.* 1870).

17 *bottom, right* Mr James Higson and his wife, Elizabeth, the Haigh Hall gatekeepers between 1866 and 1891. He had served in the army in the Xhosa wars and later in China (*c.* 1890).

18 *below, left* One of the coachmen at Haigh Hall (*c.*1920).

19 *bottom, left* The Haigh Hall Fire Brigade on their Merryweather fire engine (*c.* 1890).

20 *top, right* Three of the Haigh Hall grooms out exercising the greys (*c.* 1900).

21 *centre, right* Mowing the lawns at Haigh was a labour-intensive endeavour. Note the horse's hind lawn boots (*c.* 1880).

22 *bottom, right* Arthur Fair (d. 1934) was the agent for over thirty years. Bal, 27th Earl of Crawford, credited him for relieving him 'from all the tedium of the dull Lancashire estate' (1902).

23 The abundant availability of coal from the nearby mines meant that both the house and hot houses were warmer than most (*c.* 1930).

the Crawfords, having done service for three earls, and opened the gates for two', before the universally popular old soldier died in the couple's jubilee year.

The Hall's new kitchens always had a Frenchman for a cook, supported by a retinue of still room and scullery maids. Jane reminisced that 'there was no "snobbishness" in the style and formality maintained in the great houses. In fact, the servants were a very happy community, well-ordered and befriended by all the village houses around – who enjoyed their company.'[9] Alexander, Lord Lindsay,[10] always made sure they joined the family each morning and came together for Sunday evening prayers.[11] For more important occasions the family would use the Crawford Chapel in Wigan Parish Church. This had long been the resting place for many of the Bradshaigh family, having been founded by Lady Mabel in 1338, and continued until Lord Lindsay was buried there.[12] His daughter, Jane, designed the east window.

Other improvements included a new laundry, dairy and kennels, all incorporating Lord Bal's innovative ideas.[13] He designed an egg-shaped icehouse, which allowed the melting ice to slide and consolidate into the centre, slowing the melt process. Whenever there was a freeze, an estate worker would collect ice from lakes and ponds to fill the forty-six cubic yard space.

24 The upper library (*c.* 1880), showing a small part of the vast collection. Nine librarians catalogued and organized manuscripts, French Revolutionary papers, Lutheran tracts, scientific and philatelic material, and oriental works.

25 Mr Edmond, Haigh Hall's head librarian, stands far right with five of his eight assistants. David, 28th Earl of Crawford, wrote that he and his siblings did not get to read many books as they were frightened of the librarians.

Further additions included cottages and houses for the estate staff, a new stable yard for twenty horses, coach houses and grooms' quarters, local schools, the Haigh Church and vicarage, workshops and sawmills – all helping turn what was previously an ailing property into the most modern, up-to-date and efficiently run operation.

The estate had thirty-seven tenanted farms, which today might seem a large number for one that was only just over 2,600 acres.[14] However, farms were a great deal smaller before modern machinery reduced the need for so many steadings. The largest had 144 acres while the smallest a little over fourteen.[15] The Home Farm was the most important, as it was expected to supply everything that the household needed throughout the year – milk and cream, veal and beef, ham and bacon, lamb and mutton, chickens, turkeys and eggs.

In 1846–7 hot houses were built near the large lilypond and enlarged later in the century, stretching to 890 feet.[16] One of these had an ancient bird of paradise flower (*Strelitzia reginae*) that Lady Anne Barnard had brought back from South Africa. It was still alive after the Second World War when the house was sold. A staff of eighteen tended the four-acre kitchen gardens and three-and-a-half acres of nurseries, where they produced bananas, figs, lemons and oranges. There were vineries for grapes, and fruits, including pineapples, peaches and pears. Cart horses, given names beginning with C or B after Crawford and Balcarres, would wear leather over-shoes to protect the lawns as they dragged great mowing machines, all maintained to the highest standards. The Plantations, which made up a large part of the gardens and where the public were allowed access, had some of the finest rhododendrons in the country.

When the family were at home, the head gardener would supervise the daily delivery of flowers, such as the orchids that were brought from the hot houses into the house on stretchers. Chief pleasures for all the children were visits to the carpenters' shop that

26 The drawing room in 1916. Haigh Hall became a military hospital during the First World War.

serviced the pits, as well as mending the houses, rebuilding gates and fences or repairing carts. Calling in on the noisy electricity-generating plant was a favourite. It had the added attraction of the old *Comet* steam engine puffing away to provide power. Equally exciting was when the house fire brigade turned out for fire drill, with its firemen drawn from the pits or estate decked out in the Lindsay livery colours with polished brass helmets embossed with the family crest.

At the outbreak of the Great War, hospitals rapidly ran out of space, so soon most large houses like Haigh were offered, or indeed sometimes requisitioned, for wounded troops. Haigh was used as a military convalescent hospital from November 1914, entirely financed by the 27th Earl, David. It was mostly for Belgian soldiers. The main ward was the sixty-foot-long ballroom, while the patients' day room was the Lower West Library, where walking cases had their meals.

After the war maintaining such country houses became increasingly unfeasible. Many were demolished, contributing in part to a social revolution that was taking place across the United Kingdom. In many cases the houses could no longer be guaranteed to provide employment, housing or even patronage for the local services. It is estimated that one in six of all country houses was demolished during the twentieth century, most of them before the Second World War.[17]

The political climate and frightening financial forecasts for the post-war period convinced David, 28th Earl, that their time at Haigh had come to an end. The combination of nationalization, punitively high taxation and the decade from 1924 during which no dividends were paid from the businesses meant much of the Bibliotheca Lindesiana had to be sold. Three thousand acres of the Haigh estate went between 1943 and 1969, while the house and its Plantations were sold to the Wigan Corporation for just £18,000 in 1947 (approximately £560,000 today). The Lindsays retreated once again to Scotland, but kept the Home Farm along with the estate's mineral rights other than coal. It means that, at the time of writing, the family still owned a stake in Haigh after 827 years.

5

'My first master in Italian art'

Alexander William Crawford Lindsay, 25th Earl of Crawford & 8th Earl of Balcarres, 'Lord Lindsay', 1812–80, and Margaret, Countess of Crawford & Balcarres (née Lindsay), 1824–1909

27 An early image of Muncaster Castle before it was remodelled in 1860. The seven-year-old Lord Lindsay was distraught when his mother's father was forced to sell.

Alexander William, better known as Lord Lindsay, or William to his family when young, was the complete antithesis of his father, Lord Bal. Here was a deeply introspective, learned academic whose chief interests lay in religious art and history. 'He was chivalrous and high-minded to a quixotic extent, courteous with the courtesy of the heart, even more than the manner, and though one of the most cultivated and learned men of his day he was patience itself with any foolish or ignorant person asking him for help or information.'[1]

Lord Lindsay spent the first part of his childhood at the home of his maternal grandfather, Lord Muncaster. His daughter, Mabel, portrayed his first home, Muncaster Castle, best:

The rolling fells and the richly wooded hillside beyond which on the western horizon gleams the open sea, all the changeful beauty of the wide landscape laid its deep impress on my father's mind, in whom the love of Nature's fitful moods of light and shade and colour ever gave the most exquisite delight.[2]

He loved his Cumbrian home deeply, but the death of his grandfather and a worsening financial burden led to the house being sold. He was distraught and at the age of seven wrote: 'Oh when, O when may I see thee, And in thy dales and meadows be, When may

28 Lord Lindsay, whom John Ruskin described in 1873 as 'my first master in Italian art'. By Thomas Rodger (*c.*1850).

I thy hills to see And play and frisk upon the lea.' It was the 'indelible impression' of that childhood paradise that remained with him forever and it was here as a small child he discovered his love of history and literature. Aged just eight, he wrote his *William's Works for Children. By William Lindsay. Second Edition revised and improved. 1821 (Price One Shilling).*[3]

The family moved south to a modest house on their Caledon cousins' estate, 'Bounds', near Tunbridge Wells.[4] From there they moved to Tyttenhanger and then Wimpole, until his seventy-year-old grandfather asked Lord Bal to move back to Haigh. Meanwhile, Lord Lindsay stayed south and joined Mr Rusden's school, which encouraged his love of languages and poetry. Even before the precocious author was ten, he had written self-improvement books on grammar and moral principles for his contemporaries. His first published work was a translation of poems from German in 1840. In the preface he wrote:

A poem fresh from the heart and hand of its author, may be fancifully compared in spirit and form to a little bird shut up in a golden cage; the translator's business is to catch the little bird and build another cage ... Too often the little bird escapes during the process.

He published many more works, most of which related to his interests in the theory of Christianity and its art, and Scottish history, particularly relating to his family's roles therein. His *Sketches of the History of Christian Art*, which appeared in 1846, was made up of a series of part-historical, part-philosophical letters introducing Italian art to a young art student, actually his future brother-in-law, (later Sir) Coutts Lindsay. But this was not some purely amateurish effort. John Ruskin, the leading art expert of the Victorian era, wrote: 'As a contribution to the history of art his work is unquestionably the most valuable which has yet appeared in England.' Until then, the study of early Italian art had been almost exclusively the preserve of scholarly, but provincial, antiquarians, whose labours went largely unnoticed. Ruskin went on to describe Lindsay as 'my first master in Italian art'.[5]

His father frowned on his son's intensifying study of art and classics, believing one should look to the future to further the family's prospects. It was not music to his ears, therefore, when his eleven-year-old boy excitedly told his parents: 'I am now in Maschus a Greek poet and Matthew and Lucians Dialogues of the Dead, Greek Grammar, Virgil, Horace, Nepos and Caesar de Bell. Gal. ... all of which I find very easy.'[6] Or: 'I have lately got a most beautiful Euripides, 6 vols for 7 shillings with various readings and uncut.'[7]

Lindsay found his time at Eton became almost unbearable. Unlike his second and third brothers, James and Charles, who were described as 'wild as hawks, active as cats, universal favourites',[8] he was neither a sportsman (he was a slight 5 foot 4 inches when eighteen years old) nor sociable, exhibiting a 'singularity about him', and consequently he was badly bullied. Things became so fraught that he was forced to bear witness against one of those he had accused of tormenting him at a hearing. Matters were not helped by his mother's ambitions to make him more like the other more extrovert young men she knew, who loved dancing, house parties and shooting. All these matters he saw as personal failings, and his terrible near-sightedness acted as a bar and hindrance, causing an inevitable and painful diffidence in society. Subsequently, he became ever more engrossed in his studies.

By the time he left Eton he had already collected over five hundred books, including incunabula.[9] His special delight was to find and buy back books that been part of the original Balcarres library, which had been created by three ancestors – David, Lord Edzell (1551–98), John, Lord Menmuir (1552–98) and Menmuir's son, David, the 1st Lord Balcarres (1587–1640). He took special pleasure in retrieving the single medieval manuscript, the 1323 *Roman de la Rose* that had originally been owned by Christian, daughter of Sir William de Lindsay, and Ada, daughter of John Balliol, King of Scotland.[10]

His keen interest in theology led him to become an intensely religious man. Leading such a cerebral life, which continued at Cambridge, where he preferred to avoid the other 'noblemen', who were

29 A happy early married life at Haigh was made uncomfortable for Min by her sisters-in-law's jealousies. These eventually calmed and strengthened her ultimate position as matriach. By Thomas Rodger (*c.* 1850).

30 Paintings in the Haigh drawing room by Pinturicchio, Botticini and Botticelli reflected Lord Lindsay's deepening interest in Christian art of the Renaissance (*c.* 1880).

neither as diligent as he nor needed to be, must have limited his social horizons and, in turn, his options for a possible wife. He immersed himself in researching the family history to such an extent that those around him worried, particularly his parents. His father declared England their home – 'Scotland is past, we have to become an English family' – and was equally disdainful of the book collecting: 'A volume can claim no additional value (beyond correct text) because it may be printed by Caxton or any other early printer ... It is some time since your family has produced a first rate man.'

His first journey to Scotland to visit his uncle and aunt, General James and Anne Lindsay, at Balcarres in 1831 was to have arguably the greatest impact on his future. Anne was daughter of Sir Coutts Trotter, partner and godson of Thomas Coutts, the founder of Coutts Bank. There he met Margaret, 'Min', for the first time. His return to the surviving historical family seat inspired him deeply and he regaled the family with stories of their antecedents' colourful past. This was when he conceived the idea of creating the Bibliotheca Lindesiana, a family library – not for flashy works or particularly fine editions, but a *reading* library. 'But I will make it *super-excellent,* not a Lord Spencer collection, but a useful one.'

His first major journey to distant lands took place in 1833 when he set off with his cousin William Ramsay for Egypt. They travelled up the Nile to the Second Cataract, spending months in the desert before crossing north to Mount Sinai and the Holy Land. Disaster struck when Ramsay came down with cholera and died shortly after. Lindsay had to oversee all the arrangements, including having his body embalmed, sealed and sent to Beirut. With the help of the consul there, a secret pact was made with the captain of a small ship, which was chartered to take them back to England without the crew being told of the contents of the chest. Had they known, they might have refused to sail. It was a dangerous undertaking as the risk of infection was high – indeed, his devoted servant Messiri became ill on the slow, four-month journey home. After quarantining off Liverpool, Lindsay had to make the last trying leg of the journey to take the body of his friend and cousin back to the family.[11]

Meanwhile, there were happier developments at home. Lady Mary Crawford, a distant cousin, had an extensive archive of papers, ancient deeds and records connected to the history of the family that she had inherited from her brother George, the 22nd Earl of Crawford. His passing meant that the title, which had gone down a separate line, was now in abeyance. Attracted by Lindsay's interest in the family chronicles, Lady Mary developed a strong friendship with her cousin and surprised him on her death in 1833 by leaving him many of her properties and chattels at Crawford Priory. This legacy transformed the family's purchasing power and ability to strengthen his and his father's successful claim to the ancient earldom of Crawford. Although Lord Bal was less interested in the Scottish element, he nonetheless recognized that the claim should be made.

The research included the Herculean task of delving into the extensive archives and frequently impenetrable documents in the Advocates Library of Edinburgh, Crawford Priory and the muniment rooms at Balcarres and Haigh. This was also instrumental in enabling him to produce the definitive family history while making the claim. For Lindsay, as an intellectual, it was not just some vanity project: 'My father had no vulgar pride of lineage – with him "noblesse oblige" was an axiom of life – and in his fresh and delightful [three-volume] *Lives of the*

Lindsays the fallibilities of his ancestors are no less dwelt upon than their merits.'[12]

His picture collecting was less focused but illustrated his ambition to amass a body of work for a museum that would demonstrate man's intellectual development in all branches of literature, art and science. Initially, he was happy to commission copies, many by the Florentine artist Vicenzo Corsi. His justification was that few of the originals of the most important works were available and that he would rather have a good copy of a great work than a second- or third-rate original. But in 1848, his cousin, travelling companion, friend and by now father-in-law, General James Lindsay started to persuade him to start focusing on quality rather than quantity. In time a catholic choice of works, many

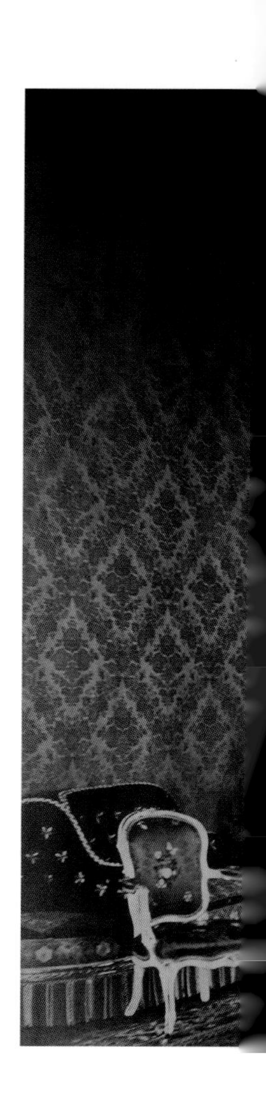

31 A 'suite of rooms suitable for receiving society in the manner that will be requisite when Alice, Minnie and their sisters make their entry upon the scene of London' was needed. Hence an Italianate house at 9–10 Grosvenor Square was built, including a ballroom (*c.* 1865).

of which showed his interest in Byzantine influences on Christian art, began to include finer pieces by Lucas Cranach, Guido Reni, Duccio, Perugino and Pinturicchio. The impression remains that his approach to picture collecting mirrored that of his historical literary quests: to build a systematic catalogue of works similar to the Renaissance tradition of private patronage rather than see and appreciate the paintings from a purely aesthetic perspective.

Alongside the obvious differences with his father, there were similarities. Both refused to exploit their many employees (over ten thousand by mid-century) and became well-thought-of, respected employers. Their shared work ethic and unquenchable curiosity propelled them relentlessly to develop, improve and perfect their knowledge of their chosen fields. They embraced their respective times: Lord Bal, recognizing the opportunities that coal and iron would offer, used all his resources and interests in technology to invest in and develop what became one of the largest corporations of its age, while his son saw that revolutionary Europe provided a golden age for the collector and a period that ultimately would help define the family's reputation in the art world. Much of their DNA must have passed down to future generations, as they continued to find the same pleasures in their leanings towards art, photography and collecting, technology and science, history and politics, travel and agriculture into the next two centuries.

While Lindsay failed to gain total support from his parents, he did develop a lifelong unbreakable bond with his cousin and father-in-law General James. This figure was 'a noble example of a high minded chivalrous gentleman, extraordinarily handsome, of warm affections, wide tolerance – and shrewd judgement, his personal influence was very great.'[13] Where his parents had shown doubt in many of his undertakings, he felt the support and encouragement from the general and shared interests and endless conversations about those academic subjects. While the latter had not benefitted from higher education, he was cultivated and had a keen love of art. His wife, Anne, was highly educated in literature and the 'perfect complement to the husband whom she worshipped almost to the exclusion of her children.'

It was this relationship that brought Lindsay out of the shy seclusion to which he was prone. His daughter, Mabel, recognized that he was diffident with strangers due to the profound distrust of his own powers of entertaining: 'However, his hearty laugh was so spontaneous that none who heard it could resist the contagion.' It was his cousin's steady influence that gave him the self-confidence and happiness that he had never had when young. Indeed, it was felt that it was the charm that emanated from the general and his wife that made Balcarres so special for all its visitors.

For years Lindsay had harboured a secret love for the general's daughter, his second cousin Min, but felt that because of their family's proximity he should let her look for a husband elsewhere. He saw in her a soulmate and always felt more relaxed in her company than anyone else's. When he conveyed his true wishes in May 1846, he was almost too late – she had accepted a proposal that very morning, but 'she ran up to him and throwing her arms around his neck burst into tears'.[14] Neither had realized how strong the sense of mutual devotion had become over the years. They married two months later and almost exactly a year after they had a son, James Ludovic.

Min may have been less visible on the social scene than her siblings but the 'grande dame' became the growing family's true matriarch, loved by her twenty-two grandchildren, allowing her husband, to whom she was devoted, to lead the sheltered life of a true academic. 'Fearless and capable' in her household management, she could show a daunting dissatisfaction for some untoward deed with just the raising of her eyebrows. Her ethics and underlying sense of purpose were typically Victorian, directed by her strongly held religious beliefs. These brought her close to regular visitor Edward Benson, who established Wellington College before becoming Archbishop of Canterbury.

The birth of Ludovic was not going to hinder their travels in search of more books and art. Travelling into Rome by carriage, with their young baby and

nurse, they arrived in the midst of the region's greatest upheavals – the revolt that was to see Austria losing its control and the eventual formation of Italy as a state. It must have been an invigorating time, while being equally worrying for the intrepid visitors. There were a number of English people in Rome at the time who had arrived for the winter and culture, among whom was Florence Nightingale, who would come to play for hours with the baby.[15] She became increasingly close to the family through Min's brother Robert. Their shared experiences of the disorganization and subsequent horrors in the Crimea War led them to work together on a number of far-reaching initiatives.[16]

If Min had thought that living at Haigh was to be an agreeable proposition, it turned out to be an uncomfortable reality. Frances and Sarah, the wives of Lindsay's brothers, Colin and James, were both older than she and had made themselves probably too comfortable. Lord Bal was keen to see his new daughter-in-law become the lady of the house, but a lack of tact and a series of slights from these two entrenched sisters-in-law became unbearable for her, compounded by homesickness and poor health after the birth of her children. In time, they were forced to become more accommodating and ultimately accepted her position. Similarly, a meeting of minds between Lindsay and his father had come about through the need to reinvest some of the enormous profits from the coal and iron companies in a northern property. Lord Lindsay had little attachment to Haigh. His sentiments were unequivocal: 'the birds, nasty little beasts are singing away quite beautifully; they enjoy this detestable drizzling soft wet-blanket moist muzzle of warm solution of soot and water which constitutes our atmosphere.'[17] [sic] Dunecht thus became the new Scottish seat.

Lord Lindsay may have been working all day, with his wife writing at her table nearby, but his daughter Mabel described how he would always allow the 'children to run in and out of his room and ask him questions without a word of impatience. The smell of attar of roses always brings irresistibly to my mind the drawer of his writing-table where he kept a little bottle, which we sniffed at, and also a box of chocolates which we did more than sniff at!'[18] Though he was not comfortable in large social gatherings, he could make those around him relax with his keen sense of fun and humour. Throughout his life he had a gift for inspiring interest in any subject close to his heart from his inexhaustible memory store. 'Anecdote and reminiscence poured forth to the delight of his hearers.'[19]

The London season and the never-ending quest for new books meant that the growing family needed a larger base than the old house at 21 Berkeley Square. They bought a site and in 1865 finished building their great double-fronted house at 9–10 Grosvenor Square.

The responsibility for the collieries was by now causing great anxiety to the young academic. The death of the manager, Mr Peace, who had exercised wise control, precipitated the decision to turn the private concern of the Haigh Collieries into a limited liability company, which would be called the Wigan Coal & Iron Co. The amalgamation with John Lancaster's Lancashire Coalfields business seemed like a well-planned, logical move. But Lancaster was

32 *top* Villa Palmieri in the Fiesole hills. From 1872 it became the base from which the Lindsays launched their book- and picture-buying expeditions.

33 *centre* Even before the Lindsays and Queen Victoria, many used Villa Palmieri as a refuge, including the ten characters in Boccaccio's *Decameron* escaping the Black Death as it swept through Florence in 1348 (1880).

a man who liked to take risks and speculate in a way that was anathema to the more conservative Lindsay. Exasperated, the former, in a display of misguided brinkmanship, offered all his stock if he could not have his way. 'Done!' was Lindsay's reply and by this brief negotiation the family became principal shareholders and would become the largest colliery owners in Lancashire, with the deepest shaft in the world and the largest joint stock company in the country after the railway concerns.

Lindsay subsequently accepted a host of responsibilities, including presidencies of various local establishments. Perhaps the most welcome was his involvement in and contribution to the building of the much-needed colliery infirmary. Many of the workers were engaged in hazardous work and the old dispensary could no longer meet their needs. He declared it 'one of those rare and precious occasions in English life when the whole inhabitants of a neighbourhood meet together for a common object, upon which there exists no difference of opinion.'[20] Two-and-a-half years later he invited the Prince and Princess of Wales to open the Royal Albert Edward Infirmary and Dispensary.

After years of staying in hotels or renting houses in Florence, they bought Villa Palmieri in 1872, overlooking the old city from the hills of Fiesole and one of the most beautifully appointed in the region. Originally called *La Fonte di Treviso* (Fountain of Three Faces), it is one of Florence's oldest.[21] In 1259 Cione di Fini built a casino that still stands in the gardens, though there is little left of the rest of the house.[22] They were followed by various families until it was bought by the apothecary, Matteo Palmieri, Cosimo di Medici's friend and ambassador.

Salvatore Cortesi best described the origins of the house's name:

Otto I came from Germany into Italy to fight against Berengarius IV and defeated him. Pope Agapitus II sent a palm to Otto as a symbol of the peace ... [who] asked the best of his knights to carry it around the town as a triumph ... His descendants, the Palmieri, went to live in Florence.[23]

34 *opposite, below* Queen Victoria was lent Villa Palmieri for two of her first holidays abroad. It entailed enormous upheaval for Lady Lindsay but it became a favourite royal destination and brought her close to the family (1887).

35 *below* Otto I, who defeated Berengarius IV, was given a palm as a symbol of peace by the Pope. His descendants became known as the Palmieri and remained in Florence. Ever since, palms have been grown at the villa (*c.* 1880).

Palms have long adorned the villa's terraces.

The house was the possible setting for Giovanni Boccaccio's *Decameron* stories of ten characters escaping the Black Death in 1348. Its heavenly sense of sanctuary is described in a way that the Lindsays could have written themselves:

The lovely gardens, with pergola, vines laden with bunches of grapes, and beds of jessamine and crimson roses, the carved marble fountains whose overflow of water was conducted by cunningly devised underground tunnels down to the plain, where it turned two mills, to the profit of the lord of the valley ... To see this garden, its handsome ordering, the plants, and the fountain with rivulets issuing from it ... that all began to affirm that, if Paradise could be made on earth, they couldn't conceive a form other than that of this garden that might be given it.[24]

Other artists who depicted the house included Giuseppe Zocchi, J. M. W. Turner, Queen Victoria and Hermann Corrodi, who painted the Queen on the terrace between 1894 and 1897 in an oil that joined hers in the Royal Collection. It was rumoured that Dante's imagination was fired by its setting; that of Alexandre Dumas *père* certainly was – in 1843, he compiled his travel essays under the title *La Villa Palmieri.* Eventually Lord Lindsay purchased the villa

from the Duchess of Tuscany.[25] It had been neglected and much work was needed before they were able to spend their first winter there in 1874.

The sight that greeted the Lindsays was a handsome house with a five-bayed arcaded open loggia, reached by symmetrically paired curved stairs from the lower south-facing terrace and lemon parterre. The outside facade was richly decorated with baroque stucco. Lindsay's daughter, Mabel, recalled how

The arrangements were very un-English. For instance, the oil and wine press and the stables were under the drawing room – Sanitary conveniences did not exist. The kitchen was on the bedroom floor – the only sleeping accommodation for servants consisted in long divans covered with leather ranged around the empty halls, upon which the men slept at night, and inside which they stored their bedding during the day ... the first thing requisite was to make passages with independent access – to provide a water supply, to introduce the ABC of necessary comfort. It was a giant undertaking – but my mother was always a most excellent architect – ingenious and thoroughly practical.[26]

Queen Victoria had mentioned to Lord Lindsay that she had long wished to visit Italy and so he offered to lend the house to her. After his death in 1880, Min renewed the invitation. Prior to that first visit in 1887, the Queen sent a message: 'Please make no special preparations for me – what suits Lady Crawford will suit me – I should like to have the house as she lives in it with all the things about.' Mabel noted that the Queen's 'personal requirements were spartan in their simplicity – a narrow iron bedstead with a mattress as hard as board and plain net curtains for her bedroom – for her sitting room her own armchair and sofa – and the only thing of beauty – a large French Louis XV writing table, with electric calls for her secretary. A crowd of photographs, among them that of General Gordon, and a few miniatures completed her personal furniture.'[27]

This Royal visit was not a simple affair. It meant a complete rearrangement of the rooms. On the ground floor, three of the fourteen rooms were converted into bedrooms for the Gentlemen in Waiting. Then there was a telegraphist's room, a private dining room, a small chapel (even though there was one in the garden), a dining room for the larger household staff. Her Indian secretary and attendant, Mohammed Abdul Karim, known as 'the Munshi', and his servants, had the top floor

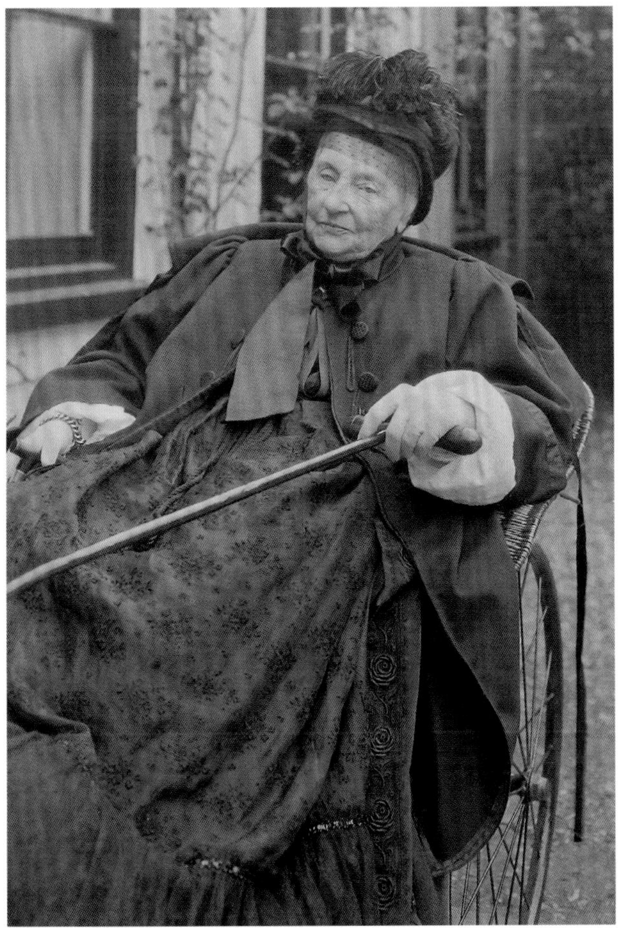

36 *opposite* Lady Lindsay visited Palmieri less frequently during her twenty-nine-year widowhood as her children found it easier to see her in England (*c.* 1890).

37 & 38 Lady Lindsay's intellect remained forever acute and intact. In 1891 she completed and published her husband's nine-hundred-page work, *The Creed of Japhet.*

with their own kitchen. Even though the Queen had insisted on no special arrangements, it was clearly a considerable undertaking. Even a lift was installed from the dining room to her apartments immediately above.

The visit was such a success that she came again in 1893. An outbreak of typhoid in the region prevented a third stay, while on a later occasion, when she asked if she might use Palmieri, Min was unwell, so another villa was taken nearby. Nonetheless, the Queen came to visit her old friend and remind herself of the happy times she had spent there.

Eventually Min found the journeys too tiring and it was decided to put the villa on the market. Her daughter, Mary, wrote: 'I have been at Florence since the happy days of long ago, but I could not bring myself to revisit the beloved place where some of my happiest days of my life were spent. I like to think of it still as a happy dream, unspoilt by improvements and still shining through the golden mists of loving memories.'[28]

In 1907 Palmieri was sold to an American, James Ellsworth, who also happened to be a collector of art and a coal-mine owner. He died there of pneumonia in 1925 while waiting for news of his son, the polar aviation pioneer Lincoln, a pilot on the Amundsen–Ellsworth Polar Flying Expedition.

Back in 1879, principally for Min's health, the couple, along with the three youngest sisters, Mabel, Anne and Jane, had sailed to Egypt for a four-month voyage up the Nile. Lindsay seemed fine on their return to Florence, but just as they were about to travel back to England his health worsened and the journey was postponed. He appeared to rally after a short period in the mountains, but on his return to the villa a chill rapidly turned to bronchitis and pneumonia, from which he died on 13 December 1880. On receiving the telegram of the news, the house steward at Haigh declared 'All is over.'[29] It was a great shock for all his close relations, who had not realized his sickness was life-threatening. He was loved by many: 'How many hearts are sorrowful now that one so dear, so noble, so generous, so sympathising, so wise, has been taken away.'[30]

39 Lord Lindsay had felt most at home at Dunecht and hoped it would be his final resting place. The horrifying later discovery that his body had been stolen marked the beginning of the end of the family's happiness there (*c.* 1880).

Lord Linday's legacy was the creation of the Bibliotheca Lindesiana; he added to the 6,000 books in 1834 to the point that it contained over 30,000 important works by his death. His son, Ludovic, would see this continue to grow to over 100,000. Additionally, as the Wigan press were among the first to recognize, he had played a major role in the town's fortune and welfare:

Among the Lindsays there have been many who have been eminent in the field, the senate and the literary and artistic world, but there will be none whose name will shed a brighter lustre on the honoured house of Lindsay than the deceased Earl. In public and in private life he proved himself a worthy scion of a noble family, and by his death the House of Haigh has not only lost an excellent and esteemed head, but the town of Wigan and its philanthropic institutions a kind and generous supporter. There was no object deserving of sympathy which had not his aid and support, and there was no appeal to him on behalf of charitable objects which had not his ready and cordial assistance. His purse was always open, and the cry of the distressed never reached him in vain. During the whole of his long life he was universally esteemed and respected, and his loss will be keenly felt by all classes in the town and neighbourhood. Gifted with a genial and kindly disposition his endeavour always seemed to be to promote the greatest good ... A Conservative in politics, he was no bigot, he allowed all to have a free and unfettered opinion, and gave credit for singleness of purpose as he expected to receive it himself ... For him politics seemed to have no attraction, and consequently his views on the home and foreign policy of the Government were unknown to the outside world except through his votes in the House of Lords.

His embalmed body was taken to Dunecht, where he was buried in the new vault under the chapel. However, months later, while Min was in Italy, horrifying news arrived. The Dunecht solicitor had received a letter, signed 'Nabob', stating:

The remains of the late Earl of Crawford are not beneath the chaple [sic] *at Dunecht as you believe, but were removed hence last spring, and the smell of decayed flowers ascending from the vault since that time will, on investigation, be found to proceed from another cause than flowers.*[31]

While the public were outraged and hugely sympathetic, many hoaxers came forward demanding money. Min wrote to *The Times* to declare that she would never give in to any ransom demand, which elicited widespread public support, including letters from Queen Victoria, who praised her courage and example. It later transpired that Nabob was in fact Charles Souter, a rat-catcher who had recently been sacked from his position at Dunecht for poaching. He claimed that he had witnessed two masked men with 'commonplace' Aberdeenshire accents. Suspicions were aroused partly due to the time he had taken to give evidence and he was sent to trial. He denied any involvement but was sentenced to five years' penal servitude.[32] His accomplices were never found.

Souter's evidence led to the discovery of the body – only five hundred yards from the chapel, now marked by a Celtic cross. Due to the embalming process, the body had not deteriorated badly. Meanwhile, Min, at the time travelling to Brighton, was confronted by 'huge placards announcing the discovery'. Jane recalled how 'she was alone, as she was I feel sure thankful to be – her terribly vivid imagination at all times redoubled suffering – how much more so then.'[33]

'I cannot remain silent', Queen Victoria wrote again to Min, 'and must express my heartfelt satisfaction and sympathy at the news from Dunecht today! Your noble self denial [*sic*] has been rewarded, and you have besides rendered a great public service thereby for which all must feel grateful ... Might I ask you for a Photograph of yourself and your dear Husband?' Special arrangements were made for Lord Lindsay's body to be reinterred, this time at Wigan. At 3 a.m. Min and her daughters, along with Amy's husband, Freddie Meynell, and Ludovic, walked to the dimly lit church where they waited for the coffin's imminent arrival on the train from Aberdeen. A blessing was

made before the body was finally laid to rest in the family vault.

Intriguingly, in February 1883, a bottle with a message was washed up on the Shetland Islands:

This bottle was thrown into the water at Stirling, in the river Forth, on the 15th July 1882, by one of the men who were concerned in the lifting of the body of the Earl of Crawford. The body is now, I think, rotted into clay. We lifted it with the intention of selling it, but it was published so soon that we buried it to get it out of the way.[34]

In Min's latter years, including twenty-nine of widowhood, she would spend less time travelling and more at the house she had built at Burcote near Clifton Hampden. She had been very much an equal to her husband's intellect and had continued his work, managing to get his weighty nine-hundred-page book on the *Creed of Japheth* published, an investigation into the origins of all languages and legends and hence the working of God's purpose.

Her daughter, Mary, described her as one of the most unselfish people she had ever come across. She could be curt in demonstrating her clear likes and dislikes while 'anything like affectation or assumption she could not abide and few people continued to show either in her presence, and for anyone who gave themselves airs, it didn't happen twice – the airs vanished with remarkable rapidity!'[35]

From 1900 onwards she would take her holidays in Torquay, where she could be surrounded by her holidaying children and grandchildren. She was forever the centre of attention until finally succumbing on 28 December 1909 to an attack of bronchitis while in London.

She had played a long and central part in the family's improved fortunes, the growth of the collections and in support of her children's broad roles in their political, business and academic fields. She was laid to rest on top of a rocky bank overlooking the river at the Clifton Hampden church on her eighty-third birthday, on a bright sunny day.

6

'A soldier in every sense'

Lt-Gen. the Hon. Sir James Lindsay, 1815–74, and Lady Sarah Elizabeth Lindsay (née Savile), 1813–90

Unlike his elder and more academic brother, James grew into a sporting and spirited individual. Later photographs show a somewhat stiff-looking officer, but behind this formal exterior was a man who set out to enjoy himself when given the opportunity. He was well regarded by his fellow men: 'a wise man of the world and a soldier in every sense and highly esteemed by all ranks who had the advantage of knowing him.'[1] Those attributes served him well in his roles both as Commander-in-Chief of the British troops in Canada and Wigan's member of parliament.

40 During his remote Canadian posting, James saw fitness as a way to alleviate boredom, managing to run one mile in five minutes and two in twelve (*c.* 1861).

He and his younger brother Charles 'were wild boys, hard riders, at home in any company – all that their brother was not, although they both loved him.'[2] After leaving school at seventeen, James joined the Grenadiers with the help of the Duke of Wellington, a family friend.[3] His first emergency and presumably a most memorable time for any young subaltern came in 1834 when the Houses of Parliament burnt down and he as officer on guard was called upon to command his thirty-five men to help organize the firefighters.

Further afield, reformers in Canada were beginning to stir to the increasing clamour for republicanism, inspired by a zeitgeist that was responding to the American Revolutionary War, French Revolution, Chartists movement and the Irish rebellion. It was into this increasingly violent environment that the Grenadiers, in which James was now adjutant, were sent in 1838.

James's position kept him busy throughout his three-year tour but though he found some of the surroundings 'nobel' (*sic*), reminding him of Scotland, he and his fellow officers were less inspired by both the hostile Québécois and their 'nasty dirty' capital. The rebellion itself did not appear to cause too much of a problem. He described 'marching about in all directions' and having 'frightened all the world considerably but killed little but cows, sheep and poultry.'[4] His fellow soldiers began to suffer from the ennui that such postings can create, but he realized that taking his men on expeditions into the wilds could successfully raise morale. Making them feel occupied but comfortable back in barracks was also important, in addition to winning admiration from

41 Sarah, dressed for the Canadian winter, became one of Queen Victoria's women of the bed chamber. Her book, *A Few Choice Recipes Collected by Lady Sarah Lindsay*, received excellent reviews (*c.* 1865).

42 Lady Sarah, according to her father-in-law, Lord Bal, 'has plenty to say for herself, seems happy to make the best of things as they are – without the nicer delicacy of feeling which often gives so much pain. A capital wife for a soldier' (*c.* 1850).

the local inhabitants. He appeared to relish challenges. Writing home, he told of 'a very foolish match he was planning.' He had disagreed with a French Canadian's assertion that the local indigenous people's speed could not be matched by any white man. Throwing down the gauntlet, he practised hard, managing to cover one mile in five minutes and one second, and two miles in twelve minutes. Unfortunately, the local champion failed to turn up. Encouraging such fitness in his troops meant that their self-esteem, discipline and self-respect were well recognized by the Québécois: 'Now the ladies will hardly speak to anyone except a guardsman.'[5]

James's first term in Canada came to an end in 1841 and he returned home to Haigh. The locals celebrated to the band's rendition of 'See the Conqueror', dragging his carriage to the Hall after removing the horses. Shortly after, he married Lady Sarah Savile, his second cousin, daughter of John, 3rd Earl of Mexborough, the Tory politician.[6] The couple had three daughters, Mabel, Mary and Maud.[7]

As an excellent speaker with long-held interests in politics, James was soon asked to stand for parliament. He supported Robert Peel and was elected to represent Wigan. He also became involved in many of the contractual issues relating to Haigh Hall, the estate, and family coal and iron concerns, realizing that his ageing father and academic brother needed a firmer hand in handling negotiations. For many years he was the 'backbone of the administration.'[8]

This was the time when the call went up for the repeal of the Corn Laws. James was not especially committed either way and was relaxed about the alternative to the protectionist taxes and the country's eventual move to free trade. It turned out to be a popular stance as, combined with the family attempts to alleviate hunger in Wigan by authorizing the bakers to supply loaves to the needy, the town's wishes for repeal meant that he was asked to continue to represent them for nineteen years, even while continuing his military career.

43 Mabel, Mary and Maud with their father, Lt-Gen. James (*c.* 1860). They were shortly to return to Canada, where his role in consolidating the newly created dominion earned him a knighthood.

He returned to Canada with his family in 1861 when the United States and Britain were on the brink of war as a result of tensions over the Civil War. He was made commander of the troops in Canada East and was joined by Colonel Garnet Wolseley, who was to become one of the foremost Victorian generals. Threat of invasion eventually passed, allowing James to return to London in 1866, where he took on command of the City of London's foot guards. In 1870 he accepted his most important role as lieutenant-general back in Canada, where he was tasked with assisting the consolidation of the Red River region into the newly formed dominion. It was a potentially costly, dangerous and drawn-out affair over six hundred miles from headquarters, but with the able assistance of Wolseley they succeeded.

Secretary of State for War Edward Cardwell was delighted with James's service, which earned him a knighthood in the newly created order of St Michael and St George. He was also awarded the colonelcy of the 3rd Foot (The Buffs). On his return, he became Inspector General of Reserve Forces.[9] However, while serving as military secretary to Prince George, the Duke of Cambridge, Commander-in-Chief of the army, a health scare brought him to Cranmer House, Mitcham, where he died suddenly from an aortic aneurysm in August 1874, aged fifty-nine.[10]

7

'So manly bold and uncompromising'

Col. the Hon. Charles, 1816–89, and Emilia Anne Lindsay (née Browne), d. 1873

Although much loved by his parents, in boyhood 'Charlie' was regarded by his mother, Maria, Lady Bal, as a 'careless, thoughtless and headstrong boy who was always losing things; moreover, he did not have an honest turned mind in viewing things and was extravagant but was regarded as ornamental but loveable.'[1] The puritanical family looked askance at the growing prodigal's diamond rings and waistcoats and worried that such affectations would limit his chances of becoming the soldier he wished to be. Fortunately, he proved he was made of sterner stuff and in years to come this charismatic figure turned into someone who would earn respect from both his men and parents: 'I was far far wrong and take my hat off to him ... all I am told of my soldier sons is most gratifying.'

44 Charles's parents need not have worried about his affectations and extravagances as young man. He went on to prove himself in the wilds of Canada and battlefields of the Crimea (*c.* 1875).

Charles joined the 43rd Light Infantry, which had fewer temptations than the Guards and where he fitted in well. Like his elder brother, James, he was sent to Canada in 1838 but they saw little of each other as they were stationed 750 miles apart. But he made friends with a Colonel Jarvis, Superintendent of Indian Affairs, who took him on his annual visit to a settlement on Lake Huron, probably Manatoulin Island:[2]

Picture yourself a very dark night and about 3 or 400 Wigwams together each with a fire blazing before the door kindled by the squaws who on hearing of our approach told their husbands (always lay sleeping inside). They instantly rushed gun in hand to the point of landing and falling in a single rank of 1,000 opened as it were a most brilliant feu de joie *as a compliment to their Father Jarvis.*[3]

He remained with them a fortnight, by which time he found the filth beyond description. However, it appears that the local people, the Anishinaabe, seemed happy with their lot and made 'chiefly expressions of gratitude for all the kindness their great mother the Queen had shown them.'[4] His colonel wrote approvingly to his mother, Lady Bal: 'I can assure your ladyship that a finer or more truly amiable young man never joined the 43rd Regiment. The more I know of him the more I have reason to admire and esteem him.'[5]

After spending three years deep in the Canadian forest, Charles was ready to return home. But he had made an impression. Even though he had been living in such a rugged environment, it was commented

45 *opposite* An accomplished artist herself, Violet became a prominent member of the Souls and model for Burne-Jones, Watts, Millais and Queen Victoria (*c.*1878).

46 Charles's career led him from Canada to the Crimea and from parliament to groom-in-waiting to Queen Victoria (*c.*1880).

that 'it is rare to meet a character at once so manly bold and uncompromising – so tender, so full of refined feelings, yet without a particle of sentimentality.' His hard work was rewarded with the adjutancy of his regiment.

In 1852 he was sent to the Crimea, where he commanded the 3rd battalion and fought in all three of the campaign's main battles as well as playing his part in the siege of Sebastopol. At the fearsome Battle of Inkerman, he was fully engaged on the frontline. One of his fellow officers recorded witnessing Charles, 'who was most gallantly leading a charge. The Russians were by now in full retreat and we kept picking up ammunition from the dead and dying, and firing it into the masses, without exaggeration, 20 times our number; we were joined by men of all sorts of regiments, and pushed on at them, slaughtering them most fearfully.'[6]

Lord Raglan handed Charles the nightmare task of setting up a supply port at Balaclava, where he was to replace its Russian governor. He wrote home:

Balaclava is a mighty chaos. Lots to eat, no end of clothes, and other comforts not eight miles off. The Army starves within reach of plenty. Balaclava, where the utmost profusion prevails, is the scene of reckless waste; potatoes and onions – the most valuable food for our poor fellows, lie rotting on the beach, etc. An extra blanket has been furnished to half the battalion and then you have to remember they have to make their bed on the hard and muddy ground. Men often eat salt pork raw.[7]

These experiences meant he later lent his weight in support of his cousin Robert[8] and Florence Nightingale in the organization that was to become the British Red Cross Society.

Prior to the Crimean War he had married the 'winning, coaxing playful thing that carried all hearts by storm', Emilia Anne Browne, daughter of the dean of Lismore. It was a successful marriage, although she died young, leaving him a widower for sixteen years and with two children, Violet and Henry. The latter joined the Gordon Highlanders, following his father's and cousins' military careers.[9]

In later years, Charles and Emilia lived at Ardington House on the Lockinge estate, which belonged to his cousin Robert. Charles served as MP for Abingdon for ten years from 1865[10] and went on to play an active role in the Volunteer Movement, in particular with the Haigh Volunteers, another of his cousin's successful initiatives. He raised and long commanded the 6th Middlesex (St George's) Volunteer Rifle Corps, which consisted mainly of tradesmen. In 1880, after retirement from active duties, he was appointed groom-in-waiting to the Queen.[11]

As a striking bearded individual, it was perhaps inevitable that he would be chosen to sit for various artists. Princess Louise, fourth daughter of Queen Victoria, painted and exhibited one such portrait at his cousin Coutts's Grosvenor Gallery in 1889. *The Illustrated London News* commented: 'The place of honour in the room is given to Princess Louise's portrait of the late Colonel Charles Lindsay … He is represented in this picture … in a very heavy suit of mail – which nevertheless, brings out in good relief his manly, but modern head.'

Their daughter, Violet, became one of the great society figures of her generation.[12] She was both a beauty and feted by critics for her artistic talent. When Charles first saw her drawings, he asked his friend,

47 Violet and her daughter Victoria Marjorie Manners, later Marchioness of Anglesey and an art historian of some note (*c.* 1886).

48 Violet lived a seemingly charmed and gilded life, but it was forever overshadowed by the death of her first son, Haddon, aged just nine (*c.* 1900).

Edward Burne-Jones, to teach her. His recommendation was: 'Do not give her lessons, let her make studies of herself before a looking glass. She will never find a more sedate model to sit for her.'[13] She became a model for Burne-Jones himself, as well as many of the other leading artists of the period, including George Frederic Watts, John Everett Millais, Sir James Jebusa Shannon, Sir Edward Poynter and even Queen Victoria in 1877.

Inevitably, she attracted many suitors, but it was Lord Henry Manners, later the 8th Duke of Rutland, 'one of the most remarkably handsome and well-favoured of men',[14] whom she married. The peerless couple appeared to be blessed but they would start to move in different directions – he preferred to hunt, fish or spend afternoons and evenings in the House of Lords. Even their daughter, Diana, later celebrated in her own right and as Duff Cooper's wife,[15] saw him as something of a philistine with no interest in or knowledge of the family history or their considerable art collection at Belvoir Castle.

The couple's emotional separation was not helped by the tragic loss of their eldest son, Robert Charles, known as Haddon, aged just nine. This led Violet to immerse herself in her other children and art, almost obsessing over one of her most accomplished and poignant pieces, a white marble sculpture of her son, that took over thirty years for her to feel it was finished.[16] Understandably, it led her to be increasingly protective over her second son, John Henry, especially in attempting to ensure that he was put in less danger during the war.

Her gender and rank limited the public's consideration for her work. However, it was displayed widely, including at the Royal Academy, the New Gallery and the Tate. She was inevitably drawn to the group known as 'The Souls'. Here was an escape from the tensions of politics; they were 'bent on pleasure, but pleasure of a superior kind, eschewing the vulgarities of racing and card-playing indulged in by the majority of the rich and noble, and looking for their excitement in romance and sentiment.'[17] Other members included George Curzon, Percy Wyndham and Henry Cust, with whom she had a long relationship and who was rumoured to have fathered her daughter, Diana. Violet would become known as the 'queen' of the Souls.

During the First World War, both Belvoir and their two London houses were made available for the war effort. No. 16 Arlington Street became the Rutland Hospital for Officers and her bedroom the operating theatre, while the ballroom and gilded drawing room were turned into wards. The castle became a military convalescent home for officers. She ran them both.

Much of Violet's legacy lies in her finely captured portraits. They depict many of the famed figures of her age, but only those whom she found interesting or relevant. Her own striking Pre-Raphaelite looks were immortalized by many artists, including George Frederic Watts, whose portrait of her was regarded as one of his most important, so it was fitting that many of her works ended up in the Watts Gallery, which is dedicated to him.[18] She held her last exhibition aged eighty-one at the Russell-Cotes Art Gallery and Museum in Bournemouth.

8

One of the 'hot headed ones'

The Hon. Colin Lindsay, 1819–92, and Lady Frances Lindsay (née Howard), 1821–97

Colin Lindsay neither inherited the privileges of his eldest brother, Lord Lindsay, who was able to lead a deeply intellectual life, nor did he wish to follow his others into a military career. But he did share both the former's scholarly approach and the latter brothers' courage by pursuing passionately held convictions for religious and social change in the face of heavy opposition.

49 Colin's older brother, Lord Lindsay, gave him the opportunity to build Haighlands near the Hall in 1854, allowing him to take a deeper interest in local affairs.

50 Colin's passionately held spiritual vocation inspired his work with the poor in Wigan. It also led him to Catholicism, much to his parents' regret (*c.*1879).

Colin was very much his mother's spoilt favourite, and her principled, religious and strictly held views on all moral matters were to have a marked impact.[1] Accordingly, after Trinity College, Cambridge, where he came under the influence of the High Church movement, Colin returned to Haigh to take an active role in local affairs, recognizing how the economic climate was having such a dire effect on so many.[2] He occasionally suffered from nerves, which at one point led to a breakdown. But he was close to his eldest brother, who cared for him and eventually gave him land to build Haighlands, near the Hall.[3] Moreover, Colin showed bravery in overcoming this setback and used his new-found vocation to set about a number of initiatives to help relieve the burden of the many who were struggling. He succeeded in persuading his father to fund a host of enterprises, including a hospital with facilities for ageing or injured colliers, schools and libraries, cricket pitches and playgrounds along with organized outdoor activities. He also initiated flower and vegetable shows and encouraged improved farming practices by founding the Haigh Agricultural Society.

The turbulent times meant many started to question faith's relevance. This inevitably altered the influences of the Anglican Church as its direction was seen as increasingly secular and intertwined with the state and politics. The Oxford Movement, led by John Henry Newman and John Keble, appeared to provide an alternative, renewed spiritual direction which Colin enthusiastically embraced. The Oxford Movement's approach led him to Catholicism, something his ardent Protestant

51 Frances and Colin went on to have seven children. She was the eldest daughter of the 4th Earl of Wicklow and granddaughter of John, 1st Marquess of Abercorn (*c.* 1880).

parents had feared, although they recognized the moral value of the Movement. His mother had referred to them as 'the hot headed ones' and never completely came to terms with his eventual conversion in 1868. His support, though, led to the Pope granting him the rare privilege of being allowed to celebrate mass wherever he was living. His convictions, often derided as popish, led him to found the Manchester Church Society, which became the English Church Union in 1860, of which he was president for many years.[4] Much to his mother's regret, he remained a staunch champion of extreme papal claims, which he included in his *Evidence for the Papacy* and other works.[5]

The parishioners of Haigh clearly felt strong affection for Colin. In 1845 over a thousand appeared at the Hall to celebrate his return from his honeymoon after marrying Lady Frances Howard. He went on to rebuild their Wigan Parish Church, All Saints', where he became church warden. But perhaps a true sign of his steeliness and their support for him came when he called on them to form a force of local men, armed with pickaxes, to fend off the larger, more aggressive mobs who had marched on Wigan intent on causing maximum damage and disruption in pursuit of the Chartist cause.

When Frances inherited the Deer Park estate in Devon, Colin's family finally moved away from Haigh, which was probably something of a relief to his brother, Lord Lindsay, who was often called upon to smooth over arguments about faith with their mother. The couple started a Catholic Mission and held what was probably the first mass in the area since the Reformation.[6] Meanwhile, their family grew to nine strong. The eldest, William Alexander,[7] remained a member of the Church of England, but the younger brothers, Leonard and (now Revd) Claud, converted from the Anglican Church to Catholicism and erected a small church near the house. This was eventually replaced with a new, simple Gothic building where there is still a Lindsay Memorial Chapel.

52 Colin was the founding president of the English Church Union, which sought to defend and propagate High Church principles within the Church of England. It later became the Church Union (*c.* 1890).

53 *above left* Leonard became chamberlain to Popes Leo XIII, Pius X, Benedict XV and Pius XI (*c.* 1867).

54 *above right* The Very Revd Claud was appointed domestic chamberlain to Popes Leo XIII, Pius X and Benedict XV (*c.* 1865).

55 *left* William Lindsay became Windsor Herald, Norroy and Clarenceux King of Arms, the senior of the two English provincial Kings of Arms (*c.* 1911).

Dunecht

'Dear Dunecht!'

56 Additions to Dunecht saw an Italianate south side added to the original neo-Greek style building. In the 1870s the French-Italianate chapel, library and tower were added. The Lindsay mottoes and armorial chequer were incorporated into the garden balustrade and tower's cornice.

Balcarres had been the principal family seat since 1588, but by the late eighteenth century Alexander, 6th Earl of Balcarres, was in need of funds and saw his only alternative was to sell Balcarres to his brother Robert in order to capitalize on the mining opportunities around Haigh Hall. However, it left some family members with a sense of yearning for their Scottish roots.

Alexander's heir, James, Lord Bal, was no romantic and initially felt strongly that his son, Alexander, Lord Lindsay, was wasting time in researching so much into the family's Scottish history. Nonetheless, by the 1840s Lord Bal became enthusiastic about investing in land. 'I had a long conversation with my father last night ... and I find him strongly inclined to purchase land *now* – and in *Scotland* – with a leaning to *Forfarshire*, the original "*country*" of the Lindsays.'[1]

Dunecht was a classically Grecian-styled, grey granite, two-storied house that had been in the Forbes family since 1469, though recently rebuilt in the 1820s. Lord Bal saw this purely as an investment opportunity and was attracted by the idea that it was 'a get riddable property'. His son felt he would have a place of his own, where he could build on the ever-growing library, away from the soot and polluted air of Haigh. Eventually, in 1845, it was bought along with its 11,000-acre estate for £117,000 (£8.225m today). Fifty-six years after leaving for England, the chief of the Lindsay clan was back in Scotland.

A cousin's wife recorded her first impressions:

The railroad is only open as far as Montrose, so you have forty miles of posting to Aberdeen through remarkably bleak ugly uninteresting country ... I am very much pleased with this place, it is very much what I expected not the least beautiful, but extremely pleasant liveable, healthy and agreeable. It is astonishing how nice they have made the house. It had always plain substantial furniture, and they have added all that is required for comfort and ornament ... Lindsay is a marvel to me he is looking so well and so free from care. He seems to have lost all feeling of shyness and to perform his part of host with the greatest courtesy and composure. He never reads or studies, but his whole time is employed in amusing himself ... He is becoming a most excellent forester.[2]

57 Lord Lindsay's dream to move his library to the new vaulted and galleried extension at Dunecht was never realized. The Cowdray family, who bought the house in 1912, referred to the room as the Ballroom.

58 Dunecht was the favourite summer destination for all generations from the 24th to 27th earls of Crawford.

And Lady Mary Meynell recalled in her memoirs:

How we loved Dunecht! Our yearly move was a big business and we all went as far as Edinburgh the first night, from Haigh in Lancashire, and on to Aberdeen next day. Oh! How dusty and dirty railway carriages were in those days! – and how the trains crept as they got farther north, and how good the Baps were at Perth Station – and how delightful it was to hear the guard's first strong Scotch accent shouting Lockerbie! Lockerbie! – and how welcome Stonehaven sounded at the last stop – and how we crawled after that till we got to Aberdeen, where a twelve-miles' drive awaited us – and then, how glad we were for Home and Tea! – and dear Dunecht![3]

In Lord Lindsay's letter to his ageing uncle and aunt, General James and Anne, inviting them to stay once more, he painted a picture of the surrounding country:

Do come and soon or all the heather will be over. The new walk and drive have succeeded to perfection, the Finnin haddocks are prime, grouse, snipe all smoking on the sideboard, new novels from Wyllies', and a decent pianoforte from Marr's, my father enchanted with the place, rambling about and discovering new beauties everywhere ... The weather is beautiful, bright sunshine, without a cloud, but a pure fresh air, almost intoxicating with its lightness, and the whole place fragrant with the pines, with long streams of light rambling up into the hills where our cuttings have taken effect.[4]

In 1855 William Smith, an Aberdeen architect, was employed to oversee considerable extensions to the house including a prominent tower. A frieze around the outside of the house was added, carved with a three-banded chequer design using elements of the Lindsay coat of arms' fess chequy along with family mottoes.

Lord Lindsay fully embraced his role as laird. He always made sure that the whole retinue of staff would join the family each morning and come together for Sunday evening prayers. 'My Father read and knelt at the central table ... All the Estate Presbyterian people loved coming to evening service and streams of chairs overflowing down the corridor were needed.'[5]

59 Dunecht photographed by George Washington Wilson in 1880. Having worked for Queen Victoria, Wilson became one of Scotland's foremost photographers of the second half of the nineteenth century. © University of Aberdeen

60 Rafting on Dunecht's Policy Loch. From left: Edith Bootle-Wilbraham, Ronald, Bal, Eddie, Gelasio Caetani, Robin and Walter (1888).

There had been a dance each year at Haigh or in London, but in 1871 a great ball was held. The family had now been there for over twenty-five years so were very much part of local society. All their nearby friends and dignitaries were invited and the local estate workers and villagers were encouraged to come and view the preparations – many of whom stayed until dawn. 'Altogether, the entertainment was of a character, as regards extent and splendour, such as, we believe, has not been witnessed in the county of Aberdeen for many years.'[6]

For some time Lord Lindsay had become increasingly unhappy with the effects of the pollution around Haigh. It wasn't just a health hazard to the family – he believed the conditions must have been damaging the rare books. He proposed to build a new wing in the 'Italico-Lombard style' at Dunecht and create a hall, some hundred feet long and fifty feet wide, capable of containing the entire library. Light would flood down from skylights on to a gallery, reached by two spiral staircases. These would run around the whole room as all the walls, apart from a large bow window, would be devoted to books. 'The Library thus constructed should bear an aspect, thoroughly comfortable indeed, but still that of a sanctuary of learning and thought, sacred to the Muses, where men and women may meet in converse on the common ground of graceful cultivation.'[7] George Street was chosen to be the architect of the library as well as a church.[8]

Other changes were also made throughout the building to modernize it. When the family had first arrived, they discovered that much of the staff's accommodation dated back to a previous era. On one side of the kitchen was a flush wall with cupboards concealing a recess which contained their beds, for example. Although this arrangement was quite likely warm and no doubt comfortable, with no air or ventilation, Lord Lindsay's wife, Min, thought it was beneath them, so she bought them new beds. 'It was a fond illusion – they came and besought her to be allowed to sleep in their cupboards!'[9] However, events out of their control meant new arrangements were forced upon them.

One night in early November 1872, a fire broke out in the kitchen wing. The butler was the first on the scene and immediately 'endeavoured to extinguish the fire by means of *L'Extincteur*.'[10] Lindsay heard cries coming from the third floor and bravely dashed in and saved two of the servants from a room filled with smoke and fire. Word was sent to Aberdeen for a fire engine to support the house's existing fire pump, desperately drawing water from the fountains, while the staff and estate workers, who had heard the alarm and seen the fire light up the sky, carried water buckets in and valuables out. By dawn the kitchens and staff wing were completely destroyed by water or gutted by flames. Fortunately, the rest of the house and new wings were unaffected.

Over this period Lord Lindsay and his son, Ludovic, were putting together what became the world's greatest collections of scientific books. As it grew, so did Ludovic's fascination and expertise in astronomy. With clear skies and long winter nights it was the perfect environment to site an observatory. Work had started in 1870 and soon recordings were being published in regular 'Dun Echt Circulars', which were distributed internationally to all the world's major observatories and centres of research.

In December 1880, after returning to Europe from Egypt, Lord Lindsay became ill and died of bronchitis and pneumonia. As was his wish, his body was returned to Dunecht, where it was interred in the recently built church's crypt. However, within a year the family received devastating news that his body had been stolen. It was not until the following year that his embalmed body was found, as if sleeping, in nearby woodland, just five hundred yards from the house. He was reburied in the family vault in Wigan.[11]

Such deeply disturbing events and their memories meant that Ludovic lost much of his love for Dunecht. Furthermore, the great library wing had not been completed when Street died in 1881 and so in the end the books were never moved north. The general economic depression which ran from 1883 to 1886 meant the family were finding it hard to maintain both great houses, and there was now a chance that he could buy Balcarres back from his

cousin, Coutts. Decisions had to be made. Which houses could they keep? Haigh was far more accessible to scholars and Ludovic also felt there would be fewer like-minded people who would make the long journey north, and so in 1886 he reluctantly decided to sell. The uncompleted library would become known as the Ballroom. He decided to buy Balcarres back.

In 1888 a plan was mooted to abolish the Royal Observatory of Edinburgh due to lack of funds. That such a central institution in the world of astronomy could be terminated was deeply troubling to Ludovic. Accordingly, he gave the entirety of the Dunecht scientific library, along with all its apparatus, to the observatory on condition that the government continued to fund its operation.

A strong bond had grown between many of the staff and the Lindsays. On their final visit to Dunecht, after Lord Lindsay's body had been recovered, some of the family paid a last visit to Mrs Yoeman, widow of their house steward. They had gone through so many changes and had shared in the memories and grief of the recent horrors. Jane described the scene:

A great cry burst from the other's lips she drew herself to her full height both arms high above her head and tottered forward to be held close in mothers arms – the dignity of sorrow in both was almost unbearable. I weep now only thinking of it.

She further recorded the family's last night in the dark building: 'in contrast with its crowded happier days they heard men and women's voices outside in the darkness. They had gathered by loving impulse and were singing Auld Lang Syne.'

Dunecht remained unsold for a further fourteen years until a local developer, A. C. Pirie, paid £97,000 for it (approximately £7.6 million today). He made a number of alterations, including a new conservatory and dining room before leasing to the brilliant engineer and industrialist, Weetman Pearson, in 1907. Eventually, the whole estate was sold to him in 1912. He, by then, had been made Baron Cowdray, before becoming the 1st Viscount Cowdray in 1917.

9

'A decided soldier'

Lt-Gen. Sir James, 1791–1855, and Anne Lindsay (née Trotter), 1803–94

One of the few surviving photographs of General James Lindsay shows an affable figure relaxing at Balcarres with his grandson, Ludovic,[1] who is seated on a small pony. As a seasoned veteran of the Napoleonic Wars and a politician during the great agricultural and reform disputes, his experiences made him ideally suited to act as mentor to his heirs.

James's father, Robert, wrote about his sons to his brother-in-law, the 3rd Earl of Hardwicke, prior to a visit to Balcarres in 1807: 'You will find them lads of a good disposition with affable manners ... Take an opportunity of sounding them as to their progress in general learning ... You will find them greatly behind boys of their own age who have had all the advantages of a regular English education ... James is ... a decided soldier. Between 17 and 18 I propose giving him a commission in the Guards, and in the meantime to improve his education.'[2]

61 Anne, General Sir James, and Lord and Lady Lindsay on the balcony at Balcarres. This collodion calotype (salt print from a wet-plate collodion negative) was taken by Thomas Rodger (1832–83), who studied at St Andrews, ten miles from Balcarres, under Dr John Adamson, who made the first calotype in Scotland. Adamson's brother Robert, along with David Octavius Hill, made the town, and Scotland, a centre for the development of photography (1855).

Later that year, as suggested by his father, James did join the Grenadiers. He soon experienced his first action in the disastrous 1809 Walcheren Expedition to the Netherlands, part of a failed attempt to aid Austria's struggle with France. While there was little fighting, the young ensign came down with the 'Walcheren fever'. Over four thousand died of what turned out to be malaria. He was nursed back to health in London by his aunt, the diarist Lady Anne Barnard (née Lindsay), who prescribed port among other remedies to prevent further outbreaks of the fever.[3] Over the years nephew and aunt became ever closer, as though he was the son she never had. 'I loved her as a mother and so did all who dwelt under her roof.'[4]

The Peninsular War followed and, although not fully recovered, James joined his regiment as it was despatched to Cadiz, where the army was besieged for two-and-a-half years. There he witnessed the dreadful conditions that were a hallmark of a campaign in which over a million people perished.[5] At one hospital he found many dying from a basic lack of medical support or food. Once the siege was lifted, it was the heat, dust and gruellingly long marches, fifteen to twenty miles a day, that took their toll on many, while the winter months were equally debilitating. The soldiers' lack of basic rations, woefully inadequate clothing and sixty-pound backpacks took their toll: 'many men dropped by the road-side and died'.[6] But his spirits remained high as did his affection for his men. He described the English soldier as someone who was 'very humane and will never take life except in the

62 Probably the earliest photograph of Balcarres (*c.*1850), showing the Burns additions to the right (west), but taken before Coutts and Bryce added the northern dining room and two-storey studio.

heat of resistance.' James was fortunate as the British consul in Cadiz, Sir James Duff, was a relation and close friend of his father: 'he then took me to the best room in his large house, and opening the door, said, "This is your room so long as you stay in Cadiz – none other than yourself shall occupy it."'[7]

James met his Field Marshal, Viscount Wellington (who would be made duke in 1814) at a dinner after the relief of Cadiz. He was much struck by being 'one of the handsomest men I had ever seen … his lordly mien would have marked him amidst a thousand.'[8] James later distinguished himself at the capture of Seville and during the bloody scenes at Salamanca. Eventually, he was wounded at the Battle of Vitoria when Wellington broke Joseph Bonaparte's army. Extraordinarily, his life was saved through his being a freemason. He was lying, unable to move, when a man came wandering among the wounded. James made the masonic sign as a desperate gesture. The man recognized this sign and immediately responded, taking him to his home where he nursed him back to health.[9] On recovering James rejoined the campaign in Holland. However, he was injured again at the siege of Bergen-op-Zoom, where his wounds were bad enough for a leg amputation to be considered, preventing him from appearing at Waterloo.[10]

Less demanding London duties followed, including a command of a detachment of the Grenadiers Guards in 1821 for the coronation of George IV. While on duty, James witnessed the unedifying attempts made by the troubled but popular Queen Caroline to gain access to Westminster Hall: 'A desperate courage seemed to animate her and unsuccessful she returned to her carriage, a malignant fury personified, her countenance quite convulsed with rage.'[11]

His regiment remained close to his heart: 'In truth I put on my red coat again as welcome as I would enter home … such are the natural interests which bind us together who have struggled through difficulties and dangers, in mutual dependence of course, for support in case of need.' His last posting before retiring from the army was to London during the Reform Bill riots in 1830, where he and his men were billeted in the then half-finished Buckingham Palace. 'A curious party – the first assembled in this far-famed palace.'

He had married Mary Anne Grant in 1819 but she died within seventeen months. In 1823 he met and married Anne ('Nan' or 'Dona') Trotter, who had 'barely left the schoolroom',[12] the granddaughter of Archibald Trotter, a partner in the banking firm of Coutts & Trotter. James's father saw her as 'certainly a distinguished being both in head and heart as well as looks. Nan's perfect independence of everybody and everything is extraordinary – everything proposed is agreeable – she is ready to work, read or walk as others are inclined.' As well as being warmly sociable, she was cultivated.

Anne's first impressions of Balcarres were not auspicious:

The manners and customs, and the standard of domestic life in Scotland, differed from what then prevailed in England, and the bride's first impressions of her Scottish home thus were not altogether favourable. Strings of herrings hung up to dry on the house walls were a shock to her refined habits; the homely family life, the companionship of rigid-minded, puritanical maiden sisters-in-law, the society of the rough witted relatives and inmates who formed the usual entourage of Scottish households in those days, were uncongenial to the young wife fresh from the polished literary and artistic circle of her father's house. But later on, she learnt to love and appreciate to the full the charm and beauty of Balcarres.[13]

On the death of his uncle, Alexander, 6th Earl of Balcarres, in 1825, James filled the Wigan parliamentary vacancy and stood unopposed in the following year's election. He would later vote for the retention of corporal punishment in the army, the 'most uncontrollable body of men in the community'.[14] Clearly, he had come around to his old commander-in-chief's point of view. When the Reform Bill, which he opposed, began to be debated, he realized that Wigan was a lost cause, so he abandoned the seat in favour of one in Fife. 'I shall glory in the fight whether successful or not, for I am

surrounded by the best of Fife, the loyal and true.' And so, even in a climate of considerable intimidation, he was elected by eighty-five to sixty-nine, though the Whigs took the country and passed their Reform Act. He was less fortunate in the 1835 election, which was even more violent. On one occasion, after he had been struck and spat on, he seized the offender, 'lugged him into the house where he was identified, examined by a magistrate and convicted of the assault ... we then let him go as "a rescue" would have been the cry had we not done so.'[15]

Having retired from the army and mainstream politics and to avoid William Burns's building works at Balcarres, he and Anne started travelling. Their son Coutts, aged fourteen, had recently become ill, so they decided that a change of climate would also do him good. Journeys between Fife and London were usually made by sea, the family sitting most of the time in their carriage, lashed to the deck. Dundee was their nearest port and thirty-nine hours to London was considered 'an excellent passage'. A typical party might have consisted of the family, coachman, two grooms, two footmen, four maids and five horses. The housekeeper and the other maids went by rail.

Anne described how they were welcomed home after their longest tour that had taken them abroad from 1838 to 1841:

You cannot imagine what a pretty sight it was. They had carried two little cannons up to the top of the Craig and you heard them firing from time to time and saw curling white smoke while the people were waving their flags and shouting – all kindness and good humour.[16]

Their carriages were unhitched from the horses' harnesses and the strongest of the seven hundred villagers vied with one another to pull them up to the house.

On the Continent they travelled by carriage, and on occasion on foot with Anne riding alongside, sometimes in the company of their future son-in-law, Lord Lindsay, to whom they had become close – 'God in heaven bless you dearest Anne' the young protégé would write later, 'spiritually – temporally – in your husband – in your children – in yourself. I always pray for you – for your earthly, for your heavenly welfare.'

It was on these sojourns that many of the artworks were bought. Italians' straitened finances drove owners to sell to the ready market. But, as Anne

63 General James with his grandson, James Ludovic, later 26th Earl of Crawford (*c.*1852).

wrote, 'we might have bought a great many more if it were not for the duties on entering England which are immense and pictures are not easily smuggled ... James thought he might put one a yard square in the back of his coat.' With prices low, they 'picked up some beautiful pieces of old furniture for Balcarres – marqueterie [*sic*], carved wood and marble tables, commodes, chairs, etc.' They had to hire a whole vessel to bring the pictures home.[17]

After years of war in Europe, crop failures and the inevitable social unrest associated with the Highlands Clearances and enclosures, much change was inevitable.[18] James felt his approach to farming needed to be as much for the welfare for its workforce as it was for the family's. He thus formed an agricultural association for the protection of property rights and ensured that agricultural instruction was included in schools which 'hitherto has been entirely neglected for Latin and Greek.' He introduced the allotment system to Scotland and led movements to improve the sanitary and social conditions of the labourers. In particular, he sought changes to the bothy system, the degrading arrangement whereby married and unmarried labourers cohabited in often filthy, wretched huts.

At the outbreak of the Crimean War in 1853, the retired general became increasingly agitated by the disastrous disorganization in the forces from the top down. The inefficiencies, particularly in clothing, logistics and supplies, as well as dire medical aid were set to destroy a great army, but no one would listen to his and others' proposed remedies, which included the dismissal of Lord Raglan. Foremost in his mind, born out of experience, was Robert's involvement in the campaign. He advised: 'Do not at present volunteer danger, especially the storming parties against Sebastopol. Do not continue that system of total disregard of danger which the Duke (of Cambridge) speaks as being your characteristic ... Recollect I do not give you leave to volunteer anything in fighting.'

In 1855 James went to visit a great panorama painted to celebrate the battle where his young son's efforts had earned him the Victoria Cross:

I did not know till this morning that I was troubled with tender feelings, or delicate sympathies, or liable to make a fool of myself from such causes. But I went today to see the panorama of the Alma, and as I first looked upon the representation of that bloody field, the Guards in the foreground, and so many of them lying prostrate ... and our gallant boy the prominent figure in the foreground, raising the standard of England in the midst of the fight, looking boldly aloft in contempt of the danger surrounding him, I began to see indistinctly, and walked away to the other side of the room.[19]

The last photograph we have of the old soldier was taken on 5 March 1855 on the balcony at Balcarres alongside his wife, Lord Lindsay and Min (see page 71). Later that year they set out for Villa Palmieri but only got as far as Genoa, where he died in December 1855. The malaria contracted on Walcheren expedition had returned.[20] It meant that he missed the chance to witness his son receive the Victoria Cross from the Queen.

James's granddaughter Jane's description of Anne conjures up the clearest picture of the strong matriarch:

She was very modest but never stopped to question what she was. Her impetuosity swept all before it. She was generous, intensely Patriotic, too narrowly a Tory, passionately sympathetic with the poor on whose behalf

64 Anne was described as intensely patriotic, passionately sympathetic, prejudiced, lovable and most rousing to live with (*c.* 1870).

she would bestir herself and everybody else – very prejudiced and determined to dislike if her instinct led her to do so. She was extremely lovable and most rousing to live with. She was very well read and a close critic ... she was not a bit feminine in the sense of how to tend a sick person, nor in any sense a 'real mother' – her kiss was a quick peck ... She didn't care a farthing about comfort and personal vanity was unknown to her ... Nature was intoxicating to her ... but unimproved by man.

Mabel was also much taken with her grandmother, whom she described as an 'ever potent factor of our lives. She was an admirable educator to young minds for she woke up the intelligence of her companions and ... was a fierce critic.'[21] 'She was an ardent and fierce politician, with a vehement dislike of Mr Gladstone's policies. Her cheek would flush and her eyes flash and she would stamp her stick in fiery wrath over his misdemeanours. She had many interests, botany, astronomy, natural science, geology.'

In her final years Anne wintered at Palmieri, with her summers divided between Balcarres, the Holford's Westonbirt or Ardington House near Robert's Lockinge, where she died in 1894 aged ninety-one, her intellect as strong as ever. Her sons, Coutts and Robert, had both followed their father into the army and worked at improving estate management while all their offspring, including their daughters May and Min, developed a similarly deep interest in fine art.

65 The seasoned soldier, politician and collector General James became the mentor of both the 25th and 26th earls of Crawford (1855).

10

'He keeps me in a constant state of terror'

Sir Coutts Lindsay, 1824–1913, and Blanche, Lady Lindsay (née Fitzroy), 1844–1914, and Kate Harriet Lindsay (née Burfield), 1850–1937

Coutts Lindsay was undoubtedly handsome, dressed unusually stylishly and clearly nurtured a romantic style of his own. This led him to follow less orthodox paths in his private life, the army and art world, though unhealthy distractions and dissoluteness threatened his lasting reputation.[1]

He was born at Brandsbury Park, owned by his maternal grandfather and namesake, Sir Coutts Trotter, who in turn was named after his godfather, Thomas Coutts, the founder of the private bank. As he had no sons the baronetcy was, by special remainder, passed to Coutts, the eldest grandson.[2] His early years were, however, not encouraging. He became spoilt and was reportedly indolent at school, so even though he had learned to read by the age of five, his lack of progress became a cause for concern. He was sent to Paris with a tutor in 1838 but contracted a serious neurological disease that caused alarming rabid-like fits, which were traumatic for the boy and frightening to the parents and doctors. Various remedies were tried – including *nux vomica*, which contains strychnine – with mixed results.

66 Sir Coutts Lindsay by Julia Margaret Cameron. Her first museum exhibition was held at the South Kensington Museum. Albumen print from wet collodion glass negative (1865).

During building work at Balcarres the family moved to Italy as part of his recuperation.[3] This triggered what became a lifelong passion for the country and its art. He had the perfect mentor in his cousin and future brother-in-law, Lord Lindsay,[4] who encouraged his artistic skills and wrote that he could 'see no earthly reason why he should not be a second Benozzo Gozzoli'. But while he often initially showed great enthusiasms for learning, he inevitably gave up. Some areas, such as spelling, he found impossible, perhaps indicating undiagnosed dyslexia.

A long-held wish to join the Grenadiers, even with the support of his father, was still going to be difficult until he properly matured, but he was finally accepted. The strict regime was exactly what was needed, although he remained inconsiderate. Coming from a strict background, reports of self-indulgences such as laziness, selfishness and even unkindness remained of concern. He was, meanwhile, proving to be an aesthete (he decorated the guard room with frescoes when stationed at Windsor), while his bohemian streak attracted him to the theatrical world more than his fellow officers, whose drunken behaviour appalled him. Having never been to public school, he had not learnt how to fit in to the officers' mess and became the outsider among them.[5] As a diversion, but with a rare streak of enthusiasm, he started to write, and even finish, some plays. *The Black Prince* was the only one that was published.

As a handsome young officer who often attended seven balls a week, gambling and young ladies became his biggest temptations. The latter got him

67 Coutts had success as a soldier but abhorred his fellow officers' philistinism. The talented artist found his métier in the company of the Pre-Raphaelite Brotherhood, William Makepeace Thackeray and George Frederic Watts, with whom he could pursue a more liberal and creative life (*c.*1860).

68 Blanche Fitzroy shared Coutts's artistic interests and brought a Rothschild inheritance to their marriage, allowing them to enlarge Balcarres and finance the Grosvenor Gallery. Inevitably, his affairs ended their marriage and his ownership of both house and gallery (*c.*1860).

into trouble; one Lizzie Chambers was left to bring up two unwanted sons, George and Coutts Lindsay Chambers. He refused to marry her, though he ensured she was taken care of financially. In 1850 his sister Min had written: 'To me he seems like some beautiful many-branched flower which straggles all over the bed ... a good gardener would tie these branches to a stake and so form a beautiful mass of colour and stand firm and united – what Coutts wants is that stake.'[6] His true love lay in art, so on his twenty-sixth birthday he gave up his commission and travelled to Italy to work under the artist Ary Scheeffer.

By early 1855 Coutts was beginning to feel frustrated that he was not out in the Crimea with many of his contemporaries. His mother noticed his restlessness and was concerned that he was spending too much time with figures such as Leighton and 'a pack of effeminate artists'.[7] Fortunately, with the backing of the Italian statesman Camillo Benson, Count of Cavour, he was asked as a foreign officer to recruit and command the Lombard Regiment in the Italian Legion. Surprisingly, he turned out to be a remarkably able officer and, employing new-found charm and charisma, managed to put together a respectful force.

His father warned that it 'would be hard to maintain discipline among these wild Italians'. Incidents that preceded his command meant mutinous tendencies had developed. But with some cunning he was able to quash a conspiracy of five hundred men and slowly turned them into a first-class unit which distinguished itself fighting the French army at the Battle of Chernaya in 1855. Their valiant effort contributed to their country's inclusion at the negotiating table at the end of the war.

Coutts had enjoyed many aspects of military life and, having proven himself, he happily accepted the command of the Fife Volunteers, a position he held for over twenty years. But his mother Anne remained concerned, writing in 1856 to Lord Lindsay:

69 The photographer David Wilkie Wynfield was the founder of the St John's Wood clique. For their own entertainment, escaping into the past, they dressed up in historical costume. Coutts was not a member but would join in, donning his own armour. Albumen print (1865).

He is very kind and affectionate in manner. But he keeps me in a constant state of terror. He is so different from all of us. So liberal minded – so full of progress – looks down upon all of us as old-fashioned, narrow-minded people who cannot keep up with the necessities of the age.[8]

He was again spending a lot of time with a group of artists who were regarded as unconventional, some of whom became members of the Pre-Raphaelite Brotherhood, William Makepeace Thackeray, Edward Burne-Jones, Alfred Tennyson, Dante Gabriel Rossetti and Julia Margaret Cameron.

While his family continued looking for a suitable bride, Coutts did his best to avoid their temptations and instead in 1857 headed to Rome to join Lord and Lady Somers, painting, photographing and writing in an ever-cosier *ménage à trois.* Lady Somers showed some of his improving drawings to Lord Lansdowne, who could scarcely believe that they were not by a great master. He then turned his attention to ceramics and provided design work for Thomas Goode (Minton's London retailers), including a plaque painted with a scene of mermaids for the International Exhibition of 1862 that harked back to Italian Renaissance majolica.

It was timely that Caroline Blanche 'Blanchy' Fitzroy appeared in about 1864 as his financial responsibilities in Scotland were mounting. She was a granddaughter of Nathan Mayer Rothschild, one of the five brothers who had, like the five arrows in their crest, been sent out across Europe. Nathan went to London, where he built up one part of the dynasty's fabulous fortunes. His daughter, Hanna, had been looking to get Blanche married and by now she was beginning to despair. Blanche may have been in denial about the much older Coutts's other female friends, in particular Lady Somers, and various illegitimate children. However, she fell in love with a man whose artistic passions matched hers and who possessed skills she could admire. Coutts' cousin, Jane, described her as 'a clever, amusing, very high spirited girl who spoke in an almost inaudible *falsetto* and would suddenly burst into shattering laugh as of a train shooting, whistling, out of a tunnel – peal upon peal emitted by a very strong sense of humour.'[9] It was rumoured that Lady Somers' encouragement of the marriage would draw a cloak of respectability over her intimacy with him, though one wonders how enthusiastic he was.[10]

Their circle of friends included many creative minds. A photograph of Coutts in shining armour taken around 1865 by Wilkie Wynfield illustrates his enthusiasm for one of his expressive group's leanings. The pioneering photographer Julia Margaret Cameron captured him too and later credited him as having had the greatest influence on her own work. He had striking looks – somewhat romantic and dashing, noble yet informal, good-looking even though now clearly beginning to age. He was very much a ladies' man, with a winning smile and an ability to make any woman he spoke to feel special.

Part of the marriage settlement allowed him to undertake even greater works at Balcarres, especially with the Italianate garden terraces and a new north wing.[11] It was not yet the comfortable home that it was soon to become. The couple's daughters Effie (Euphemia) and Helen lived on the top floor with

70 After consulting William Holman Hunt and Sir John Millais, Coutts and Blanche employed the Balcarres gardener, Robert Adamson, to transform the south-facing terraced gardens to David Bryce's designs (*c.* 1890).

71 Blanche never fitted in with 'Old Scotland' and instead would invite her artistic friends to stay, including W. S. Gilbert's writing partner, Arthur Sullivan (*c.* 1875).

72 For a period, Coutts and Blanche were at the heart of society and entertained frequently at Balcarres. His artistic talents were in demand, while his Grosvenor Gallery's electricity generators allowed regular evening soirées in its uniquely lit rooms (*c.* 1865).

a French governess, where they were made to have baths in sea water brought up in casks from Elie.[12] When it was cold, they had to break ice in the jugs to wash in the morning. Fortunately, steady improvements meant that the family were able to start to entertain more comfortably.

Blanche found it hard to share the house with her widowed mother-in-law, particularly with the little support she received from her husband, and as she did not fit in with 'Old Scotland', she filled the house more with her entertaining and society types than family. For instance, none of Coutts's family were invited for the visit of Queen Victoria's youngest son, Prince Leopold, which saddened Coutts, even though he found him the least interesting member of the royal family. The visit was particularly wearying as this guest was only amused when flattered. The composer Arthur Sullivan (the dramatist W. S. Gilbert's partner), another regular guest, was loath to keep playing for the demanding prince, but relief came with a message from Queen Victoria, who gave orders that her son should not dance due to illness – a relief to Coutts, too, who was tiring of being made to repeatedly rearrange the furniture to make space. In 1874 Sullivan returned to Balcarres where, on the marquetry piano that is still in the school room today, he composed the comic opera *The Sorcerer*, as well as 'I Would I Were a King' for *The Pirates of Penzance.*

Louise Jopling, one of the most prominent artists of her generation, described Blanche as a 'very attractive young woman, with hair of a rich brown colouring and beautiful blue eyes. She was very clever and witty, but as I used to laugh and tell her, her chief delight was to appear foolish.'[13] Blanche was highly possessive and jealous, especially of her husband's early close attention to their daughters. This may have accounted for his increasing distance from them over the years. While Coutts and Blanche were brought together by the Balcarres developments and their new London concern, the Grosvenor Gallery (opened to some fanfare in 1878), stresses at home mounted. Their age difference and being forced to come to terms with his illegitimate sons, including the third, Arthur Madley, who started to call himself James Lindsay, did not bode well. (Blanche refused to allow James to stay at Balcarres.)

The gallery was the culmination of Coutts's years of studying art. As patrons of art, the couple gave a platform to painters who wished to be less stereotyped than the Royal Academy allowed. It shared similarities with Paris's *Salon des Refusés* and drew in artists from the Aesthetic Movement and Pre-Raphaelites who had nowhere else to go. It rapidly grew into a destination for evening events, lit through the magic of new electric lighting, as its basement was the home of his cousin Ludovic's embryonic electricity generating system, from which the country's first grid emanated. The exhibitions were important to the careers of many of their friends, including James Abbott McNeill Whistler, James Tissot, Walter Crane and Lawrence Alma-Tadema. Oscar Wilde described the interior as having 'walls hung with scarlet damask above a dado of dull green and gold; there are luxurious velvet couches, beautiful flowers and plants, tables of gilded and inlaid marbles, covered with Japanese china and

73 Coutts's sister May had married the fabulously wealthy Robert Holford, who built Dorchester House. Coutts was involved both in overseeing the redecorating as well as painting the Red Drawing Room's frieze (*c.* 1865).

74 Blanche contributed more than forty pictures to the Grosvenor Gallery exhibitions but after her divorce from Coutts turned her attention to writing poetry and fiction (*c.* 1875).

the latest "Minton", globes of "rainbow glass" like large soap-bubbles, and ... everything in decoration that is lovely to look on, and in harmony with the surrounding works of art.'[14] This was a significant development in the changing role of galleries as this setting magnified the attention on the surroundings and the way in which work was displayed.

Coutts's artistic talents were also used nearby as he was helping with some of the decoration at Dorchester House, the palatial home of his sister May Holford on Park Lane. Watts was so taken by Coutts's efforts that he even suggested going into partnership with him, especially after his success with his murals in the house.[15]

However, while trying to ignore her husband's infidelities, Blanche went overboard in entertaining. Soon she had a staff of fourteen in London. But all of this made her ill. Coutts felt steadily more hemmed in as she became more possessive. In 1882 she finally left Balcarres with her daughters for good. The combination of his behaviour and her high-flying society life had caused a rift between the two. Separation and ultimately divorce did not stop her social play; if anything it propelled it. She was lent a studio by the Burne-Joneses and dined out regularly with Millais, Robert Browning, Arthur Sullivan and Lord Leighton. But in 1884 she fell headlong down some stairs, causing her to be invalided for over two years in a quiet darkened house in St John's Wood, where she was devotedly looked after by her daughter Helen.

After recovering, she continued entertaining the artistic world from her home at 41 Hans Place for the next twenty-five years. Her intelligence appeared wasted by lack of true ambition or direction, although she did write a great deal of poetry and several books, some of which included her own illustrations. She died after a short illness in 1912. The latter part of her life was spent suffering head and eye pain owing to another bad fall on her romantically draped staircase. After her death Helen went to

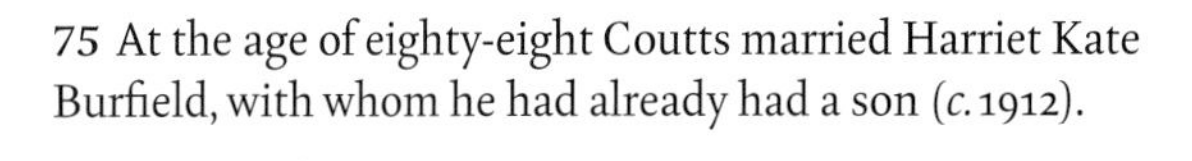

75 At the age of eighty-eight Coutts married Harriet Kate Burfield, with whom he had already had a son (*c.* 1912).

China to work as a missionary. Sadly, the daughters dislike of their father meant that they rarely, if ever, saw him after 1882.

By now Coutts's earlier ascendancy was very much on the wane. His niece Jane wrote how her mother had

loved Coutts with ineradicable tenaciousness of heart, rooted in the early pride which had gloried in the brilliant promise of his youth – but there are few things so sad when reviewing her happy life as the steady growth of disillusionment as his character emphasised its failings ... He was always selfish ... We of the younger generation felt great antipathy for our handsome Uncle – his manner was so suave, his remarks cast in a superior tolerant fashion – yet it was undeniable: his conversation was full of knowledge and charm so that socially he was of marked value. How we disliked him; mainly I suppose because we resented the pain he inflicted smilingly upon our beloved elders.[16]

In the end, many of his leading artists were starting to take umbrage at a change in direction at the gallery and after a disagreement with two of his fellow founders, J. Comyn Carr and Charles Hallé, many moved to the New Gallery set up by the disgruntled directors at the lower end of Regent Street. This was to be the undoing of ten years of important work and, following the withdrawal of Blanche's investment in the company, it had to close, leaving Coutts with an overdraft of £100,000 for his troubles (approximately £8,200,000 today). Facing social disapproval, and the end of his heady times in Bond Street, he became less sociable and rarely visited his old haunts and friends.

He was tiring. He was seen as a noble, dashing and attractive man when younger, but a relation now saw in him 'a wasted life. Too versatile, too fond of experiment, he never allowed himself to master the theory of work, too impatient ever to get beyond the ambit of the dilettante and amateur.'[17] (Nonetheless, his cousin, Bal, the 27th Earl of Crawford, fondly commented that he was 'alternately distinguished and enterprising, always original and interesting yet his labours were never crowned with success. Lack of patience and steadfastness marked his career throughout, except in the ceaseless and unchanging devotion he lavished on Kate'.[18]... 'Nevertheless, with all his faults he was one of the most attractive personalities I ever met. I shall never forget his dignity and charm – they outbalanced all his human shortcomings. He was a good man who assuredly ought to have been a great one.'[19]

Coutts finally sold Balcarres back to the senior branch of the family to alleviate his precarious finances. Less than a year before he died, he married Harriet Kate Burfield, the last of his loves, a servant's daughter, artist's model, mistress and mother of his third son. He died in 1913 and was buried at St Andrew's, Ham. Kate lived until 1937.

Coutts probably would have accepted the description that accompanied his portrait by Jopling in *Vanity Fair*: 'Sir Coutts owes much to the ladies ... a man well fitted to be popular; without being conceited, he has a proper opinion of himself; he speaks well without ever being tiresome or garrulous; his knowledge is considerable, and his manners, charming.'[20]

Balcarres

'This pleasant retreat, not inferior perhaps to the Temple of Thessaly'

Balcarres commands one of the finest views over Fife's rolling East Neuk from a gentle hill that runs south down to the small village of Colinsburgh and two miles on to the sea, looking out far across the Firth of Forth, the Bass Rock and the hills of North Berwick. It is a panorama that has long drawn generations of Lindsays back to this mostly dark basalt house that was transformed throughout the late eighteenth and early nineteenth centuries. That evolution included the latest fashionable baronial features and terraced gardens, but they conceal a history that goes back more than half a millennium into the past.

In the early twentieth century, work creating a series of walks was under way when on the southern side of the Craig hill to the east of the house five late Bronze and early Iron Age stone coffins were uncovered. Dwellings were found nearby, some discovered by Mary, Countess of Crawford, in the 1960s and 1970s, often by using her favoured divining rods or swinging pendulum. Pictish and Celtic tribes settled here, too, while later Viking invasions caused devastation, slaying many, including the ecclesiastics taking refuge on the Isle of May, which is visible from the hills above the house.

The earliest records of the house appear in the thirteenth century. The last earl of the MacDuff clan, Duncan, Earl of Fife, listed in 1288 his possessions around the 'Schtra de Ryrays' or 'the shire of Ryrys' included place names that are still part of the estate, such as Balnackcrois (or Balcarres, the town of the cross), Balniel, Rires Farm and the mill and coal pits.[1] In time, the spelling altered slightly and when James II granted the lands to Robert Hunter in 1465 it was described as 'the landis of Balkerous and the myln of the sammyn landis in the schirefdome of Fiff'.[2] An early incarnation of the house in 1511 describes a hall, chamber, barn, stable, byre, garden, apiary and doocot. A vaulted room with gun loops, now filled in, lay at the heart of the current house.

76 The Panel Room's plaster ceiling was one of only five in houses in Scotland to have the assent to show King James VI's arms.

Over this period the Lindsays held courts in over twenty baronies and lordships across Scotland from Inverness to Dumfries. Finaven and Edzell castles were their Angus strongholds, where a 'magnificence that would have benefitted a monarch' was retained.[3] The first of the family to live at Balcarres was John Lindsay, in 1588. The house had been settled on his first wife, Marion Guthrie, by her late husband, David Borthwick. John, son of David, 9th Earl of Crawford (who lived at Edzell), rose to secretary of state and held the office of privy seal, having become Lord Menmuir when lord of session in 1581. His descendants have much to be grateful for. As Alexander, Lord Lindsay put it in his *Lives of the Lindsays*:

Lord Menmuir, in fixing his residence at Balcarres, bequeathed to his descendants the enjoyment of pure and fresh air, of proximity to the sea, and a prospect embracing rock and meadow, island and lake, river and ocean well-nigh boundless, and for which they have great reason to bless the merciful Dispenser of all things, who has cast their 'lines of life' so pleasantly.[4]

Throughout his life there was a great deal of tree planting, some of which still live today, including the old ilex near the house.[5]

John's son, David, the 1st Lord Lindsay of Balcarres, in the early seventeenth century started the construction of a four-, partly five-storey building to the east of the Rose Garden later to be known as the Dower House.[6] He also erected the pretty chapel in 1635 that stands, now roofless, in the garden (and where he was buried in 1641).[7] The future Panel Room was given a fine plaster ceiling with the arms of King James VI at its centre in about 1605 as in his reign Balcarres became one of only five houses in Scotland assigned as royal court chambers when required. In 1651, shortly after King Charles I was crowned at Scone and before the battle of Worcester, he attended a banquet here hosted by Alexander, 1st Earl of Balcarres. By now the house had become a significant establishment and was said to have had the finest library in Scotland, but siding with the Stuarts incurred the wrath of Cromwell and almost drove the family to penury.

77 Balcarres from the north-west (*c.*1870).

78 The drawing room (*c.* 1900).

79 The drawing room, with Connie, Walter, Mary (Robert's wife) and Emily (*c.* 1900).

By the time of the Restoration the house was in a sad state and only through the financial support of Lady Anna Mackenzie, the widow of Alexander, 1st Earl of Balcarres, did matters improve. Her son, Colin, soldier and later commissioner of the treasury, had great ambitions to turn Balcarres into something on the lines of Drumlanrig. However, Alexander's support for the Jacobite cause forced him abroad and put paid to any architectural ambitions – although he did build the village of Colinsburgh at the foot of the estate.

Finances by the late 1780s were so bad that Alexander, 6th Earl of Balcarres, offered the house to his brother as he wanted to invest in the nascent coal-mining endeavours at Haigh Hall recently inherited by his wife. The Hon. Robert Lindsay had made a fortune in India and on his return in 1789 took on the family seat. He made few changes to the exterior but transformed the now spartan interior with fabrics, new fireplaces, furniture and art. In 1793 he added new stables and a coach house. The gardens and greenhouses were further improved with everything from melon pits to a host of experimental plants. With the architect and builder James Fisher, in 1813, Robert built a gothic folly in the form of a round, four-storey, castellated basalt tower on top of the Craig hill above an old quarry and visible for miles.

Dominating the whole demesne, a lofty precipitous rock, from the summit of which a soul-stirring prospect spreads around. Beyond the rich woods and fertile plain lies the blue Firth of Forth, bearing on its bosom the massive Bass Rock. The smooth outline of the Lammermuir [sic] *forms the southern horizon, within which Auld Reekie rears her dusky canopy.*[8]

Furthermore in 1817 he embarked on a great planting exercise of almost twenty-five thousand trees.

Around this time the Fife architect Robert Balfour broke through to the north of the house and added a billiard room, connected by a door from what became the Panel Room. Improvements were made to the surrounding farms and cottages that led Sir Walter

80 In 1651, shortly after the Scots crowned King Charles II at Scone, he attended a banquet hosted by Alexander, 1st Earl of Balcarres, in the room that would later become the Panel Room.

81 The architect David Bryce added a new wing to the north that included the dining room (seen here). This became the main library after Haigh was sold in 1947 (*c.* 1880).

82 Balcarres, when painted white, from the lower terraces, with parterres modelled on those seen in *Les Jardins du Roi de Pologne* (*c.* 1860).

83 The lower terrace centred by the Japanese fountain (*c.* 1900).

84 Robert Adamson (left), here with Coutts, was employed to transform the gardens into Italianate terraces (*c.* 1860).

85 Summertime at Balcarres. A view down the newly built drive near Lorimer's North Lodge (*c.* 1897).

Scott, visiting in 1823, to declare: 'I never saw so many good houses of people of family and fortune nestled so close together as in that part of Fife.'

Robert's son, General Sir James, was to make the first significant changes to the exterior with the help of the most eminent architect of the day, William Burn. They first turned the new south-west room into a library, a well-lit room with far-reaching southerly views. A new entrance was built which included a theatrical stairway that led up into the picture gallery. A further extension was built on to the east of the house, which became the family wing. One experiment, completed in 1843, was painting the outside walls white, as the family had not liked the new harsh, almost black whinstone. It was reversed soon after.

The general's son, Coutts, in 1864 had married Nathan Mayer Rothschild's granddaughter, Caroline Blanche Fitzroy. On inheriting the house, the couple started entertaining on a grand scale, which required the house to be made even larger. Unfortunately, Coutts was a serial womanizer, but before Blanche left him in 1882 he was able to use much of her fortune to have William Burn's protégé, David Bryce, architect of Fettes College, make a number of major additions. These included a new wing to the north that incorporated a new dining room (which would later become a second library), a studio (now the billiard room) with a specially designed tall window to enable large canvases to be brought in and out, and a host of baronial features around the house that were far less understated than earlier additions.

In 1893 the Panel Room was transformed with two large plate-glass windows at either end. Until now, the walls had been panelled with a light painted wood and hung with pictures. Bryce fitted Coutts's newly acquired oak panelling portraying, among other iconographic scenes, the Labours of Hercules, which he purchased from the palace or abbey refectory of Bishop Levi in Louvain in the Low Countries. A fine set of oak and ebony bookcases dated 'Anno 1625' from Peter Paul Rubens' library in Antwerp were fitted into Burn's southern library.

86 The Craig folly flying the Lindsay fess chequy; armorial colours dominated 'the whole demesne' (*c.* 1880).

87 The west wing, designed by William Burn, completed in 1843, was coloured white due to the family distaste of the almost black whinstone.

Coutts discussed the garden plans with Holman Hunt and Sir John Millais but eventually Bryce and Jesse Hall, an architect from St Andrews, oversaw the day-to-day work and between them and Robert Adamson, his gardener, started the transformation of the gardens into the terraces that remain today. The terraces have box and rose gardens, dense yew hedges (which took ten men ten days a year to trim), and small flower gardens, each with their own distinct character, divided from one another by buttresses of yew. Three of the parterres came from designs in Emmanuel Héré's 1753 book *Recueil des Plans, Elevations et Coupes des Chateaux et Jardins que le Roi de Pologne Occupe en Lorraine.* Each level was centred by ponds with Nuremberg and Japanese fountains, while the west terrace had an ancient pillar sundial carved with sixty-six facets on a Sir Robert Lorimer-designed base.[9] A croquet lawn that doubled as grass tennis court was made to the south of Coutts's studio. The gardens were described in 1902 as 'second only in Scotland to those of Drummond Castle. Their character is truly magnificent, and they make, with double and single descents, a noble approach to the quaint and beautiful box garden and the splendid circle and enclosing hedged rectangle.'[10]

The walled kitchen garden, started by Coutts's grandfather, continued to flourish and records kept by Adamson showed that quantities of soft fruit were produced for the house, including peaches and grapes. He was delighted when in 1853 Coutts built him a cottage nearby.

After Blanche left Coutts, his finances were strained. His grandfather, Robert, had always preferred the head of the family to live at Balcarres and so it was offered back to his cousin Ludovic, the 26th Earl of Crawford. In April 1886, after paying £150,000 (approximately £12.3 million today), Balcarres returned to the senior branch of the family.[11]

From then on, no major alterations were made and the house has remained very much the same to this day. Surprisingly, for a family which had been at the forefront of the revolution in its use, electricity was not installed until 1948.

88 The Scottish Arts and Crafts architect and furniture designer, and a neighbour, Sir Robert Lorimer, designed Balcarres' North Lodge and gates (*c.* 1897).

David, 28th Earl of Crawford, remembered how life in the house was run on fairly strict lines. His father took great pride in his fires, for instance, and insisted that the wood for them was sawn into rectangular pieces and laid down with shavings (no newspaper was ever allowed). The servants were under strict orders not to remove any of the ever-growing mound of white wood ash. Meanwhile, fire continued to be a constant hazard at Balcarres, especially as they had to rely on light supplied by gas and candles.

The nearby stable yard was always busy. Various pony and governess carts and a fine barouche-landau, each with the Lindsay crests in gold, discreetly painted on the sides, were forever being tended to by the grooms in their wooden-soled, knee-high waterproof boots. The carriages were all painted dark blue with a thin red line, matching the men's livery until the twentieth century, when they started wearing black. The whole family rode; some from necessity, others for the thrill of the chase.

In 1896, a drive was built up through the rocky Den to what became the North or Balniel Lodge, designed by Lorimer in the Arts and Crafts style. Rich with Lindsay heraldic symbolism incorporated into the stone and pierced metal work, Lorimer modestly described it as 'rather snippy in the Scots-French style à la Queen Mary's baths.'[12] The success of this work meant that in 1903 he was asked to design the estate office near the Italian 'Golden Gates' of the South Lodge on the Colinsburgh road. From there a more informal drive replacing a previous straight avenue had been fashioned in 1853, snaking up through rolling parkland.

A burn flows from above Lathallan Mill to the Balcarres Mill dam and on through the deep narrow valley beneath climbing walls of rhododendrons, eucryphias, beech and birch, lending an air of apparently untamed forest wilderness. The planting has rarely halted and it has matured into one of the outstanding stretches of mature and diverse plantings in Scotland with much of it classified as Ancient Woodland.

The feathered tribe seem proud of pouring forth their various melody in this pleasant retreat, not inferior perhaps to the Temple of ancient Thessaly. Balcarras [sic] *is no less fertile than beautiful, the fields are properly divided and inclosed, and in the highest state of cultivation. The late Earl of Balcarras (Earl James) a nobleman distinguished by the benevolence of his knowledge, particularly in history and agriculture, was among the first that brought farming to any degree of perfection in the country.*[13]

11

'Balls were held of dazzling brilliancy'

Mary Anne, 'May', 1823–1901 and Robert Staynor Holford, 1808–92

While it may appear that Mary Anne Lindsay, otherwise known as 'Mayflower' or simply 'May', lived in a gilded cage, surrounded by beautiful objects in palatial splendour, she nonetheless made her own contributions through talent and intelligence. She was at the heart of the social scene, but she was also very much a partner in her husband's artistic, literary and even sylvan pursuits.

She had never been short of suitors: Sir Thomas Erskine, Lord John Manners and Lord Dufferin had all been possible matches but, like her mother, she found in Robert Stayner Holford a man who was 'very good-tempered and pleased everybody and everything about him in his ordinarily entirely comfortable completeness.'[1] Her younger brother, Robert, who was out in the Crimea and about to go into battle for the first time, wrote to his sister Maysie how he 'liked all he had seen and heard of the man.'[2] Her father had asked of him his means. 'Holford began by saying that he was sorry to say his income had sunk to £35,000 a year [approximately £2,806,000 today], after which James inquired no more.'[3]

Robert was once reputed to be 'the richest commoner in England', and a contemporary writer, A. N. L. Munby, described him as 'a collector with an eye for quality and the means to indulge it without stint'. The considerable fortune of around £1 million (£60 million today) that Robert had inherited from his uncle Robert was created principally by the New River Company, which supplied London with fresh water. He also took on roles as a magistrate and became high sheriff of Wiltshire as well as Member of Parliament for Gloucestershire East.

Robert set out to build a Roman-style palace on the site of the Earl of Dorchester's eponymously named house on London's Park Lane with the help of the architect Lewis Vulliamy. Dorchester House was greatly influenced by Peruzzi's Villa Farnesina and the Palazzo Braschi, which Holford had visited in 1855, inspired by the views through the screens of columns on each floor.[4] On completion in 1860, it was described 'without hyperbole ... the finest private dwelling in London.'[5] It was decorated at enormous expense, including a famed and vast central marble staircase that led up to a vaulted gallery surrounding the great hall. The dining room had a spectacular fireplace sculpted by Alfred Stevens (now the centrepiece in the Victoria and Albert Museum Gamble Room café). Various artists were brought in, including May's brother, Sir Coutts, who painted a series of panels in the dining room.

Here Robert could house some of his exceptional art collection, including works by the greatest masters, and build one of the country's finest libraries. Frequent balls were held of unsurpassed 'dazzling brilliancy'; the house, full of magnificent pictures, was brilliantly lit: 'From the further gallery the dance would be visible through the arches across the well of the hall, and from the ballroom could be watched the gay throng crowding the staircase, while

89 Robert Staynor Holford by Camille Silvy (1861).

90 May Lindsay became a central figure in English society as Robert Holford's wife and chatelaine of Dorchester House and Westonbirt. By Camille Silvy (1861).

91 Dorchester House was described as the finest private house in London (*c.*1860).

92 From a vaulted gallery one could watch visitors arrive below in the great hall (*c.*1860).

the ringleted and crinolined nymphs and whiskered Guardsmen conversed in the gallery arcades.'[6]

May's niece, Jane, was more candid in her views of Robert and his collecting:

Uncle Holford, distinguished in looks, tall, lean, utterly unselfconscious, intensely downright unimaginative much pre-occupied by his own enterprises, building, decorating, terracing, planting ... One would see him dumped in a chair indoors or out, analysing and arguing whether a cornice was too narrow or broad, whether a tree should be planted 3 yards or 2½, to the right or left of a group of shrubs. Whether its autumn colouring would be too lacking in colour for its neighbour. He painted as it were in Things, not paints. He bought pictures to suit the walls of the architectural beauties of Dorchester House – more than for the actual artistic work. The same with books, I fancy he valued them most as perfect furniture. Her [Mary's] taste was instinctive – in colour and textiles, wherever she lived these abounded in old velvet damasks embroideries – having great spaces, there was no oppression of stuffy fuss.[7]

The Westonbirt estate in Gloucestershire had come to the Holford family through marriage in the mid-seventeenth century. The previous Georgian house had replaced an earlier Elizabethan one. Lewis Vulliamy was brought in again to design and build its successor over seven years from 1863. The new Westonbirt House and gardens were rebuilt in an Elizabethan style on an even grander scale. The interiors were in a classical style and fitted with the latest technology, including gas lighting, central heating, fireproof construction and iron roofs. The couple felt that the existing village of Weston Birt spoiled their view, so they had the entire village torn down and rebuilt a quarter a mile away.

93 A Westonbirt house party with left to right, standing, Prince de Clermont-Tonnerre, Earl Grey, the 26th Earl of Crawford, May's daughter Lady Grey, and neighbour George Escourt and Robert Holford and seated, George Holford, Mrs Grosvenor and the Countess of Crawford (1884).

While his father had started planting a few ornamental and interesting trees, it was really Robert who, from the age of twenty-one, and later with May, created one of the country's finest arboretums. Outdoor entertainment was taken care of in the grand style. Near the stables with the finest horses, the kennels housed some fifteen brace of working pointers, deerhounds, terriers and a pack of thirteen couples of the finest spaniels. This was the period that set new standards for field sports and the Holfords were ready to oblige with the most generous levels of hospitality.

May shared her husband's passions in the gardens and art but was creative in her own right too. She wrote a well-received novel, *Strathrowan: A Tale of Modern Life*, a three-volume love story that was published in 1879 but, as modesty demanded at the time, pseudonymously under the name of 'M.H.'[8]

Robert and May had three daughters, Margaret, Evelyn and Alice, and one son, George. The daughters married, respectively, the 3rd Earl of Morley of Saltram in Devon, the banker and art critic Robert Benson, and the 4th Earl Grey of Howick. After May was widowed in 1892, she spent more time with her sister, Minnie, who had moved south to live on her brother Robert's estate near Wantage. She died two weeks after Queen Victoria's funeral in 1901.

George Lindsay Holford continued to support international seed- and plant-collecting expeditions after his parents' deaths. Indeed, he was probably even more passionate about the gardens than they had been and so the whole concern continued to flourish under his tenure. As equerry to various members of the royal family, George spent much time at court. He married late in life, to Susannah Menzies, but died childless in 1926.

94 May's creative talents complemented her husband's grand endeavours. In 1875 a Westonbirt guest, French diplomat Charles Gayard, observed: 'The most original room in the house is the one painted by Mrs Holford, in a bizarre fanciful style, something between Delacroix landscape and Rouen pottery' (*c.* 1860).

12

For Valour

Lt-Col. Sir Robert James Loyd-Lindsay, 1st Baron Wantage of Lockinge, VC, 1832–1901, and the Hon. Harriet Sarah Lindsay, Lady Wantage (née Loyd), 1837–1920

Robert Lindsay's childhood presented few hints of his later years' achievements both on and off the battlefield. He was the youngest of four children who came from a family with a long and distinguished military tradition. His father, who had served throughout the Napoleonic Wars, showed little confidence in his son's chances of gaining a commission and worried about his 'vile habit of sleepiness and laziness and want of inclination to learn'.[1]

However, the general was not devoid of affection: 'Robin is so full of health and joyousness that he is almost overpowering. He cannot walk, he leaps and flies and squeaks with spirits.' Robert was originally destined to join the East India Company, not a prospect he relished. Fortunately, a steady stream of officers visited his father, including General Simpson, who later succeeded Lord Raglan as Commander-in-Chief in the Crimea, and who opened up a different world of possibilities and excitements. It was through an admirer of his sister, May, that he took a step forward into this new career after leaving Eton. Thanks to Col. the Hon. Alexander Gordon, ADC to Prince Albert, he obtained the commission into the Scots Fusilier Guards in December 1850.[2] His mother, Anne, commented:

I wonder how much his beautiful face helped him, and his pleasing manners ... Bob is slender and straight as an arrow; his forehead, brow, and eyes are beautiful; his mouth is like a statue, with a delightful mixture of gentleness and scorn; there is a look of calmness and power about him that is very striking. He is graceful in his movements and excels in all manly exercises such as shooting, riding and skating he seems to fall naturally into them without any trouble.[3]

These seem to be attributes that stayed with him for life.

One of Robert's first public duties as Ensign of the Guards was to stand as one of the four mourners on guard around the Duke of Wellington's coffin as it lay in state at Chelsea Hospital prior to the state funeral on 18 November 1852. Shortly after, he was summoned to active service when his regiment was sent to the Balkans as part of the West's attempt to consolidate the defeat of the Russians after their failed efforts to control the Danubian principalities. One early dawn, he left Balcarres after what turned out to be the final farewell from his father.

Robert had recently had a serious riding accident and caught rheumatic fever, so he was not in the best of health when he marched past Buckingham Palace on 29 February 1854 before steaming off the next day to join the allied forces in Scutari and eventually the Crimea. Although he avoided the cholera epidemic

95 Captain Robert Lindsay was granted his first leave from the Crimea to see his mother in Florence in January 1856, following his father's death a month earlier.

(there was by now a daily average of thirty deaths in the British sectors alone), he was struck down with dysentery, which weakened him further. His experiences of the appalling conditions and the medical staff's management of similarly afflicted men left a marked impression on him. The old pensioners who were supposed to take care of the sick were useless and drunk on the brandy supplied for the sick. The oppressive heat and unsanitary conditions also took their toll. The almost non-existent logistical management meant many of the supplies remained on the ships as they returned to Scutari with the sick. On disembarkation, troops were only given three days' provisions and had no shelter but their cloaks. It was months before Robert saw his chest with a change of clothes or even a tent to sleep in.

It was in such a state that the twenty-two-year-old found himself chosen to lead his company as the Queen's Colour Ensign. Their goal was Sebastopol, but the route was blocked by the Russians with their hundred field guns lined along a natural defensive position above the River Alma. Robert, as inexperienced as the rest of his regiment, was about to be thrown into the bloodiest mêlée with its chaos and hand-to-hand fighting at the first battle of the Crimea on 20 September 1854.

Amid the mass confusion at the start of the Battle of the Alma, the Duke of Cambridge's 1st Division, which included the Guards' Brigade of which Robert's Scots Fusiliers Battalion was a part, advanced into a scene of deadly turmoil – one that was already looking ominously like it would end in a defeat by the Russians, who outnumbered the allies three to one.[4] The Light Brigade were in disarray, having already lost more than a thousand men (many more than in its later, more infamous charge at Balaclava), and came rushing back down, temporarily breaking Robert's line. His company battled on, often so close to the enemy that they could only use bayonets, and steadily progressed up the slopes. Their goal was the Great Redoubt at the summit above the River Alma. Climbing on, they came under a tremendous volume of grapeshot and cannister fire from both flanks, then direct attack from the front by the Vladimir Regiment. The situation rapidly became desperate – they were now almost entirely surrounded.

Robert would later write that, as senior subaltern,

I was left alone with the Colours, standing on the hill. The noise of the firing was so great it was in vain to call to the men. I firmly planted the Colours and waved my bearskin ... I cannot say how long I remained alone, but it must have been a full five minutes at the very least. Then the men began to rally round me ... and not more than a company were up with the Colours, when a volley from the Russians cut down the three colour sergeants and shattered the Queen's colours in my hand.[5]

But he had stood firm, rallied the troops and, neither drawing his sword nor firing his revolver, was the first up into the Russian earthworks. Captain Hugh F. Drummond, his adjutant, described their actions:

As for the two ensigns Lindsay and Thistlewayte [sic], *they were my children ... their coolness, steadiness and deliberate courage were admirable ... They never moved or flinched, but went steadily on, as if on parade; a species of cool bravery in such young fellows as I think only exists in Englishmen.*

The Duke of Cambridge reiterated this to Robert's father:

I can tell you, General, your son is a very fine fellow, a most gallant soldier amongst men, for they are a noble set of fellows. How we escaped has been a marvel to me. I watched him with the Queen's colours at Alma – at one moment I thought him gone, the colours fell and he disappeared under them, but presently he came out from below them, the flagstaff had been cut and the colours fell over him, but he raised them again, and waved them over his head. He has my highest approbation.[6]

It was recognized that without this stand the British regiments would have been overwhelmed.[7] His actions earned Robert his first citation for the newly created Victoria Cross, the highest award for gallantry. He was less involved at Balaclava, where he witnessed the failed and fabled charge, but Inkerman was to have greater significance in the war. As he wrote to his

96 Robert was the first soldier to receive two citations for the Victoria Cross. The investiture by Queen Victoria was held in Hyde Park in 1857.

father: 'The loss on both sides you will see was enormous; the list of killed in the brigade will be most melancholy to you.'[8] The Russians used the country's unusual mists in which to make their surprise attack. Robert's company was involved throughout in hand-to-hand fighting; at one point he was almost bayoneted as he ran one Russian through with his sword. But all understood the peril they were amidst – any wounded would be finished off by the enemy.

He wrote to his father:

A shot struck the toe of my boot on the sole and stung most tremendously. I thought my toe was off at first … A battle is the most exciting thing in the world, I think much more confusion than one usually imagines, and as for all the nonsense the newspapers write about unbroken lines and columns, it is all stuff. Those who funk lie down or get out of fire, and in a charge if you get ten or twelve men to follow you it is as much as you can do. As for colonels or mounted officers, one never sees them, or takes any notice if one does. In fact, it is just like boys snowballing one another at school. Some battles, of course, are different, and the troops, until they come to close quarters, preserve very decent order. I often longed for you at Inkerman, as I know how you would have enjoyed parts of it. I pursued some Russians so far down the hill when they were routed, that I was as near as possible being taken prisoner or rather bayoneted. I had to run for my life, for the rascals had got between me and the top of the hill, so I had to skirt along the bottom. I caught a pony and galloped him some way till he tumbled, and then I had to run again. I arrived in safety at last, so beat that I could hardly move one leg after the other.[9]

He gained similar recognition at Inkerman as at Alma, giving him the unique distinction of being the first soldier to have two Victoria Cross citations for separate acts of valour.

The 'inexpressible miseries' during the winter of 1854–5 began immediately after the Battle of Inkerman, with a storm which knocked down or flooded the tents, including those used as hospitals, and wrecked supply vessels in Balaclava harbour containing essential stores for the troops. Temporary relief came for him when he was appointed ADC to General Simpson, the officer he had met as a young man at Balcarres, who was now chief of staff. He felt that this posting might further his cause to alleviate the problems afflicting his men: the severe lack of food, clothing and shelter. Throughout, he wrote a steady stream of letters home describing the unacceptable conditions his men had to bear. With just a blanket at night, feet bound in rags and often suffering days of rain or snow with no shelter, it was little wonder that frostbite and cholera set in. Many died needlessly. Inefficiencies and the actions, or inaction, of many officers meant that starvation was never far away, even though all the necessary supplies were nearby. Frequently, overworked men would have no energy or fuel to cook their food and would simply eat their pork raw. Mud and rain, with famished horses dying by the dozen every day, munitions failing to get to the front, all contributed to the unnecessarily drawn-out affair. 'In fact, never was an army in such distress or so badly off for everything', Robert wrote. When he had arrived in the Crimea, his Brigade of Guards numbered over two thousand. By the end of the war it was down to three hundred.

97 Harriet's only brother had died in infancy. She was reputed to be the richest heiress in England (*c.* 1860).

98 Harriet's father, Samuel Jones-Loyd, 1st Baron Overstone, who was cultured and forward-looking, was regarded as one of the foremost figures in nineteenth-century monetary history. He was the guarantor for the 1851 Great Exhibition (*c.* 1865).

These were some of the worst conditions the British army has faced in modern history. Many of Robert's letters were passed to the Duke of Newcastle, then minister for war, contributing to the groundswell of opinion against the minister, Raglan's woeful administration and the conduct of the war.[10] But letters written home by many officers became controversial as they were perceived as unpatriotic and dangerous to the campaign.

On being made adjutant, Robert was able to return to his regiment in the final stages of the siege of Sebastopol. Finally, after months of bombardment, the Russians gave up the city and retreated north. Robert was keen to enter but dangers lay everywhere:

I rode through all the principal streets, which are, or rather were, very fine, the public buildings equal to anything in the provincial towns of England or France. The explosions becoming rather frequent, I felt rather nervous for the top of my head. At length one great house going off within a hundred yards of me, and scattering large splinters of stone all round, decided me to gallop out of the place, which I accordingly did, as hard as ever I could. The panic in the main street became general, and the rush of the crowd tremendous, drunken soldiers and sailors, French and English, tumbling over one another, and those on horseback riding over them. I put my head down and my spurs in and scoured up the street as hard as ever I could go, regardless of everyone except myself, for one mine was connected with another, and after the first explosion a succession of smaller ones followed. I got out all safe, though covered with dust and powder.[11]

When the war ended, Robert returned home a hero. There could not have been a prouder family in Hyde Park on 26 June 1857, witnessing their young officer being awarded his cross of gallantry by their Queen. He took on the role as equerry to HRH the Prince of Wales (later Edward VII) until he became engaged to the Hon. Harriet Jones-Loyd, the only daughter of Lord Overstone and reputedly the richest heiress in England.

They had met in 1850 when her father was chairman of what was then the London and Westminster Bank (later the National Westminster

99 Lockinge was run successfully as a model estate on a cooperative basis with profit-sharing initiatives. On the death of Lord Overstone, Robert and Harriet took on his other estates in eleven counties, managing over fifty thousand acres. The burden of double death duties saw Lockinge House demolished in 1947.

Bank). Robert proposed to her on 30 June 1858 at a great party given by her parents at the Crystal Palace (Lord Overstone had been the financial guarantor of the 1851 Great Exhibition)[12] and they were married later that year. Shortly after, he retired from the army as a twenty-six-year-old lieutenant-colonel, to manage the estate at Lockinge, near Wantage, given to them by his father-in-law.[13] He also now changed his name to Loyd-Lindsay.

Overstone, a trustee of the National Gallery, was regarded as one of the outstanding collectors and lovers of art of his age. He had amassed a great collection, especially pieces by Italian and Dutch masters, including works by Rembrandt, Cranach, Claude and Turner. Robert and Harriet continued to add to the collection.[14] Julia Margaret Cameron, whom he probably met through his brother Coutts, was keen to photograph them. Her artistic skill in photography was perhaps at its best in her series influenced by Tennyson's *Idylls,* and she was wont to say that Robert was nearer than anyone she knew to her ideal of King Arthur.

Robert never lost his interest in military matters and the welfare of the common soldier. Army reform was necessary, but he was also forthright in his support for reorganizing the aid to those other victims of war, the innocent civilians. Using his experience and wealth of connections, he and his wife became founders of the National Society for Aid to the Sick and Wounded in War. In 1870 he was made its first chairman. Contributions flooded in after his letter to *The Times* on 22 July that year proposing the creation of a neutral, impartial aid organization to help the wounded on both sides. The Queen became patroness of the society and was supported by a large element of her family. Henry Dunant had recently instigated the Geneva Convention, paving the way for the Red Cross movement. Accordingly, in 1905, Robert and Harriet's society was renamed the British Red Cross and fell under the convention's rulings.

Florence Nightingale, who had long been a family friend, became involved in the work of the society and a close cooperation and friendship developed between the two veterans of the Crimea. Her own experiences, fame and knowledge lent great weight to her advice in all matters. She was adamant that improvements to procedures such as sanitation, training and ward management – things that are taken for granted today – should be foremost in the guiding principles.

100 A Lockinge house party, including Harriet's mother seated between Robert and Lord Overstone. Others include the uniformed Sir Paul Hunter, Harriet in a floral hat and Robert's cousin Col. Charles Lindsay on the far right (*c.* 1860).

101 Florence Nightingale believed Robert epitomised the true qualities of chivalry (*c.* 1900).

Harriet was already a noted philanthropist and took great interest in hospital and nursing work and as a result she became highly respected in this field. When Queen Victoria instituted the Order of the Red Cross, Harriet was one of the first to receive the honour.

In 1871 the Franco-Prussian War was at its worst, with reports of the sufferings on both sides attracting great public sympathy. Both sides were allied to Great Britain – the Prussians due to their ties to the royal family and the French had been allies in the Crimea – hence donations to the society poured in. By the end of the war, the society had raised over £250,000 (approximately £11.4 million today). Robert found himself travelling to the palace of Versailles, which by then had become the headquarters of the Prussian army, with £40,000 of financial aid, which he delivered to Bismarck for their medical needs and was then given passage, while escorted with a large white flag, into Paris, where the French were handed their share. However, it was not without serious risk, as on two occasions he was captured by French soldiers who thought he was a Prussian spy. It could have turned very unpleasant – others had not been so lucky – but he was released after some tense negotiations.

The society's work was again called on for the next wave of Balkan troubles. Robert set up a British Red Cross hospital in Belgrade independently of the Serbian government.[15] The intelligence he gained allowed him to report back on Russia's objectives in the region, highly valued information for Great Britain's policymakers.[16]

In 1877, now the Conservative member for Berkshire, he was asked to become financial secretary

102 Robert (centre) in his Berkshire Rifle Volunteer uniform with Lord Bury (left) and Sir Paul Hunter, Brussels, 1866. All three were closely involved in establishing the Volunteer Movement (later the Territorial Army).

103 Harriet remained friends with Robert's contemporary officers, here with three of the most distinguished field marshals; from left, Lord Grenfell, Earl Roberts, VC and Sir Evelyn Wood, VC (1908).

104 The Prince of Wales (left) and Duke of York with Lady Wantage at Lockinge for a shooting party. Their grandfather, King Edward VII, had done much to support the Wantages' endeavours (*c.*1910).

to the War Office in Disraeli's ministry. He only remained in this position for three years but was repeatedly called on for advice, even after the change of ministry when he had to vacate the office. Lord Salisbury offered him the surveyor-governorship in the War Office in 1885, but Robert declined due to ill health, but he was elevated to Baron Wantage of Lockinge. During the same period, he was made Lord Lieutenant of Berkshire, a position he held until his death.

His interests in military matters never left him, leading him to co-found and support the Volunteer Movement. He became Berkshire's first colonel and in 1888 was appointed brigadier-general for the Home Counties. In time, the force became what is now the Territorial Army. It was only his failing health in 1900 that prevented him from sailing to South Africa to work with the Red Cross during the Boer War.

Back at home, the Loyd-Lindsays were running the huge Lockinge estate on the most progressive lines. They had set about building a school for each village and a profit-sharing scheme was introduced to help farm employees. They also went from farming 4,427 acres to over 20,528 on the estate, as well as Lord Overstone's other properties scattered over the country totalling over fifty thousand acres.

The couple held strong ethical beliefs that drove them to alleviate suffering among their rural communities. Robert set up and chaired the Small Farm and Labourers' Land Company, created to enable the less advantaged to buy land for themselves rather than be beholden to the large estates. Ultimately, this initiative did not succeed, but it was a measure of the efforts they went to with their relatively unorthodox social philosophy to help those who had lost out due to the Enclosures Acts.

105 Florence Nightingale declared that Robert 'realised the ideal of martial beauty and chivalry attributed to the knights of old' (*c.* 1900).

Meanwhile, his brother Coutts[17] had been building on the success of the Grosvenor Gallery and, on the advice of his cousin Ludovic, 26th Earl of Crawford, had installed electric lighting, but he needed further investment. They became shareholders in Sir Coutts Lindsay and Co., creating one of the world's first electricity grids.[18] This eventually became the London Electricity Supply Corporation and soon its supply of over 10,000 volts made it by far the world's largest electricity provider.

Their support for the creation of a technical college, initially for agricultural sciences, at Reading under the auspices of Oxford University in 1892 meant that Robert became the first president of Reading College (later Reading University). Harriet's inheritance included a number of properties across the country. One of these was Abington Park in Northampton, which the town feared would be sold for housing. Instead, in 1892, Harriet offered the twenty acres of land to the corporation, to be called the People's Park. It remains Northamptonshire's oldest surviving municipal park, dating back to the seventeenth century, hosting the Northampton Show among other events.

Robert's extraordinarily full life came to an end shortly after he attended Queen Victoria's funeral and heard of the death of his much-loved sister May. Florence Nightingale wrote:

Lord Wantage is a great loss but he had been a great gain. And what he has gained for us can never be lost. It is my experience that such men exist only in England. A man who had everything (to use the common phrase) that this world could give him, but who worked as hard, and to the last, as the poorest able man and all for others for the common good. A man whose life makes a great difference for all. All are better than if he had not lived ... That is the true estimate of a great life ... In form and feature his appearance was the visible expression of his character and marked him out as no ordinary man. As he moved in a crowd, people turned instinctively to gaze at the tall, soldier-like figure, the noble head, the finely chiselled features, the fair hair that waved and curled triumphantly over the broad brow, the calm power and nobility of purpose conveyed in look and movement. Stately in bearing and distinguished in manner, he realised the ideal of martial beauty and chivalry attributed to the knights of old.[19]

Harriet continued supporting Robert's philanthropic initiatives after his passing.[20] Those endeavours and their broad reach of friends meant that Lockinge remained an attractive destination for the great and good. Her strong-willed exterior was captured equally successfully by photographers and artists, including Philip de Lazlo. She outlived Robert by almost twenty years and died in 1920, aged eighty-three, leaving a estate of approximately £1,300,000 (roughly £58.5 million today). As well as writing the definitive memoir on Robert, Lord Wantage, she financed and founded the first hall of residence in his memory at Reading University, Wantage Hall. Up on the Ridgeway above Lockinge she erected a monument to him, with a Latin inscription which translates as 'Peace in passing away. Salvation after death. Light after Darkness. Hope in light.'

13

'The most professional amateur I ever met'

James Ludovic, 26th Earl of Crawford & 9th Earl of Balcarres, 1847–1913

James Ludovic, known intimately as 'Udo' as a young man and latterly Ludovic, was surely one of the family's most colourful figures of the last two centuries, both in his pursuits and appearance.[1] Images show a man with an imposing, even Arthurian, presence while a cursory glance at his array of enterprises belie the fact that he only lived for sixty-five years. It would be an understatement to say that the list of the offices he presided over, thanks to his insatiable curiosity for artistic or scientific knowledge, was extensive. His remarkable intellect meant that he reached the highest positions in almost every one of his chosen passions.

106 The striking images of James Ludovic, Earl of Crawford – whether in his Knight of the Thistle robes, at work in his great library or aboard a yacht wrapped in a sarong – are of a figure who seems to belong to a more heroic age.

Ludovic's father was prescient enough to recognize early in him an intelligence and worthy successor. As a child he showed an interest in collecting and a wish to add to what his father had so effectively begun, the building up of the Bibliotheca Lindesiana, one of the most important private libraries in the world. Ludovic's quest, in which he had some success, was to match the greatest scientific libraries in existence. It brought him into contact with many of the leading minds from that field, which only reinforced his wish to add to or learn from their new discoveries, whether they were from the natural or New World, history, art, technology or, his deepest passion, astronomy.

Ludovic was described as a 'highly spirited child, resilient, intelligent and curious with a sense of mischief. Later at school he is continually getting beatings but they have not had the slightest effect on him.' Perhaps it was the influence of Florence Nightingale, who would come to play with him in his nursery when his parents moved to Rome during part of his childhood.

Another figure who had an impact was his cousin, General James Lindsay.[2] He had inherited Balcarres, the family home that his father had bought from his brother, Alexander, 6th Earl of Balcarres, who had needed the capital to develop the Wigan coalfields. The family's Scottish roots were impressed upon Ludovic by this retired general and elder mentor – in 1855 a kilt was ordered for the eight-year-old and he was subsequently photographed by Mr Rodger, the 'daguerreotyper' from St Andrews (although the image was actually a calotype). They remained close throughout their lives.

107 General James encouraged both his son-in-law Alexander and grandson Ludovic, shown with him here, to embrace their Scottish roots (1855).

108 Ludovic's art, book and stamp collecting began in earnest while still at Eton (*c.*1860).

Ludovic divided much of his time between Haigh Hall and Dunecht. His affection for the latter began to wane in the late 1870s with the economic downturn and the fraught case involving the theft of his father Lord Lindsay's body from the crypt. But in 1886, after a lengthy series of negotiations, he was able to buy Balcarres back from Coutts, who had fallen on difficult times since the divorce from his wife, Blanche. He returned with his family to his true spiritual and much-loved home.

Ludovic's collecting bug began with stamps while at Eton. Aged thirteen, he had met the great bookseller Bernard Quaritch, whereupon they embarked on a lifelong and resoundingly fruitful symbiotic relationship. A tutor would describe Ludovic as 'remarkably intelligent [with] a very unusual degree of aptitude for *anything* that takes his fancy.' By the time he left Eton, he had, like his father before him, amassed a collection of over five hundred incunabula.

While some portraits indicate a bookish sort, others portray a statuesque and imposing figure – an impression reinforced by his splendid red beard. He was actually tall, athletic and surprisingly strong. He went up to Trinity College, Cambridge, but did not enjoy it, so he left and went on to an army tutors' school. Here he relished the healthy lifestyle, winning the long jump and hammer – disciplines that would seem to require opposite physical attributes – before taking a commission in the Grenadiers. When canvassing in Wigan in his late twenties, he was challenged to jump against the local champion over a pit. He was still more than able and made the leap, though still in his riding boots and breeches, and by defeating his opponent was said to have won the votes of a whole street. He retained his military links until 1900 as lieutenant-colonel commandant and honorary colonel of the 1st Volunteer Battalion, the Manchester Regiment.

A side interest saw Ludovic rise steeply through the ranks of the masons, joining as freemason before becoming senior grand warden of the United Grand Lodge. He was incurably curious and added to his ever-broadening range of interests by

109 Ludovic was strong and athletic, though asthma became the bane of his life in later years (*c.* 1870).

110 From 1876 to 1900, Ludovic rose to become lieutenant-colonel commandant and honorary colonel of the 1st Volunteer Battalion, the Manchester Regiment.

travelling in his early twenties to Italy, Waterloo, Cologne, Hanover, Stockholm and St Petersburg (including a long river trip down the Volga and Don to Sebastopol), Constantinople, Trieste, Vienna and Paris.

The striking Emily Bootle Wilbraham, granddaughter of the 1st Baron Skelmersdale, had come into Ludovic's life on New Year's Day 1868, when they met at a great ball held for his coming of age at Haigh. She 'has made a great conquest of Udo who was her devoted slave all the time she was there', recorded his sister, Alice. They married in the summer of 1869 and went on to have a daughter, Evelyn, and six sons: David, known as 'Bal', later the 27th Earl of Crawford, Walter, Robert (known as Robin), Edward, Ronald and Lionel. All of them achieved much in their own lives, whether in their work or war.

Marriage, however, was not going to stifle his yearning to travel in search of art, books and furthering of his budding research in astronomy.[3] This went down well with his father, who recognized the shortage of such material in the growing library at Haigh. Ludovic went on to lead a series of important expeditions around the world to witness and record some of the key observations possible at the time, always kitted out with the latest and finest equipment for him and the eminent scientists

111 Ludovic was incurably curious. In his twenties he travelled throughout Western and Eastern Europe, initiating a lifetime of travel (1875).

112 Ludovic and Emily at his sister May Holford's Westonbirt House for a shooting party (1884).

who accompanied him. Meanwhile, with an apparently insatiable but systematic approach, and the learned and invaluable help of Quaritch, he was able in time to set up what was probably the world's greatest scientific library. He had sought to equal, if not better, the Tsar's library in St Petersburg. He succeeded. Thus, at the precociously young age of around thirty, he became the president of the Royal Astronomical Society, purely on merit, and in the same period fellow and later vice-president of the Royal Society. In the meantime, he never missed the chance to fill a gap in the ever-increasing manuscript collection and library. His stamp collection alone became the most outstanding ever compiled. His son, Bal, wrote:

He was a collector born. Every collection he ever made was about the best of its kind – stamps, bibles, manuscripts, French State papers, French revolutionary iconography. When my father took up some particular branch he concentrated his efforts on securing the finest examples available. He was the most professional amateur I ever met, a dilettante with profound insight and an unerring flair, a buyer of promptness and pertinacity and always able to withstand buying a cheap or second-rate thing. Dealers all over Europe used to ask his opinion on doubtful items. He would concentrate his force, master his subject, analyse it to its last degree, deriving every attainable advantage, benefit or recreation and then he would drop it perhaps never again to give one thought to the subject.

As an MP between 1874 and 1880, his contribution to politics was less apparent. The records show he rarely spoke. It appears the only reform he introduced was for the right for MPs to be able to play chess. He recalled a rare occasion when he did join a debate: 'While speaking on the railway Bill I was absent-mindedly gazing at the Ladies' Gallery and said "There is one more important point I should like to lay before your Ladyships' notice." Lord Salisbury who was sitting immediately below me turned round and said, "Why Crawford, which party are you addressing now?"' In 1907 he attended the Chamber during the visit of Mark Twain, who had

113 Ludovic, far left, as part of the delegation to welcome Mark Twain, sixth from left, on his visit to parliament in 1907, while in the country to receive an honorary degree at Oxford.

come to England to receive an honorary degree from Oxford University. Nonetheless, his experiences with the family electricity company, along with his other technological interests, gave him the knowledge and undoubted understanding which he brought to the Board of Trade on the Patent Commission in the late 1880s.

In 1888 he was horrified to learn that the Scottish Universities Bill proposed the abolition of the Royal Observatory of Edinburgh. With the possible demise of Scotland's position in the world as a leading centre for astronomical research, he offered the entirety of the apparatus and scientific library from Dunecht to ensure its survival. His observatory had the finest equipment and leading astronomers had visited it from around the world. It was agreed that the institution could continue if, in addition to his donation, he as Royal Astronomical Society president chaired the reorganization committee. He entrusted his own astronomer, Dr Ralph Copeland, with finding a new site. Blackford Hill on the south side of Edinburgh was identified and Copeland was subsequently appointed the third Astronomer Royal for Scotland.[4]

Ludovic's broad array of interests did not mean that he treated any area lightly, nor was he some profiteering absentee proprietor. On the contrary, overseeing his stake in his cousin Coutts's Grosvenor Gallery along with the London Electricity Supply Corporation threatened to become all-consuming. There were meetings to be chaired at the British Museum, while the family's industrial concerns led him to represent the interests of the Coal Traders' Association, to say nothing of managing his estates and other investments.

114 Ludovic aboard the *Valhalla*, Malacca, 1908. He led scientific expeditions and quests for books and maunscripts around the world from the age of twenty-three. Wa-Wa, the silver gibbon, lived with him in his study at Cavendish Square.

None of his ventures or ability to keep growing the collections would have been possible without the successful operation of the vast Wigan Coal and Iron Company. Additionally, he always had an eye on the welfare of his employees and passionately supported the formation of trustworthy benefit societies, including taking on the presidency for twenty years of the Central Association for Distress caused by Mining Accidents and chairmanship of the Lancashire and Cheshire Mines Permanent Relief Society. But he was hard on himself and his health suffered. It was not helped by his time at Haigh, where smoke and soot from the burgeoning industries and mining concerns caused so many to suffer. His chronic asthma was also compounded by smoking (though he did reduce that to '10 and 1/10th cigarettes a day') and had been exacerbated by a bad bout of tropical fever he had contracted in Mauritius in 1874.

He increasingly only felt well at sea and subsequently his collecting concentrated on items that he could study and catalogue while on board, as well as developing new ways of cataloguing his stamp collection. The Middle East attracted him as the climate helped reduce his asthma attacks and he could hunt down great numbers of Greek, Coptic, Kufic and Arabic manuscripts and papyri. Photography became one of his more relaxing pastimes and by 1888 he had a Kodak No. 5, which he used with the new Eastman film. This he took on his regular trips to sea. He owned four of the finest private yachts of the time, the schooner *Venus* and two that were named the RYS SS *Consuelo*, before finally buying the fully rigged three-mast 1,490-ton RYS SY *Valhalla*, which sometimes had a crew of more than one hundred.

His position as Hereditary Standard Bearer, Great Steward and Premier Earl of Scotland resulted in fulfilling important roles in the coronation of George V. After being dressed by his faithful butler Poldo, he appeared at Westminster Abbey:

Somehow or other Father came into view rather unexpectedly, and I do not exaggerate when I say that the sight of him brought one's heart into one's mouth! Knowing where our seats were he looked straight up towards us and enveloped the whole gallery in a rapid glance, making a tremendous impression on the people round us, none of whom I imagine knew him by sight. 'Simply terrific', as one man said. Some of the foreign representatives in the choir got up in their places to get a better view of him in the procession.

Dozens of people have told us they thought him by far the most striking personality in the whole procession – in fact, he has become the topic of conversation in smart society. He was carrying a huge silver staff as big as a broomstick, which he held very high up, so that his hand was high or perhaps higher than his head. Though much bowed he nonetheless gave one the feeling that he was a gigantic in frame, and with his long hair, a kilt adorned with every conceivable appurtenance, and a piercing gaze, he really made a combination which was dominating and arresting.

In the long wait in the Abbey he almost fainted but was saved by a spoonful of whisky from Lord Abercorn 'which set me right in a moment.'

From then on, he spent much of his time in his London house working on his huge collection of thirteen thousand French Revolution papers. His inner sanctum was a large book-lined room built over the garden.

In his memoirs, writer Gabriel Stanley Woods recalled in 1912:

I was confronted by a tall imposing figure, already somewhat emaciated by constant bouts of asthma. His tweed suit hung loosely about him, his piercing but kindly eyes seemed to look right through me; he wore a straggling beard – so much the fashion in the period following the Crimean War. He told me later that in his day only actors were clean-shaven and he did not approve of the modern fashion. During those last months of his life Ludovic seldom left his study and was constantly racked by severe fits of coughing, the sound of which penetrated to my small room. His only relief was to be found in the cylinders of oxygen, which were in continual demand.[5]

His grandson, David, described what he saw:

The building in the garden at 2 Cavendish Square ... [had a long passage containing] the famous stamp collection, and this led into the very large room where he sat, and which I remember. It was filled with instruments, lathes, etc., and he sat at an enormous desk, filled with books with which he was working. He was always delighted to welcome us as children, to give us presents, including surprisingly good stamps (e.g., proofs of the penny black). There was a parrot in the room, and roaming without doing damage, a silver gibbon which he had brought home from some tropical island. He was the most impressive person I had ever seen: but we were never in any way frightened of him.

Ludovic's vision for the Bibliotheca Lindesiana was for it to contain the totality of human knowledge. He had attempted to create a catalogue so that its contents might be known, widely available and useful for all. The Libraries Act, which he supported, encouraged the growth of public libraries but also had the unintended consequence of making his library's original purpose obsolete.

115 Ludovic's position as Hereditary Standard Bearer, Great Steward and Premier Earl of Scotland meant he played a prominent role in the coronation of George V (1911).

116 Ludovic (centre) with Eddie, Walter, Robert and Lionel before leaving for the wedding of their cousin, Roffredo Caetani, later 17th Duca di Sermoneta (October 1911).

On his death in 1913 his eldest son noted 'the chorus and esteem and love which his death evoked, and I can never forget the poignant grief shown by humble people in his entourage – valet, commissionaire, housekeeper, doctor and so forth. The funeral was at Balcarres, one of the most stately and solemn ceremonies I ever witnessed.' His coffin had been taken on the night train from London to Kilconquhar Station, where it was covered in a Lindsay tartan and drawn by four horses the two-and-a-half miles up to the chapel at Balcarres. A telegram from the King read: 'I have lost an old and valued friend of many years standing, for whom I had the greatest respect.' At 12.30 p.m. on 4 February there was a memorial service in the Chapel Royal; at the same hour Ludovic was buried beside the roofless chapel at Balcarres.

14

The Chatelaine of Balcarres, Haigh, Palmieri and Dunecht

Emily Florence, Countess of Crawford & Balcarres, (née Bootle-Wilbraham), 1848–1934

The Bootle-Wilbrahams were prominent Lancashire landowners whose family could be traced back to Sir Richard Wilburgham, Henry III's sheriff of Cheshire in 1259. As they lived near Haigh Hall at Lathom Hall, Skelmersdale, it was inevitable that two neighbours in their twenties with similar backgrounds would meet, and so it was that at a great ball held at Haigh on 1 January 1868 to celebrate his twenty-first birthday Ludovic met his future wife.

Shortly after meeting, he travelled to Rome with his parents, but he knew she was going there too, and soon after he proposed to her. At the time, he was still serving as a lieutenant in the Guards and it was deemed inappropriate to rush into marriage immediately. But the couple were very much in love and a year later, in the summer of 1869, they were married at St George's in Hanover Square. Once his commission had finished the following year, the young family moved up to Haigh Hall with their baby daughter, Evelyn. They went on to have six sons.

117 *right* Emily's mother, also Emily (née Ramsbottom), spent much of her widowhood at Balcarres after the death of Col. the Hon. Edward Bootle-Wilbraham (*c.*1895).

118 *opposite* In 1875 Emily travelled to Rome with her daughter, Evelyn, for a fancy-dress ball held by her sister, Ada, wife of Onorato Caetani.

Emmie was considered one of the best-looking women of her age, famed for her figure and youthful appearance. Some young officers 'swore she was not a day over seventeen, little suspecting that there were seven squalling children'. Some years later a contemporary said that 'her figure is as straight as if she were eighteen, surrounded by six boys looking quite young enough to be their sister.'[1]

She was close to her sisters, in particular Ada, who went on to marry Onorato Caetani, who, on the death of his brother, became Principe di Teano and 15th Duca di Sermoneta. Frequent travels to

10210

119 'Rory won't jump.' Eddie, Emily and Lionel at Elie (1892). Generations of the family have been repeatedly drawn to the rocks and beaches around Elie, four miles from Balcarres.

120 Missionary work, prospecting and diplomacy would take Eddie, Lionel and Ronald abroad for much of their younger years. Here they are seen as teenagers with their mother in the Balcarres garden (1892).

Italy included one memorable trip in 1875 for a great fancy dress ball in her sister-in-law's Roman palazzo, to which she was accompanied by her daughter, Evelyn, who was also suitably attired. Onorato and his sons, Leone and Roffredo, became great friends of Ludovic and would occasionally join him on his yachts *Valhalla* and *Consuelo*.

Meanwhile, one of her sisters, another Evelyn, who married Sir John Kennedy, had a daughter, Kathleen ('Yone'), who married the Crawford's youngest, Lionel. This closely-knit family would later frequent Balcarres when it came back into their family.

Emmie was strong-minded, less of an intellect, and particularly thrifty – to such an extent that her

121 Four generations. Mrs Wilbraham, Emily and her daughter Evelyn Mason holding Violet (1896).

122 Ada's husband, Onorato, became Principe di Teano and 15th Duca di Sermoneta on the death of his brother. Ada remained close to her sister, Emily (right), (*c.*1870).

husband was enraged to find that over a period she had saved something like £20,000 from the household allowance (approximately £1.3 million today).

The house had been run on exceptionally frugal lines – I never saw wine on the table for instance, except for my father, and everything in the house was managed at the minimum of cost and lowest standard of comfort … anyhow he was furious to learn that the meagre household allowance wasn't spent, and ultimately the investments were distributed among my brothers.[2]

Ludovic's taste and appetite were far less austere and so he would frequently repair to the Carlton Club. Emmie's concerns rose considerably when he decided to buy Balcarres back from his uncle Coutts at a time when their finances were less robust. She also worried that the burden of Ludovic's work at the British Museum, the Board of Trade, the estates and the electricity company was increasing while his asthma got progressively worse. Her protectiveness of him meant that she often referred to 'that dreadful Electric Light business'.[3]

In widowhood other concerns emerged as her sons came of age and started travelling abroad, both in peace and war. Nonetheless, fortified by an independence forced upon her by Ludovic's long voyages abroad, she had become matriarch of a family whose responsibilities included maintaining a paternalistic tradition and sense of duty. She had strong religious convictions, which led her to encourage initiatives to improve housing and also lend support to local charitable institutions, clothing societies, Sunday and church school, and sick clubs.

Electricity

'That dreadful electric light business'

Among the diverse group of brilliant minds engaged in the wide range of enterprises the Lindsays became involved with in the latter part of the nineteenth century was a young inventor called Sebastian Ziani de Ferranti. For a while, a collaboration between the two parties saw them lead the world as they embraced the new technologies that harnessed the power of electricity for the benefit of all.

An enthusiastic polymath, Ludovic, the 26th Earl of Crawford, was as courageous as he was curious. While visiting the 1881 International Exposition of Electricity in Paris in his role as British commissioner, he had witnessed Edison's incandescent lights and immediately became enthused about the endless possibilities of electricity. His first experiment, in May 1885,[1] was to install lighting in the Bond Street gallery of his cousin, Sir Coutts Lindsay,[2] which would help the Grosvenor Gallery become one of the more fashionable evening venues, uniquely able to entice visitors to enjoy the paintings at regular soirées illuminated by the 'new smokeless electricity'.

The initial foray into this uncharted territory saw Messrs Gaulard and Gibbs install one of the new generators in the gallery's spacious basement, powered by a coal-fired steam engine. The modest demand of the gallery's lighting meant that they were soon able to harness the excess capacity of its one-thousand-kilowatt output to supply neighbouring properties, launching the AC revolution in England.[3] In 1886 Ferranti was appointed the company's chief engineer and immediately replaced the system with transformers and switch gear of his own design, doubling the voltage to 2,400 volts – enough for ten thousand ten-candle-power lamps. This first incarnation of the company, and one of the first owners of an electricity grid in Great Britain, was Sir Coutts Lindsay & Co. Other investors included Coutts's brother, Robert, Lord Wantage and Robert's father-in-law, Lord Overstone. Within three years the electricity supply extended from St John's Wood to Lincoln's Inn Fields and from Eaton Place to Euston.

Soon the small power station was outgrowing its surroundings. A new company, the London Electricity Supply Corporation (LESC) was registered in 1887. This was to be the vehicle, open to public investment, that would allow the operation to enlarge. Deptford was identified as the ideal location: the land was cheap, the river Thames provided water for cooling, and it was close to railway lines along which they could run cabling and where coal could be readily delivered. No longer did the Mayfair residents have to put up with the noise and vibrations from generators, endless lorries bringing coal and equipment

123 *above* The nascent Sir Coutts Lindsay & Co. electricity company was struggling until Sebastian Ziani de Ferranti, one of the great innovators of the age, was appointed company engineer in 1886. © The Science and Society Picture Library

124 *right* Ferranti's improvements meant that by 1887 the company was the country's largest supplier of electricity. This 1887 map shows the extent to which the family's London Electricity Supply Corporation grid extended over London. © The Science and Society Picture Library

OVERHEAD SYSTEM - 18
2400 VOLTS.
REGENT'S PARK
MARYLEBONE
CAVENDISH SQ.
OXFORD CIRCUS
SOHO SQ.
HOLBORN
LINCOLN'S INN FIELDS
GROSVENOR SQ.
GROSVENOR GALLERY
ADELPHI WHARF
TRAFALGAR SQUARE
ST JAMES'S SQ.
GREEN PARK
ST JAMES'S PARK
ST. MARTIN IN THE FIELDS
RIVER THAMES
ST. GEORGE HANOVER
EATON PLACE
WESTMINSTER

125 By 1888 the 1,000-kW alternators in the Deptford power station, all designed by Ferranti, were producing over 10,000 volts, far exceeding any other supplier worldwide.

126 After Ferranti set off on his own in 1891 he continued to supply equipment to the Lindsay family's London Electric Supply Co.

or removing ash, nor the unpleasant smoke from the premises' tall chimney. Instead, the gallery would be downgraded to a distribution centre for that area.

The great 'Battle of the Systems' that lasted long into the future was fought most fiercely in the United States, where George Westinghouse saw the high-voltage Alternating Current (AC) system as the viable route, believing it safer and more efficient, while Thomas Edison advocated the lower-voltage Direct Current (DC) alternative, with smaller power stations dotted all over an urban area. In Britain, Ferranti was almost alone in supporting AC power over DC, so it was thanks to that brave group of investors that the undertaking got as far as it did.

For two years Coutts remained as a rather ineffective chairman, leaving it up to Ludovic and Robert to handle the difficult task of negotiating with the Board of Trade, suppliers and customers. Emmie, Ludovic's wife, was less enamoured of the ground-breaking company, referring to it as 'that dreadful Electric Light business'.[4] However, Robert suggested that he take over the role of chairman, which he did in 1889, while Ludovic's increasingly poor health meant that they handed over the day-to-day running to James Staats Forbes, who had already cut his teeth as chairman of the Edison & Swan United Electric Light Co.[5]

Within a year the generators on the south bank of the Thames were producing thirty thousand horsepower – enough to light the whole of London through a series of substations and cables running over eight miles away along with the unheard-of pressure of ten thousand volts – exceeding by many times any other electricity system in the world. Ferranti was alone in believing in such a scheme.

Being at the forefront of innovation meant that the company's own engineering abilities and initiatives were constantly being put to the test. They could not rely on outside suppliers of equipment, which led them to experiment and devise their own. This included a lathe to turn the largest castings ever produced, shipped down from Scotland, into the seventy-ton shafts that would be fitted into the vast forty-two-foot diameter dynamos. Of course, there were no suppliers of cabling at that time, so the company had to manufacture what became known as the 'mains' themselves. These twenty-foot lengths were laid along the railways and new District Line underground service routes to small substations before radiating out to customers. Ferranti's designs would prove to be the world's first viable high-tension line. The entire system was, by 1890, the largest anywhere and would only be superseded by the Niagara power station in the late 1890s. And for a while, it was profitable.

But all was not well. Considerable and continued investment was necessary, which allowed less pioneering competitors' projects to become more profitable, simply by being less encumbered by debt. Dividends started to dry up and Ludovic and Robert were reluctantly forced to invest further. As the latter remarked, 'I thought, as a director, I had some responsibility for driving the coach into the ditch, and I was not going to ask anybody else's help to pull it out again.'[6] The passing of the Electric Lighting Act of 1889 introduced twelve new companies into the market, all vying for the same district allocations. Competition became intense. A disastrous and costly fire at the Grosvenor Gallery and legal issues over patents were followed by a catastrophic equipment failure at Deptford. An improperly repaired transformer had transferred its load to an already fully loaded one and persisted until they all burnt out. With three months of repairs necessary, it was inevitable that three-quarters of the customers transferred their business to other, smaller companies.

127 One of the generating engines under construction for the Deptford Power Station by Hick, Hargreaves & Co. (1890). © The Science and Society Picture Library

128 Digging a trench for electric cabling near the Haigh wind pump in 1940. Although Ludovic was a member of the Select Committee on Lighting in 1879, it is strange that it was not until 1898 that a generator was installed at Haigh. The Hall had 124 storage batteries, more than the whole of the Wigan Corporation at the time. More surprising is that Balcarres did not get electric lighting until the late 1940s.

The Board of Trade compounded their woes by limiting the company's area of operation. Investors additionally were concerned that local authorities had the power to buy back electricity companies within only twenty-one years of their founding, in effect revoking their licences. By 1888 these rules were relaxed by increasing that period to forty-two years, but, combined with the financial losses, confidence in Ferranti's ambitious but costly vision had evaporated.

The two parties finally went their separate ways in 1891. The principles behind Ferranti's ideas were seen as bordering on reckless. But his genius was, in time, finally appreciated. Before long, his use of AC was universally adopted and remains the system used worldwide today.

For a while the LESC continued in its previous guise, even though by 1894 the company was in poor shape. Its competitors had started offering far cheaper rates. A receiver was appointed to tackle the rival operators head-on and threatened: 'If you persist in your policy, I shall simply reduce our rates by one half; and remember you have got your shareholders to whom you must render account. I have only myself. Today I am the Company.'[7] It worked. In 1900 Robert oversaw a series of upgrades and prospects improved with the new supplies of 6,600 volts for businesses and a similar amount for the London, Brighton and

South Coast Railway, the UK's first electric train line.[8] It had taken less than thirty years to go from the small seed of an idea to lighting up an art gallery to powering a mainline railway in 1909.

Ludovic's knowledge had, back in 1871, seen him appointed as the first vice-president of the Society of Telegraph Engineers (renamed the Institution of Electrical Engineers in 1887) under the presidency of Sir William Siemens.[9] The society's first *Conversazione* was held in his laboratory in 1872, where he showed off the largest electromagnet that had been made up to that time and various other scientific apparatus.[10] He was thus at the centre of the greatest technological advances of the age. Additionally, he played a pivotal role in the founding of the Electrical Standardizing, Testing and Training Institution, later known as Faraday House, serving as chairman of its governors from 1890 until his death. The college uniquely provided its graduates with opportunities to study and work in the field before electrical engineering had become respectable in universities.[11]

Ludovic had long recognized that his mines could benefit from electricity. Here was a source of power that could be harnessed to power pumps, fans, winches and other equipment with a ready source of fuel. The power station built at Kirkless near Wigan in 1908, one of the first in the industry, was fired by waste gas from their own coke ovens and supplied five thousand volts to its nearby collieries, the iron, tarmacadam and engineering works, offices and washery.[12] Concerns over gas explosions down below, easily caused by sparks from early electric lighting equipment, meant some applications took longer to implement. For instance, electric cap lamps were not fully approved until the 1930s.

Those long, round-the-world expeditions aboard Ludovic's yacht, the RYS *Valhalla,* made the vessel a prime candidate for using electricity in various innovative ways. She was fitted with Marconi telegraph, electrically powered navigational devices, a desalination system and lighting, and she was the first to have electric-powered steering.[13]

Ludovic saw that high-speed communications could bring wide-reaching benefits for shipping, commercial, military and strategic interests and also be of considerable assistance to meteorologists. The Pacific Radiotelegraphic Company, of which he became the first chairman in 1909, proposed a wide chain of stations across Oceania connected by wireless telegraph. 'Messages have been received from a distance of 2,500 miles. A thoroughly competent operator can send as many as a hundred words a minute through the air, but the average sending speed is 30 words a minute.'[14] By the end of the year stations were being set up 'and within a few months the dots on the map which are now geographical mysteries to the junior class in geography will become as much within the ken of civilised countries as Sydney.'[15]

Ludovic's son, David, 'Bal', the 27th Earl, was less interested in the science but he was, as chairman of the North of England Institute for Electrical Engineers, fully aware of its importance. He ensured his industries and mines all benefitted from the many new developments – even though, ironically, Balcarres would not see electric lighting until the late 1940s, some fifty years after the first light bulbs had lit up the paintings at the Grosvenor Gallery.

15

'Handsome, clever, impetuous and satirical'

Lady Alice Frances Houblon (née Lindsay), 1849–1915, and Col. George Bramston Archer Houblon, 1843–1913

Alice Frances Lindsay was Ludovic's eldest sister, putting her in an assertive position, which would in later years lead her to being described with the mixed compliments of 'very handsome, impetuous, clever and satirical,'[1] and 'loveable, queenly, observant, missing nothing' though 'a kind-hearted lady with a patronising manner.'[2]

It was in London that the twenty-three-year-old Alice fell 'blindly in love with the very antithesis of our family characteristics', wrote her less than impressed sister Jane. 'The inexpressive handsomeness, the unimaginative prosaic commonplaceness of admirable George Eyre ... Dull, Dull, Dull, George [*sic*] how he bored even little schoolroom me, near whose ears every family groan was carefully suppressed. But I remember wondering how Alice could bear the humiliation of seeing him sitting whole mornings and evenings lolling in an armchair Doing Nothing! Supreme marvel. For never did any member of our family do nothing!' But in April 1873, presumably to her sister's chagrin, they married.

In spite of Jane's misgivings, George was actually popular and respected in the army as well as among his own workforce and local communities, becoming Colonel of the Buffs[3] from 1870 to 1874, the Royal Berkshire Regiment in 1898 and High Sheriff of Essex in the same year. On the death of his father in 1891, George had his Eyre surname legally changed to Archer Houblon[4] as part of the agreement in his inheritance. This came with three substantial properties: Culverthorpe in Lincolnshire, which they did not use; Hallingbury Place, the main Archer Houblon family home in Essex, where they lived until 1909; and Welford Park in Berkshire, which had been in the family from the mid-seventeenth century. All were used as hospitals during the Great War.

George's relations became increasingly endeared to Alice and she wholly embraced their history, writing an exhaustive two-volume book, *The Houblon Family, Its Story and Times.*[5] Other works included *By the Way: Essays on Various Subjects* and a collection of poems entitled *Love as Pedlar and Other Verses*. Her sense of duty drove her to support local and national communities; she held the presidencies of the Arachne Club (for training girls in domestic sciences) and the Essex branch of the Soldiers' Help Society. In 1904 she became the first president of the National Union of Mistresses, an organization that ruled that 'Members shall endeavour to make conditions of service pleasant, healthy, and moral for both men and women servants.'[6]

In 1912, just before his seventieth birthday, George experienced a fainting fit in church, which caused a broken rib followed by a throat infection. He never fully recovered and died a year later. In

129 Alice standing with her sister Mary (Amy). She was described by her younger sister, Jane, as 'very handsome, impetuous clever and satirical' (*c.*1860).

130 A shooting party at Lockinge. From left: George and Alice Houblon, Jim Majendie, Lady Louisa Charteris, Aline Majendie, Lord Ebrington, Lord and Lady Wantage, Lady Ebrington, Capt. Erskine and Alice, far right (*c.* 1900).

131 All of the 25th Earl's daughters were creative and artistic. Alice is seen here playing the guitar at the Villa Palmieri (*c.* 1870).

132 Alice's husband, Col. George Eyre, was descended from Sir John Houblon, the first governor of the Bank of England, whose surname they adopted (1901).

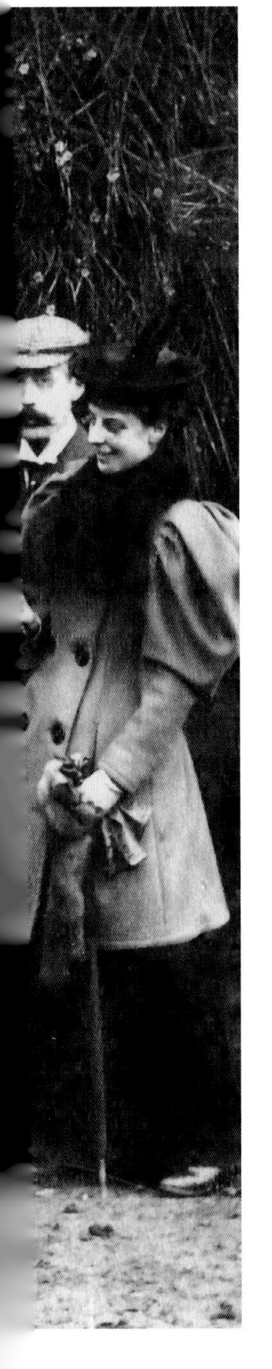

line with his express wishes, he was buried not in the Houblon family vault, but in an ordinary grave in the newly consecrated extension to the Hallingbury churchyard, which he himself had given to the church, and in which he was the first occupant. In his obituary in the *Herts and Essex Observer*, the 'Good old Colonel'[7] was described as one of 'nature's gentlemen' and very much a representative of the old order. Alice died three years later at Howe Green House on 28 September 1915. Her funeral, unlike her husband's, took place very quietly – as most did during wartime.[8]

Alice and George had nine children, adding to their more than thirty first cousins on the Lindsay side of the family alone. The eldest, Margaret Mary Anne, born in 1873, became a sculptor of note and exhibited her *Royal Artillery Team and Gun* at the Walker Art Gallery in 1901. Their sons, Henry Lindsay Archer Houblon, born at Villa Palmieri, and Richard both served in the army, the former in the South Africa War and both in the Great War, each being mentioned in dispatches, with Richard earning the DSO. In just seven years, grief must have haunted Richard, as his twenty-nine-year-old brother, Francis, died in 1909; two similarly aged sisters, Sybil and Alice, passed away two years later in 1911; his father in 1913 and then his mother, Alice, in 1915. Henry was happiest while alone in the country, a keen shot, big game hunter and fisherman. He died in 1954, fittingly after a day spent shooting.[9]

16

Sunshine and Shadows

Lady Mary Susan Félicie Meynell (née Lindsay), 1852–1937, and the Hon. Frederick George Lindley Meynell, 1846–1910

We are fortunate to have the fullest account of Mary Lindsay's life from her own pen. Her reminiscences, *Sunshine and Shadows*,[1] paint not only the most candid portrait of her family, but also of the changing world around her. She was resigned to the inevitable, believing that, however nobly the great estates had been run, they had had their heyday and would no longer be supported by the legions of staff or host the long house parties or the frequent dazzling displays of opulence.

133 Amy remained single until she was twenty-six. In the preceding years, she travelled widely throughout Europe (*c.* 1878).

Her times at Dunecht were clearly her happiest. Away from the school room, learning to cook oatcakes, finding strawberries and raspberries in the kitchen gardens or even recalling the smell of the apple rooms seemed so long ago by the time she put pen to paper. Visiting the keeper and kennels to see his magnificent St Bernard dog, meeting the foresters, or the long walks to the shop for barley sugar could never be forgotten. She recalled how she always missed the crisp clean, fresh Scottish air when they had to come south once again to their Lancashire home near Wigan.

London, on the other hand, had its own attractions. As a young girl, Mary admired the different carriages with their portly, white-powdered coachmen as they drove their matching horses, stepping high in perfect unison in brightly polished tack:

They were easily recognised by their colours and liveries, coal black prancing steeds or brilliant bays with their bunches of coloured ribbons at the ears, or the silver and blue liveries of the French Ambassador, or the yellow carriages of the Fitzwilliams, the mulberry and grey, or brown, or black and white, one saw them all and enjoyed the sight.[2]

Streets may have been noisier than today with the ever-present sounds of iron-shod hooves on cobbles pulling all manner of commercial carts and the grandest carriages, broughams to landaus, phaetons to cabriolets and barouches to coaches. With so many horses it is unsurprising to learn that the busier streets had crossing-sweepers and that it was best to avoid the frequent hay carts delivering fodder

134 Amy's childhood reminiscences in *Sunshine and Shadows* give some of the most revealing impressions of life at the Lindsay houses (*c.* 1862).

135 Amy, Minnie and Alice with their mother, Min, Countess of Crawford, at Villa Palmieri (*c.* 1860).

to the mews. Then there were organ-grinders to whom Mary and her siblings flung pennies and rolls; trips to Hampstead Heath from their great double-fronted Grosvenor Square house in their small double pony carriage to ride on white linen-covered saddles on the donkeys for hire; or excursions to Fulham to see the market gardens.

The most stressful time for young ladies of Mary's background arrived with the daunting initiation into the social scene, including the occasional 'Drawing Rooms' held at Buckingham Palace, when they were presented to the monarch. At 3 p.m. on the appointed day mothers would line up with their debutante daughters, dressed in low-necked white dresses, white veils and long trains, possibly adorned in great ostrich feathers. They would then enter, curtseying up to the Queen, who might deign to kiss those above a certain rank before the nervous girl would perform a backwards walk, somehow manoeuvring her four-foot-long train, before curtseying once more and retiring, relieved that she had avoided a terrible faux pas.

The debutante year was supposed to be one in which parents could ensure their offspring found a suitable spouse, but in the 'fresh, delicious fun loving, amusing, immensely admired'[3] Mary's case that would not happen until she was twenty-six. Instead, she travelled widely in Europe, having begun when she was twelve when she and the family crossed the Alps by Mount Cenis in three *vetturini* carriages on their way to Florence. Italy remained a favourite destination and over the years they holidayed there frequently, most often at Villa Palmieri.

In 1878 she eventually fell in love with and married the 'very good looking, with excellent brains'[4] Hon. Frederick 'Freddie' Lindley Wood.[5] The couple made their home at two of his inherited houses, Hoar Cross Hall and Temple Newsam, which they shared with his widowed sister, Emily, Mrs Meynell Ingram. She was immensely rich and clever, though her sister Jane, in her more unreserved memories, believed her to be over-controlling and authoritarian.[6]

Notwithstanding reservations about Emily, Mary and Freddie's relationship with her was initially a happier one and they readily accepted an invitation to join her on her yacht the *Guinevere* in 1884, even though Mary concluded she was the only member of her family who did not like the sea, describing herself as 'a shocking sailor'.[7] The leg down to Gibraltar in a passenger steamer failed to raise her spirits, taking eight rather than the expected five days. She had to endure storms, cockroaches and unpalatable food that had that 'same peculiar steamboat flavour'. Once they were on board the *Guinevere* they sailed on to Algiers in hideous weather. When it did calm down, they witnessed the extraordinary sunsets that were being experienced around the world as a result of the catastrophic eruption of Krakatoa in Indonesia, which had ejected many millions of tons of dust into the atmosphere a year before. From there they sailed on to Palermo and Messina, but she felt it was too much for her and decided she could not continue on to Constantinople.

Leaving the party and travelling up through Italy did, however, have its compensations as she was able to visit Pompeii and Rome before returning to her much-loved Palmieri. For some inexplicable reason, Mary elected to go on another yachting adventure four years later with her husband. However, the conditions were even worse – and the voyage lasted four months.[8] There would be another memorable expedition in 1890 when she relented once more and joined her sister-in-law Emily in Egypt, but this time on the *Horus*, a luxurious *dahabeah*. This time she was able to fully enjoy the tranquil, steady pace as they sailed up the Nile, visiting all the great wonders over the next two months.

While staying with her Uncle Bob, Lord Wantage,[9] they were shown around a medieval and Victorian Gothic manor house that was coming on to the market, The Abbey, near Abingdon, not far from her mother's house in Burcote. They quickly sold the small London home that they had by now outgrown and bought it in 1890, eventually using it principally as their holiday home where they could enjoy rowing along the upper reaches of the river Thames while being close to her cousins and mother.

But the relaxed life that Mary had long known was now less light and easy as she found herself in far more complicated and trying environment caused by her sister-in-law's decision-making. Thus far they had been able to bring up their five children at Temple Newsam and Hoar Cross Hall as well as the Abbey, but much was turned upside down when Emily died in 1904, leaving a will that was complicated and obscure. It allowed other members of his family to contest the settlement, which included disputes about much of the valuable contents of the houses that they had been assured by Emily would be theirs. Eventually, they gave up the Abbey, and Hoar Cross Hall became their principal home. They changed their surname to Meynell as it was about to die out and Freddie felt it was one that should be retained since it dated back to the Norman past.

Life now appeared more settled. Freddie and Mary travelled up to Scotland, her first return visit for seventeen years. They stayed at Glamis, where they enjoyed a dancing display by Lady Strathmore's little daughter, Elizabeth, who would later become the Duchess of York, and later still Queen and Queen Mother. Their last happy trip came to an end when they returned to London with Freddie beginning to feel unwell. He died shortly after from a brain haemorrhage in 1910, aged sixty-one.

Mary's London home, 8 Lennox Gardens, became a hospital during the war. It had only twenty-three beds, but the operating theatre was in constant use and eventually Lady Mary Meynell's Hospital for Officers attracted a surprise visit from the King and Queen. The wards were named after her children: Francis, Robert, Everard, Charles and Mary Margaret Desiree (known as Daisy). Harold Macmillan, the future prime minister whose mother was a friend of Mary's, was cared for there after being wounded at the Battle of Loos.

In 1910 Mary had concluded her chapter on the death of her husband with words that could have been the epitaph of her own full life:

136 *opposite* Five of the wards at the Lady Mary Meynell's Hospital for Officers were named after her children, Francis (known as Fra), Robert, Everard, Charles and Mary Margaret Desiree (known as Daisy and not included here), (1896).

And now that chapter of my life was ended. I had written closed – but I was wrong, for it never has been closed and shafts of sunlight have ever since that day of dark shadow been penetrating into the new life and times which were to follow and continue to this day. But – I had to begin again – and that is always hard to begin again – alone. When I say alone, though, I am almost ashamed for there rise before me the loving eyes of my children, whose tenderness and care for their mother have been an unending source of thankfulness – I may almost say of surprise – to me ever since that dark November day. Peace and contentment and happiness, too – have come back to me, I can say with truth. Indeed, how could it be otherwise with all the blessings that have been showered on me with open hand? Deo gratiae! *– and there it ends – till yet another life begins.*[10]

137 *above left* In 1878 Amy married the very good-looking and intelligent Hon. Frederick (Freddie) Lindley Wood. They later changed their surname to his old family name, Meynell (*c.*1895).

138 *left* Amy was instrumental in the creation of the Heartsease Guild, which promoted needlework for the welfare of the widows and unmarried daughters of the clergy and of army and naval officers (*c.*1895).

17

'A writer who possesses an excellent gift of humour'

Lady Margaret Majendie (née Lindsay), 1850–1912 and Lewis Ashurst Majendie, 1835–85

Margaret, also known as Minnie or little Min, was born at the Lindsay's Aberdeenshire retreat, Dunecht, and would eventually leave home and move to Essex, where she became the chatelaine of Hedingham Castle and, like her father, Alexander, Lord Lindsay, a prolific writer.

Minnie was seen as 'brilliantly clever, very ambitious, full of intense admiration for everything noble and great and with boundless energy and spirits and appreciation of all that was beautiful and artistic.'[1] She was the first of her siblings to get married which, according to her sister, happened rather suddenly.[2] Staying with Canon Charles Courtenay, Queen Victoria's chaplain, she and the much older Lewis Ashurst Majendie fell for one another instantly. But even with their age difference there were few reservations from either family as they saw him as an 'excellent man', full of energy with his involvements in politics, the church and his family home, Hedingham Castle.

Minnie's life with Lewis started so promisingly. His political career appeared to be in the ascendant and high office assured, but his health soon started to falter, gradually turning him into an invalid. Inevitably, this affected their finances while they made every effort to travel widely in France and Germany in search of a cure. They also ventured to the more clement Isle of Wight, where they became close to Alfred, Lord Tennyson, who would often read them his poems and introduced Minnie to writing. Her immediate family had all been immersed in

139 *right* Hedingham Castle has one of the finest and best-preserved Norman keeps in England, dating from around 1100.

140 *opposite* Minnie Lindsay was regarded by her sister, Mary, as 'brilliantly clever, very ambitious, full of intense admiration for everything noble and great', while Lewis was described as 'an excellent man' (*c.* 1870).

141 Field Marshal Lord Francis Grenfell with his and Aline's son, Pascoe, born in 1905 (see page 144). Grenfell was the popular polymath veteran of the Zulu and Boer wars; he studied Egyptology while commanding the Egyptian army and became president of the Royal Horticultural Society (*c.* 1907).

literature, either writing or collecting, and so it was no surprise that she would start putting pen to paper, becoming prolific. Her first book to be published was *Giannetto* in 1874.

A year later, Minnie moved into a smaller, more viable farmhouse near the castle where she continued to write novels and short stories until 1889.[3] *Dita*, her 1877 novel, led *The Graphic* to describe Minnie as

one of the most promising among rising novelists, but it seems out of place to speak of promise when performance is already so rich and assured. Nothing can be brighter or more touching, as occasion requires, than this charming little story, which will meet with a hearty welcome from all who can appreciate careful and highly finished workmanship.[4]

Not all her reviewers gave her such high praise. *The Pall Mall Gazette* described her oeuvre as

what may be called the solid pudding of fiction. There is a pleasant domesticity about them which is grateful to the palate for once in a way, after a course of more highly-spiced dishes. [Her book] Precautions, *like its predecessors, introduces us to a large 'set' of pleasant, well-dressed, well bred, very fair representatives of a certain not very interesting section of English society. Lady Margaret Majendie neither satirizes, idealizes nor philosophizes.*[5]

However, the *Spectator* reviewed *Once More* somewhat more favourably as 'A pretty volume of pleasant tales by a writer who possesses an excellent gift of humour and an easy, refined style.'[6] *The Pall Mall Gazette* later wrote how her 'books have always shown considerable inventive power, while she has gradually learned much more of the technique of novel-writing than she at first displayed.' Some were well received, even enjoyed by the Queen, and were the financial success that was so necessary for the upkeep of the much-loved Hedingham, which consisted of both a fine Queen Anne house and castle, arguably the finest and best preserved Norman keep in Britain, all of which were continuing to be a drain on the family.

142 Queen Victoria had enjoyed Aline's company when staying at Villa Palmieri and subsequently made her maid of honour. Here Aline is seen with her brother Jim, who inherited Hedingham (1901).

143 Horton the Hedingham butler with Billy the Donkey (*c.*1890).

The lack of funds did mean that she was not able to give their daughter, Margaret Aline, her ball. In spite of this, the girl was to see herself launched into society, having met Queen Victoria when the latter was staying at her Crawford grandmother's Villa Palmieri outside Florence. Each day Aline had been asked over from the villa they had temporarily moved into to act as a sort of maid of honour, the unofficial beginning of her court life.[7] The following summer she was officially appointed maid of honour, which came with the courtesy title of 'Honourable', a position she held till the Queen's death.

Aline, like her mother, married a man somewhat older than her. Field Marshal Lord Francis Wallace Grenfell was a highly decorated officer who had seen action in South Africa that included taking part in the final defeat of the Zulus at Ulundi in 1879.[8] He became famous for having taken command of the Anglo-Egyptian army in its most turbulent period at the end of the century. He went on to command the 4th Army Corps, becoming general and commander-in-chief in Ireland and eventually field marshal. In 1902, at the coronation of King Edward VII, he was made Baron Grenfell of Kilvey. His popularity, both in the army and in society generally, never waned. He was an elderly sixty-two when his son and heir, Pascoe, was born, but he would outlive Aline by fourteen years, dying at Windlesham, Surrey, on 27 January 1925.

Margaret's younger son, Bernard, was rising up through the naval ranks when he had an unfortunate skating accident, fracturing his skull and dying soon after. Tragedy struck again when Aline was taken ill and died within the year. The combined losses with the ongoing financial difficulties must have affected her own health as she, too, became sick and in 1912 finally passed away at her aunt Harriet Wantage's Lockinge home. Those Hedingham finances became an even heavier burden, leading James Henry Majendie, her surviving son, to be declared bankrupt. Of his two sons and a daughter, it was Musette who would eventually return to save Hedingham Castle, where she lived with her friend and companion, Dr Margery G. Blackie, until her death in 1981.

144 Musette Majendie as a child (c.1910)

145 Musette inherited Hedingham and successfully preserved the house and castle.

146 Jim Majendie's initial promise was overshadowed by the burden of running Hedingham, a mental breakdown and bankruptcy (*c.* 1900).

147 Jim Majendie pole-dancing with a friend.

18

'She might have become a great engineer'

Lady Mabel Lindsay, 1855–1936

In every generation there have been talented, loved and well-thought-of sons or daughters destined to worry their parents through their failure to find someone to marry. Often, the reasons were unexplained, but the anguish remained. In the case of Mabel ('May'), her sister Jane blamed it on her extreme short-sightedness, an issue that was the 'bane of her noble life, giving rise to an extreme pride preventing her from feeling at ease with young contemporaries, chiefly men.' There wasn't a great deal of encouragement from her mother who 'was the very, very last person to point a finger towards a matrimonial path'.[1] The sadness was that May was gifted, energetic and generous to a fault, but the least known by her descendants as she left no family nor obvious legacy. However, she played a pivotal role in supporting her mother, wrote beautifully and had rare ability.

148 Mabel, right, suffered from extreme short-sightedness, which her sister Jane, left, blamed for her insecurities with men. She never married (*c.*1868).

May was the fifth of the seven children of Alexander and Min,[2] and for much of her life until young adulthood would find herself being paired (almost by default) with her elder sister, Amy.[3] She was, perhaps, the most intellectual of the girls and the most appreciative of the learned world that she grew up in. She was seen as intensely eager with the ability to master any subject of the moment. 'Had she been a man she might have become a great engineer, or an equally great administrator.'[4] Meanwhile, those powers of management came into their own when she took on the responsibilities of Villa Palmieri, as well as their mother's house near Burcote in Oxfordshire and its later transformation into a wartime hospital.

She clearly appreciated her father and brother's bibliomania:

every room ... and every lobby and passage was lined with bookcases. All through our childhood and youth we had shared in the excitement caused by the acquisition of a long sought treasure whether by the exquisite tiny book of hours of Mary, Queen of Scots – the companion of her sorrows with her delicate autograph ... or the grand Mazzarine bible or the Koran on vellum – or the Landino Dante *or the 5 volumes of the* Colonna Missal *with its marvellously beautiful miniatures of the very finest period of art.*[5]

When her mother was ordered to recuperate in the heat from an attack of rheumatic fever in 1879, it was on Egypt they set their sights.

They were fortunate in that the country had 'not yet woken from the sleep of centuries'. They sailed as far south as the Second Cataract in what was then

149 Mabel's reminiscences remain some of the family archives' most colourful, though she only wrote about others, sadly never about herself (1872).

Nubia, just south of Wadi Halfa, where they were able to witness the

multitude of black and shining islets, among which the river, divided into hundreds of separate channels, spreads far and wide ... Foams, and frets, and falls; gushing smooth and strong where its course is free; murmuring hoarsely where it is interrupted; now hurrying; now loitering; here eddying in oily circles; there lying in still pools unbroken by a ripple; everywhere full of life, full of voices; everywhere shining to the sun.[6]

While it proved a curative exercise for her mother, it was to set off a steady decline for Lord Lindsay,[7] who found the heat of the last few days of March 1880 unbearable and exhausting. They returned to Italy, but after a spell in the cooler mountain air of Mugello, where he appeared to strengthen, he deteriorated once back at Palmieri and soon contracted bronchitis and pneumonia and died that December. It was another few weeks before they could finally lay him to rest at Dunecht.

From then until her mother's death almost thirty years later, May was her constant support. Her steadfastness became invaluable when she had to help support her mother after the horrifying discovery that her father's body had been stolen from the house chapel's crypt a year later in 1881. It was an enormous shock to all the family – as well as the country, including Queen Victoria, who wrote letters of sympathy, support and encouragement. It was not for another six months that his remains were found in woods not far from the house. It had been an exhausting two years for them all.

Those engineering skills that her sister Jane had once alluded to came into their own when May, in an enterprise quite unusual for a lady of her time, invented a cycle rack that enabled seven bikes to be transported at once. 'Not only did she want the freedom to pedal, she wanted to take her friends along for the ride.'[8] Three patents were granted for her 'New or Improved Vehicle or Cart for the Conveyance of Velocipedes from Place to Place', followed by a device with 'Improvements in or connected with Vehicles for Carrying Bicycles' for

which Morgan & Co. of Long Acre and 10, Bond St. became the licensed builders[9] and, eventually, 'A New or Improved Adjustable Grip or Clutch Device for Ropes, Flexible Cords, or the like, applicable for the Suspension of Bicycles, and for other Suspending Purposes'.[10] Sadly, however, it appears that the genius in these designs remained unrecognized.

The year 1904 was still early in the history of the automobile but safety concerns were becoming an issue. May, while staying at Ridley Hall with her sister, Anne Bowes-Lyon,[11] was being driven one day with her sister's mother-in-law, Frances, Countess of Strathmore, and niece, Muriel Bowes-Lyon, when the driver got into difficulties. Descending a steep hill, the vehicle swerved and turned over, ejecting its occupants. May suffered a broken arm and Muriel was concussed, but the seventy-three-year-old Lady Strathmore received the worst injuries, including concussion, a broken wrist and arm, having been thrown fifteen yards from the car. The driver was found practically uninjured beneath the overturned vehicle.[12] This was not May's first road accident. In 1878 she was out on the roads near Dunecht in a carriage with her sister-in-law Emily, Lady Lindsay. A farm horse kicked out and set their pair of horses off in a gallop – throwing Emily into a ditch, where she was knocked out and suffered a broken arm. It must have been particularly alarming as the coachman and May were then dragged a considerable distance, the carriage having lost one of its fore wheels – although they miraculously avoided serious injury.[13]

With her mother, she helped complete her late father's enormous tome, the heftily titled *The Creed of Japhet – That is of the Race Popularly Surnamed Indo-Germanic of Aryan as held before the Period of its Dispersion; ascertained by the aid of Comparative Mythology and Language.*[14] Perhaps it was this exercise that gave her the inspiration to write her own weighty two-volume *Anni Domini: A Gospel Study.*[15] This was her treatise on the First Testament and further evidence of May's broad range of talents and deep interest in theology.[16] She finally moved to Thorny House in London's Smith Square, where she died, aged seventy-six, leaving her diarist sister on her own. Jane lamented her passing by recording how she 'was so reliable, so clear headed and so devoted to those she loved, that she had something of the nature of a rock about her, which in these days one can ill afford to lose.'[17]

150 After their mother's death, Mabel and Jane continued to live at Burcote House, which Ludovic had bought for them before they eventually moved to Smith Square in London. (*c.* 1920).

19

A Marriage Within Two Ancient Clan Rivals

Lady Anne Catherine Sybil, 1858–1936 and the Hon. Francis Kenneth Bowes-Lyon, 1856–1948

It is an unfortunate truth that however loving and inspirational a child's upbringing may be, there are no guarantees that they will experience an equally happy and fulfilled later life. Anne, or Nan, was born into the most nurturing of families, often noisy with the sounds of laughter when cousins visited, though there would be a hushed air of expectancy when her father showed some newly acquired rare volume or manuscript. She herself developed some mastery in her creative endeavours, got married to a man she loved deeply and was blessed with seven children. But with the loss of her eldest son and a marriage to someone who became increasingly reclusive, life's earlier optimism and freedoms faded, to be replaced by a new, less agreeable order that progressively wore her down.

151 Anne (Nan) with the keepers at Haigh Hall (1861).

Until Nan reached her mid-twenties there was little talk of love and marriage. The combination of deeply religious parents and such an academic environment discouraged such thought. Indeed, her two sisters closest in age, May and Jane, never married at all. It was therefore a great surprise when she told Jane that she intended to accept the Hon. Francis Bowes-Lyon, known to all as Frank.[1] It appears that his brother's mother-in-law, Mrs Harry Scott, had been trying to kindle the relationship for some time – and with success.

He was very tall, nice looking, a perfect Rider and Dancer with a store of good spirits – but as I said I had not a speculative eye – so when I learnt that Frank was driving over on the morrow from Glamis Castle to convey her there for the day – I still suspected nothing!!![2]

Frank had all the attributes that would attract any young lady. He was 'said to be one of the best shots in Scotland, a beautiful rider, keen sportsman and generally popular, a young fellow full of life, good looks and charm, and withal the most wonderful friend rather than trainer of dogs I ever saw! They would do anything for him.'[3] He and his brother Claude, who would become the 14th Earl of Strathmore and Kinghorne, were from a family of eleven siblings. Claude and his wife, Cecilia, went on to have ten children, one of whom was Elizabeth, who married the future King George VI.

Frank's family story had parallels and connections with the Lindsays', who often held equally high roles in matters of state and also had less agreeable times when they fought over neighbouring lands. Even

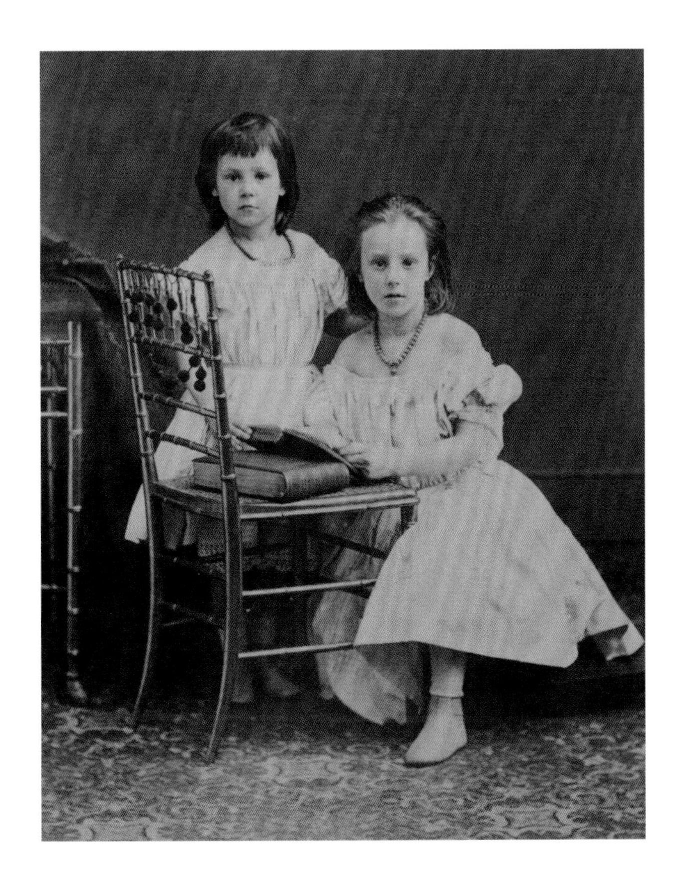

152 *opposite* Anne and Jane at Villa Palmieri. Much of the year was spent travelling between Dunecht, London, Haigh Hall and Palmieri (*c.* 1872).

153 *left* Jane and Nan, the 25th earl of Crawford's two youngest daughters (*c.* 1866).

today the ghost of the 'Tiger Earl', Alexander, the 4th Earl of Crawford, famed for his anger and more often known as 'Earl Beardie', is reputed to haunt Glamis Castle, playing cards with the Devil, who took his soul and will continue their game until Doomsday. Another connection was through Frank and his eldest son Charles's regiment, the Black Watch, which was originally raised and commanded by John Lindsay, the 20th Earl of Crawford. Geoffrey also joined the regiment while their youngest, Ronald, joined the navy, later becoming ADC to George VI.

Frank preferred the seclusion of Northumberland to London and increasingly harboured jealousies that meant that Anne became isolated from her own family, gradually depriving her of self-confidence. Lilian, the youngest in the family, felt similarly suffocated but sharing her mother's creativity and, taking control of her own life, she went up to Oxford University and started to write novels and poetry. Though she suffered from major health issues, her critically acclaimed *Collected Poems* was praised by Cecil Day-Lewis as 'gnarled and formidable verse.' But it would have been her poem, 'Battlefield', in memory of her lost brother, Charles, that would have resonated most profoundly with her parents.

By the late 1920s, back in Northumberland, with most of her children either dead, fledged or unable to travel due to sickness, Anne, a talented musician and singer (with a low voice), developed crippling arthritis and deafness.

It is sad to see them now in their lovely home, Ridley Hall, Northumberland, both quite unfit for a noisy battling world, with their devoted daughters [Muriel and Winifred] *living for their well-being and to bring what light and happiness they can into their lives, but it is good to know that some merry little grandchildren came there from time to time with their own atmosphere of brightness and life.*[4]

154 *left* Frank Bowes-Lyon was, above all, a countryman though his preference for a secluded life meant Anne felt increasingly isolated (*c.* 1890).

20

The Family's Most Accomplished Artist

Lady Jane Evelyn Lindsay, 1862–1948

Jane, or Jeanie, the youngest of the Crawford's seven children, followed the same path as most of her siblings. However, she was somehow influenced to a far greater degree by her childhood surroundings, inspiring her to paint, sculpt and candidly record her life and the immense, sweeping changes to society in her diaries.

She remembered her earliest years on the nursery floor fondly, being looked after by nannies and maids including the 'tall as a Grenadier' Mlle Mollet, the spirited and engaging French governess, to whom she was devoted and forever grateful for having had any shyness knocked out of her. The children inevitably became close to the house staff, of which there were rarely fewer than two dozen. Jane later lamented how they were to be some of the last times that her family and the many who worked for them were able to maintain such bonds. She deeply regretted how employees were taught by those with radical tendencies to hate their employers, especially in domestic service.[1] The period's chaotic political changes brought about such lasting and irretrievable gaps and even mistrust between those she had described as 'mistress and maid and man and master'. That old order, in which the great houses were viable communities, was coming to an end with the revolutionary changes spreading across Europe: the Great War, taxation, transport and modern amenities all conspiring to bring a centuries-old system to an end, for better or worse. But Jane felt she had been fortunate to experience some of the last great events of that gilded age.

The year's highlight was when they decamped to Dunecht, though London would always offer treats and its own excitements. When her parents took her up to town, they normally stayed at their 21 Berkeley Square house until the rebuilding of Nos. 9 & 10 Grosvenor Square had been completed, creating one great house.

Ours and the Fitzwilliam's carriage and horses used to occupy much of that corner of Grosvenor Square – in the afternoons – enlivening it with splashes of colour, the leather linings of their carriages was brilliant yellow, ours were blue. Our carriage horses in their London harness bedecked with gay broad satin ribbons of blue and scarlet at the ears and upholstered little saddle cloths and gilt metalling. The Head Coachman when driving the high barouche wore his grey curled wig and always in fine weather the coachmen and footmen sat on their folded overcoats which hung downwards glittering with brass buttons. How funny to write these common-place things! I only do so because these days are so different those were not so crowded as these.[2]

During the summer season of 1887 Jane, then twenty-five, received an invitation to stay at Windsor Castle. She was collected from the Windsor train station by an open carriage with a postillion and a pair of greys that took her up to the castle, where she was given a room in the Lancaster Tower. Even though the overall atmosphere was one of great formality and somewhat daunting, she found that the Queen was 'extraordinarily nice to me'. The next morning, they

155 Jane, or Jeanie, became a prolific writer of personal, and often extremely candid, reminiscences (1899).

156 Jane never married and spent much of her time caring for her mother, Margaret (Min), Countess of Crawford, here with her nephew David, 'Bal', later 27th Earl, at Villa Palmieri (*c.* 1890).

157 Jane frequently returned north. Here she is seen with neighbour and architect of many of Balcarres' improvements Sir Robert Lorimer, Bal's lifelong friend, Cosmo Gordon Lang, archbishop of Canterbury, and her great-nieces, Barbara and Mary (*c.* 1926).

attended prayers together before breakfast, followed by a tour of the state rooms and a visit to the mausoleum at Frogmore, where Prince Albert had been laid to rest some twenty-six years before, a special favour for the young lady.

Jane's experience left a lasting impression:

Inside the castle the quietness – immense significance of things – the absolute absence of showiness or glitter – no dawdlers – no hanging about – the atmosphere bespeaking Power as though one stood in a vast Engineering building filled with superb machinery – not working at the moment – buy potentially mighty – the unostentatiousness of the Queen herself – the latent Power in her Presence and simplicity of good breeding – Everything was in keeping and most impressive.[3]

When Jane got to know her a little better, especially after the happy times the Queen had had in Italy, she felt many great injustices had been done to the monarch's likeness and, as an observant, talented and skilled sculptor, when sitting close beside her, she noted with some astonishment the Queen's cheeks were not 'the swollen curve we subjects were accustomed to see portrayed but a face full of detail – full of interest to a sculptor, with structural hollows and salient beautiful nose and superb eyes clean cut and extra observant – not a dreamer's.'

Jane became close to her uncle and aunt, Lord and Lady Wantage at Lockinge, and in the winter of 1897 joined them on a fact-finding expedition to Egypt. The country was beginning to attract more visitors after the turbulent period of the eighteen-year Mahdist Revolt between the Mahdist Sudanese and Khedivate of Egypt, supported by Britain, and the danger of a threatened invasion by the Dervishes was subsiding. She was part of an auspicious group as they were accompanied by Wantage's old friend from the Crimea, General Sir Frederick Stephenson. He had been Commander-in-Chief of the British army in Egypt and had led the frontier force that had temporarily defeated the Dervish army.

They chartered a stern-wheel steamer, the *Toski*,[4] spending two months visiting the sites as they travelled up to Aswan, where they were held

158 Among many of Jane's skilled designs was her mother's headstone at Clifton Hampden, completed by Robert Bridgemann, who worked for her sister's family at Hoar Cross (*c.* 1910).

159 A marble bust of her uncle by Lady Jane Lindsay (1904).

up due to Dervish raids. Finally they got through and steamed on in a military post boat with accompanying barges of supplies for the Camel Corps. They eventually arrived at the British garrison at Karoska from where they could visit Abu Simbel under the protection of a guard of Sudanese soldiers. Egypt was an important ally, particularly since the Suez Canal had opened in 1869. It was imperative that the threat by the Sudanese forces in the Upper Nile was contained and thus developments were followed keenly by many back home. This fact-finding mission strengthened Wantage's successful plea to enforce the British and Egyptian garrisons, enabling Sir Herbert Kitchener to achieve his final crushing defeat of the Dervish forces at Omdurman.

As a peer's daughter Jane was entitled to sit in the nave of Westminster Abbey for the coronation of George V in 1911, but her cousin, Leonard Lindsay, an usher, found her a hidden seat high above among the gargoyles, giving her a unique view of the choir, north and south transepts, and high altar – which are not all simultaneously visible at ground level. Among the dazzling sea of tiaras and coronets, she was able to witness her brother, Ludovic,[5] dressed in his coronation robes, bearing the Sword of Scotland ahead of the Prince as they slowly progressed up the nave, attended by his grandson David and cousin Humphrey Lindsay. Ludovic's height, red beard and attire made a great impression and, for many, was the highlight of the procession. Having suffered an asthma attack and tired by the ceremony, he slipped away quickly afterwards and returned home by the Underground – 'a most incongruous passenger!'[6]

Jane was one of the most prolific and talented artists in the family. Unencumbered by a young family, she was able to devote much of her time to developing an array of skills. The white marble bust of her uncle, Lord Wantage, that now looks down a long passage at Balcarres is as fine as any by a leading sculptor and a testament to her skill. Her watercolours, painted on her journey up the Nile in a style close to Edward Lear's, are now in the Victoria & Albert Museum. She was a fine portrait artist with a delicate touch in her drawings and throughout her life was commissioned to illustrate novels and poems. Her largest piece was a design for the four stained-glass windows in the east transept of the Crawford Chapel at Wigan Parish Church, made in memory of her father.

After her mother died in 1909, Jane and her other unmarried sister, Mabel, continued to live at Burcote House, near Clifton Hampden, overlooking the Thames, which her brother Ludovic had bought for them. As soon as the war broke out, they turned it into a hospital and moved into a smaller house nearby as well as retaining their London house in Smith Square. There she died in 1947, aged eighty-six, the last surviving member of her immediate family, and was buried at Hedingham Castle, then owned by her sister Margaret's granddaughter, Musette. One newspaper report described her as someone 'who figured brilliantly in social life.'[7] Jane left perhaps the definitive account of her family's story from the period, one that is still amusingly informative and candidly revealing.

Astronomy

Astra, castra, numen, lumen, munimen[1]

Lord Lindsay had long known that the Bibliotheca Lindesiana's weakness lay in its paucity of scientific literature. He was thus relieved to see his son, Ludovic, take a keen interest in astronomy from a young age. This developed into something more than amassing the greatest collection of scientific books the world had seen, but a true passion for all things celestial on a practical level. Ludovic became one of the 'grand amateurs' of the Victorian era; in time, his knowledge and contribution to the science would see him elevated to president of the Royal Astronomical Society.

In 1864 the seventeen-year-old Ludovic wrote: 'I am in daily expectations of a notice from S&B Solomons that my telescope is ready ... How pleasant it will be at Echt [Dunecht]. I quite look forward to the long evenings to examine there, in that clear atmosphere.'[2] His studies at Trinity College, Cambridge, added to his growing knowledge while at the same time the precocious stargazer embarked on building his first observatory at Dunecht. This was to be no passing fad. Sir Philip Grey Egerton, a distinguished scientist himself, when visiting in 1870 was much impressed by the boy's 'new arrangement of spectroscope with telescope and sidereal mounting' for solar photography.

In the same year, the first of Ludovic's expeditions took place: a voyage to Cadiz to coincide with a solar eclipse, during which he was able try out his new spectrograph. He set up an observatory at the Maria Luisa vineyard, where they recorded every detail of the event for the Royal Astronomical Society. He was clearly moved by the experience: 'At the moment of totality a feeling of loneliness and sadness seemed to come over one, and I could distinctly hear the subdued murmur of voices at hand while the

160 *opposite* Ludovic's quest to build one of the finest scientific libraries began with purchasing Charles Babbage's collection. His target, in which he was successful, was to better the tsar's library at Pulkova (*c.*1890).

161 *below* The observatory at Dunecht (1919).
© The Royal Observatory, Edinburgh

162 *below* Dr Blackley, David Gill, Ludovic, and Dr Copeland at Belmont in Mauritius for the transit of Venus. While that phenomenon took the headlines, it was Gill's expertise and ingenious decision to observe the asteroid Juno that proved superior in measuring of the size of the solar system (1874).

reappearance of the Sun seemed to bring a feeling of relief.' While there were mathematical measurements to be taken, his lyrical descriptions were evidence of his passion; the moon 'had, moreover, the colour and appearance of pearl, with a bright phosphorescent tone about it … whereas the rest of the corona had a faint violet colour, tinged in places with faint green and faint red.' He was fortunate in its timing as moments later clouds blew over and the sun disappeared for the day. A gale ensued, leading him to write: 'The elements seemed to say, We have up to the present held ourselves in check for your pleasure and for the success of your observations, and now that these are satisfactorily accomplished, we will have full play for our bottled-up energies.'[3]

David Gill was a watchmaker by profession (with a royal warrant as watchmaker to the Queen) and a pioneer in astrophotography.[4]

I was in business for 8 years, had married, was making £1,500 a year, and working at night in my own observatory when Lord Crawford offered me £300 a year to take the directorship of Dun Echt Observatory … in 24 hours Lord Crawford had my answer – yes. I never regretted that decision – my life became full of interest, and has so continued ever since.[5]

The young horologist would become one of the most renowned astronomers of his generation. Gill's first job was to bring the observatory up to world-class standard. In 1873 he embarked on a tour of the major European observatories. In each he met the foremost instrument makers and ordered a wealth of equipment that would enable the observatory to become one of the finest in the world. At home, employing Gill's watchmaking skills, they embarked on their own designs for a new driving clock for equatorials, which would be of great use for astrophotography, allowing the long exposures to perfectly track the shifting stellar objects.[6] New equipment included a fifteen-inch refractor by Grubb and a large forty-foot focus solar telescope.

In 1871, now elected to the Royal Astronomical Society, Ludovic's passion was unstoppable and he immediately set about planning his most ambitious expedition – a voyage to the East. He took a 398-ton three-masted schooner, the *Venus*, and set sail for India for another eclipse. But the principal motive for the mission was to have his telescopes in place on Mauritius to record the 1874 transit of Venus. Such an event, taking place in pairs eight years apart (the second part of this transit would be in 1882), occurs once every 243 years, so transits are among the rarest predictable astronomic phenomena. They allow trigonometric readings from different locations to

163 Ludovic adjusting Gill's 12-inch reflector telescope. A. B. Brown (left) was helping develop the spectroscope for studying the solar corona (1870).

164 An array of telescopes and devices was used to observe, photograph and measure all aspects of the eclipse (1870).

165 Preparations for the eclipse by the foreign scientists at the Maria Luisa Observatory of Cadiz inevitably attracted curious onlookers (1870).

help calculate the astronomical unit (AU) – the distance between the earth and sun – essential for the advancement in astronomy and the calculation of the size of the solar system, and the distances to other planets and the stars. The team's role was part of the British effort as it joined an international plan to have seventy-five observing stations distributed worldwide. It was masterminded with military efficiency and anticipated as 'probably the most important astronomical event of the century'. Ludovic was accompanied by Dr Ralph Copeland, on leave from his post at the Dublin Dunsink Observatory. The expedition to Mauritius, where they stayed for three months, would result in over 280 photographs. A separate steam ship had sailed earlier with Gill, who accompanied a specially crafted forty-foot solar telescope and many highly specialized pieces of equipment, including the Dun Echt Heliometer, constructed in Hamburg for Ludovic.[7] Gill was further assisted with domes and huts for the observation site by the Dunecht observatory carpenter.

Ludovic's journey around South Africa took longer than expected and left him and his crew in poor health, but they arrived to find that Gill had already successfully erected the observatory. However, the cloudy weather could have been a disaster for Ludovic's expectant party, meaning a return home empty-handed. Fortunately, other experiments were undertaken, including a hitherto untried and unorthodox method of obtaining solar readings in conjunction with the recently discovered 170-mile-wide asteroid, Juno. The results of these observations turned out to have greater accuracy and significance to astronomy than the transit of Venus itself.[8]

Gill had brought out fifty-two chronometers, which may have seemed excessive to the less knowledgeable. Long into the twentieth century, astronomers, navigators and cartographers relied on these exceptionally accurate, but ultimately delicate, timepieces to establish longitudinal differences. By bringing so many, Gill and Ludovic were far more likely to record

166 The helioscope used to observe the sun during the 1870 Cadiz solar eclipse, with Dr Ralph Copeland, seated on the left.

an accurate time for any event. Gill spent a further month travelling through the Indian Ocean and the Mediterranean, where his readings enabled him to correct the latest maritime charts by determining the longitude more accurately than ever before. This brought about immeasurable safety improvements for seafarers for years to come.

The significance of young Ludovic's role, with its wealth of fresh astronomical measurements and their contribution to science along with the improvements for navigation, was not lost on the scientific community and public.[9] An indication of the fame of the expedition was that his return was a major event for the people of Wigan, who flooded the streets to welcome him home with a band and, removing the horses from his carriage, pulled him through the streets up to the house.[10] The expedition has been described as 'perhaps the most completely equipped one ever undertaken by a private individual in the interests of astronomy'.[11]

Ralph Copeland replaced Gill in 1876 and continued the regular reports for publication by the Royal Astronomical Society as well producing over one hundred of their own 'Dun Echt Circulars', which were distributed to every major observatory around the world. These were not simple pamphlets with observational updates. The report describing the longitudinal calculations taken by Gill after the Mauritius expedition alone filled some 520 pages of volume III of the publications.[12] The value of this body of work and contribution to science meant that in 1878 Ludovic was made a fellow of the Royal Society of London and president of the Royal Astronomical Society.

Meanwhile, Ludovic's bibliomaniac tendencies never wavered. His quest to equal, if not exceed, the importance of the tsar's scientific library at Pulkova remained his long-held ambition. One of the first great collections he was able buy was that of Charles Babbage, the mathematician and inventor of the first calculating machine, who had died in 1871. Securing this collection of over two-and-a-half thousand books in 1873 made the 'Library rich at once in a department where it was once poor'.[13]

Ludovic went on to obtain a copy of a first edition of Nicolaus Copernicus' *De Revolutionibus* (1543), one of the greatest astronomical treatises of the sixteenth century. That copy has been called the most important in existence, the work's significance being that it helped alter the perception of earth's place in the universe and hence of humanity itself. Then there were copies of the sixteenth-century Danish astronomer Tycho Brahe's works and Galileo Galilei's *De Proportionum Instrumento* (1612), the mathematician's proposal for a mechanical calculator. Other exceptional purchases included a wealth of pre-Copernican material and later works, including a first edition of Johannes Kepler's

167 *below left* David Gill (later Sir David) joined Ludovic on expeditions to Cadiz for the eclipse and Mauritius for the transit of Venus. A pioneer in astrophotography, he later became president of the Royal Astronomical Society.

168 *below right* Dr Ralph Copeland would become the third Astronomer Royal for Scotland.

169 *bottom* In 1896 the 15-inch telescope from Dunecht, along with all the astronomical equipment and fifteen thousand works of scientific literature, were moved to Edinburgh. © The Royal Observatory, Edinburgh

170 *opposite* The new home of the Royal Observatory, Blackford Hill, Edinburgh, soon after construction. © The Royal Observatory, Edinburgh

Tabulae Rudolphinae (1627), the standard source of astronomical tables for more than a century, and his important earlier work of 1619, *Harmonices Mundi*, which includes his discovery of the third law of planetary motion describing our planets' elliptical orbits. There were also works by Isaac Newton, including the first edition of his revolutionary *Principia Mathematica* (1687) with an imprimatur by Samuel Pepys, president of the Royal Society, that included his laws of motion, and most importantly, universal gravitation.[14]

Ludovic's sister, Jane, was no less fascinated and intrigued by these wonders and discoveries:

We used to love on privileged occasions to go and lie under the huge telescope watching the stars frantically racing past when unharnessed from the clock control which counteracted the speed of the revolving globe, no particular star had to be kept in view – there was always something enthralling happening there. Learned visitors

used to come to stay at Dunecht, the tall lean Professor Struve of Yerkes Observatory for one, the Russian who discovered Epsilon Aurigae, a trifle, a star 3,000 times as big as the Sun; its radius that is 20 times greater than the distance from the Sun to our Earth.[15]

In 1888 Ludovic was dismayed to discover that the Scottish Universities Bill proposed the abolition of the Royal Observatory of Edinburgh due to years of lack of investment. His first reaction was indignation, his second sorrow and his third that 'it shan't be!'[16] He recognized the very possible demise of Scotland's position in the world as a leading centre for astronomical research so he offered to the nation the entirety of the apparatus and scientific library, numbering over fifteen thousand items, to ensure its survival. The government agreed that the institution could continue if, alongside his donation, Ludovic chaired the committee to re-evaluate and reorganize it.

Calton Hill above Edinburgh's New Town was increasingly affected by the city's smoke, so Copelend identified Blackford Hill on the south side of Edinburgh as the ideal site. It was close to the university, protected by the southern prevailing winds that would drive the greater part of the city's pollution away and had a strong geological base for the heavy telescopic equipment. It finally opened in April 1896.

With some sadness, Ludovic wrote to Copeland:

I can hardly think without a sigh of those foundations at Dun Echt which I laboured to make so satisfactory and sound – all swept away – and yet I am sure it is for the best interests of science that it should be so. You have a grand chance, with all your experience, to plan a splendid observatory – and I am sure you will.[17]

Copeland was subsequently appointed Scotland's third Astronomer Royal.

The legacy, born at Dunecht, continues: the ROE plays a vital role in the United Kingdom's part in the European Space Agency while undertaking projects linked to NASA and observatories around the globe. As part of the sesquicentenary celebration in 1972 the Crawford Room, where Ludovic's unique collection is now housed, was opened by the 28th Earl of Crawford and is in continual demand by researchers from around the world.

21

A Marriage of Mining Families

Lady Evelyn Margaret Mason (née Lindsay), 1870–1944 and James Francis Mason, 1861–1929

Ludovic and Emily Crawford's firstborn was Evelyn, named after her mother's sister.[1] She was to become a strong, civic-minded figure and would be decorated for the contribution she made to the welfare of injured soldiers from the Great War.

Evelyn was born a year after her parents married and returned to Haigh Hall, where she spent most of her childhood with her six younger brothers. As the only daughter, she frequently accompanied her mother on her travels, including a trip to Rome when aged just five for the magnificent fancy-dress ball held for her mother's sister Ada, married to the 15th Duke of Sermoneta. Other highlights included acting as bridesmaid to her father's first cousin, the beautiful and charismatic Violet Lindsay, for her wedding to Henry Manners, the future 8th Duke of Rutland. She was called on again for the same role, aged twenty-two, by Princess Mary of Teck, who was planning to marry Prince Eddie, the Duke of Clarence & Avondale. Unfortunately, 'he flashed into Princess May's later life as her fiancé, only to leave it six weeks after for the tomb.'[2]

171 Evelyn had a busy social life. Here she is seen at Lockinge standing between her cousins, Ladies Hilda (left) and Susan Keppel, daughters of William Coutts, 7th Earl of Albemarle (*c.* 1892).

In 1895 she became a bride herself, marrying a man who fitted in well with her family's business concerns. The Haigh Ironworks had been responsible for over one hundred and fifty locomotives, while James 'Jim' Francis Mason's interest in steam led him to become a director of the Great Western Railway. His father, James Mason, a mining engineer and scientist, had made his fortune from copper, sulphur and iron in Spain and Portugal.[3] With profits from Mason & Barry Limited's vast San Domingo mining operations, the father had bought Eynsham Hall in Oxfordshire in 1866, from where he started a range of experiments in order to improve agricultural techniques.[4] Thanks to the success of the mining, King Carlos I of Portugal made James the first Baron de Pomarão, followed by granting him a viscountcy, before making him Conde (count) in 1897, a title that Jim inherited. Demands on the mines rose sharply during the Franco-Prussian War, which further increased his fortune. He died in 1903, leaving the house and 10,000-acre estate[5] and over £750,000 (approximately £92 million today).[6]

After Eton, Jim started working under his father in Portugal, where he had a brief affair with the King's daughter.[7] He returned to join the Oxfordshire Hussars, in which he served as captain and honorary commandant of the Oxfordshire Volunteer Regiment from 1916 to 1918, though he was too old to fight.

Eynsham had been rebuilt twice over the previous hundred years by both Sir Charles Barry, best remembered for the Palace of Westminster, and Owen Jones, famed his role in decorating the Crystal Palace for the Great Exhibition. But the couple

172 In 1875 Evelyn accompanied her mother to a fancy-dress ball held in Rome by her aunt, Ada Caetani (later Duchessa di Sermoneta).

173 A vivacious Evelyn in theatrical pose (*c.* 1892).

decided to demolish it in 1904 and eventually moved into a new Elizabethan-style house designed by Sir Ernest George that remains today. In line with its more modern approach, they embraced the latest in conveniences, including a gas plant, electricity generator for its own supply of power and a telephone system connecting them to the whole estate.

Evelyn was fortunate to escape with only bruising from a frightening accident in 1897 while staying with cousins, the Earl and Countess of Lathom at Lathom House. Returning to the house, Alice, Lady Lathom,[8] got into difficulties when one of her reins got caught under the tail of one of the horses. The horses swerved, causing the phaeton to overturn. Lady Lathom was thrown into a water-filled ditch and the carriage fell on her. She was then repeatedly kicked by one of the horses while her head remained under water. They rushed her back to Lathom House, but she died shortly after from her head injuries and near-drowning.[9]

Once the rebuilding of Eynsham Hall was completed, they had just six years in which to enjoy their new home before the outbreak of war. They promptly turned one of their London Mayfair houses into a hospital.[10] All thirty beds at 16 Bruton Street were occupied by December 1914. In time this would increase to fifty and would be affiliated to Queen Alexandra's Military Hospital at Millbank. To the patients it must have seemed that this was a luxurious place to recover, but the expense of running such an operation with twenty-four-hour care and increasingly hard-to-find medicines, fuel and food meant some officers found it less agreeable.[11] As commandant of the hospital, Evelyn was also regarded as autocratic by some and was referred to in one account as 'Lady Economy', but many found that her hospital achieved exactly what it set out

174 Jim Mason was popular with Evelyn's family. He shared her brothers' mining and military background while also embracing technology and culture (1907).

175 Evelyn, Haigh Hall, Christmas 1907. Seven years later she became an indominable commandant of the Lady Evelyn Mason's Hospital for Officers.

to do and helped in their recovery. Meanwhile, Jim and Evelyn also made Eynsham available to the war effort. It was used by the Air Ministry as well as a maternity hospital for the period.

With the 'menace of the talkies' came a movement in 1925 to help strengthen theatres. Their large Bruton Street house in London was turned into the 'Bruton Club', with a five-hundred-seat theatre, art studio, exhibition gallery and roof garden. It was to be a nursery to develop new dramatic works and writers – but supported by the theatre-goers rather than the theatre industry itself. Additionally, Evelyn led a tireless life in taking on a host of duties, bringing up four daughters, Violet, Rhona, Doris and Joan, and a son, Michael, while running a large house, as well as canvasing for her husband's election as MP for Windsor in 1906.[12] She became involved in Robert Baden-Powell's Scout and Brownie movement from the start and formed the Eynsham Hall Troop, becoming its first District and County Commissioner. Other roles saw her become president of the Oxford Nursing Association and found the North Leigh WI in 1919. She was made Lady of Grace, Order of St John of Jerusalem in 1919, appointed OBE in 1920, awarded the Silver Jubilee Medal in 1935 and the Coronation Medal in 1937. She died in 1944 aged seventy-three.

On leaving Eton, Michael joined the army and became its boxing champion in 1918, before travelling throughout Canada for three years, where he became an experienced explorer, completing two summers in the Arctic.[13] He married Annette Baird, the daughter of Lord Stonehaven and Governor-General of Australia and together they sailed widely. In 1938, having by now inherited Eynsham, he was recruited by the director of naval intelligence and took on a number of undercover roles throughout the war in Europe.[14]

176 Jim with Star, Eddie Lindsay, Evelyn and Ronald Lindsay at Freeland. In 1885 his father had bought Freeland Lodge adjoining Eynsham Hall, making one large, coherent estate.

22

Endure Fort

David Alexander Edward Lindsay, 27th Earl of Crawford & 10th Earl of Balcarres, 'Bal', 1871–1940

It's impossible to briefly describe the range of roles and positions that David Lindsay, 27th Earl of Crawford, was associated with, whether in politics, business or the arts.[1] From the carefree portrayals of a young man, better known as Bal, to the later, more sombre portraits of the uniformed medic who experienced the horrors of the First World War, few images can illustrate the weight of responsibilities this most distinguished figure was to carry.

If the collective wisdom of the nation should one day decide to appoint a chief director of public taste, whether it be in connection with the arts of building ... the choice might well fall upon David Edward Lindsay, twenty-seventh Earl of Crawford and tenth Earl of Balcarres, an accomplished critic and man of affairs, the inheritor of great family traditions, which he nobly upholds.[2]

He always considered his childhood a happy one. He excelled at Eton and Magdalen College, Oxford, becoming both a scholar and budding politician. He was elected as president of the Union, a position which in those days carried considerable prestige. But that time at university, from where he graduated in 1894 with honours in History, introduced him to another side of life, one to which many of the aristocracy were rarely exposed and which left a deep impression on him throughout his life.

Oxford House in Bethnal Green was established in 1884 as the first 'settlement house' where students and graduates could volunteer to spend time learning first-hand about the realities of urban poverty. They initiated a host of projects – setting up youth clubs, providing legal help, labour exchanges and adult education classes. This became a lifelong concern of Bal's and, until old age, he kept in touch with many he met there. 'They are lovable people and the lower one descends in "the scale" the more brightly do certain qualities shine forth.'[3] Working there and with a host of other charitable organizations throughout his life strengthened his profoundly held religious views and liberal conservatism. He would forever bridle at the pompous and became irritated with those who felt entitled. He was far more comfortable carrying out work for the poor and destitute than he ever was at church tea parties for the middle class, abhorring their genteelness.

Bal's politics were often at odds with his fellow landed gentry, especially the absentee landlords and those he saw as lazy politicians. While in Bethnal Green he had got to know the labour leader and Liberal cabinet minister, John Burns. Although from vastly different backgrounds, they worked hard together on the future of the South Kensington Museum and became firm allies. Bal's experiences

177 Bal volunteered to work at Oxford University's Bethnal Green project, set up to help alleviate urban poverty. 'To myself this knowledge has dispelled many dreams, shattered many illusions, blighted many hopes' (*c.*1897).

178 Bal considered his childhood, spent between Haigh Hall, Dunecht and later Balcarres, a happy one (*c.*1878).

as an employer of thousands of miners, foundrymen and farmers taught him to maintain an open-minded approach to such liberal and left-leaning figures. The two men became lifelong friends, forever bouncing ideas off each other in healthy debate. Thus, while he recognized his position in Wigan still had a near-feudal element, it was one which he felt had a benign influence which worked for both sides.

He had never been distracted by the bright lights of Mayfair and instead, after Oxford, set out on a not so grand tour, guided by his friend and mentor Cosmo Lang, who would later become Archbishop of Canterbury. Before long he was back in the East End, where he spent much of the following year among some of the capital's most wretched and diseased, which gave him an even deeper insight into the problems and, for much of his political career, the tools and arguments with which to rally against those who were less exposed. It would leave him with a deep sense of enlightenment – and disappointment. 'To myself this knowledge has dispelled many dreams, shattered many illusions, blighted many hopes.'[4]

By the time he was twenty-three, his life was already fuller than most. On any given day he may have had lunch with Burne-Jones at the Grange or William Morris at Kelmscott, later recalling how the former prayed that French impressionism would pass in 'ten years, and fifteen years hence there will scarcely be a relic of the abominable stench.' Or he may have met with Princess Mary of Teck,[5] whom he became deeply attached to, or Viscount Goschen, the First Lord of the Admiralty, whom he described as 'blind, voiceless, and singularly uncouth in appearance and gesture: but a commanding intellect and most sympathetic.'[6] In the same year he became the youngest member of parliament, representing Chorley, the constituency around Haigh.[7]

His first official role at Westminster came a year later when he was made private secretary to Gerald Balfour, the chief secretary for Ireland (brother of Arthur, later to be prime minister). These were formative times for developing his understanding of land ownership and agricultural issues as Ireland was beginning to come out of the long depression

179 As with the eldest sons before and after, Bal's coming of age was celebrated at both Balcarres and Haigh Hall (1892).

180 Every generation of the Lindsays has enjoyed climbing the challenging coastal rocks at nearby Kincraig, near Dunecht. Here Bal is being helped out of difficulty by brothers Robert and Walter (1892).

181 Bal, standing as David Lindsay, won the local Chorley seat seven times for the Conservatives from 1895. He stood for the last time in 1910 and subsequently moved to the House of Lords (1910).

182 A postcard, possibly published for the 1906 election, with Margaret (later Illingworth), Connie, Bal and David being chauffeured with their dog at Haigh Hall.

brought on by cheap imports. He was appalled, though, by the Queen, who refused to see a royal residence established there on account of what she saw as its unhealthy climate. Her refusal to agree, even though encouraged by many of her advisors, compounded the problems he saw developing, while doing nothing to encourage the absentee landowners to fulfil their obligations.[8]

At the same time, he took on a host of roles that included guiding the select committee that divided what he saw was a chronically badly managed South Kensington Museum, transforming it into the Science and Victoria & Albert Museums. In order to safeguard the nation's artworks, particularly from the great US collectors, he became the first chairman of the National Arts Collection Fund in 1903.

He then became the youngest minister in the Commons when he accepted the offer of junior lordship of the Treasury. He took his parliamentary responsibilities seriously and energetically but often found them tiresome, regretting that he was not able to meet more people outside the Westminster machine. But his diaries are full of the many leading lights of the day whom he spent time with in conversation and debate, lunches and dinners: the pages are filled with figures such as Lord Salisbury and Cecil Rhodes, Asquith and Arthur Balfour, the Roseberys and Rothschilds, Curzon and Chamberlains, Rudyard Kipling and Sir Edwin Lutyens. Normally scrupulously diplomatic in public, he could be scathing in his writing about some he had little respect for: 'A long sitting during which Churchill succeeded in disgusting his friends and foes indiscriminately. What a cad he is.'[9]

His position as Unionist chief whip from 1911 lasted two busy years until he succeeded his father in 1913 and took his seat in the Lords.[10] However, this meant that he lost his connection to the heart of the political scene and found that retirement from public life gave him less pleasure than he expected. Entering that quieter chamber he no longer looked at a political career with great enthusiasm, believing that the soporific and atrophied Lords had become deeply 'emasculated.'[11] He felt disappointed that he had not been asked to take on some other task as he had been successful in the work he had already done and had gleaned a great deal of experience. But he would not go begging. All he could do was offer himself up as a knowledgeable contributor to debates. Eventually, though, he was made Lord Privy Seal, giving him the responsibility for the organization of government business in the House.

Death duties became a constant thorn in his side (he calculated that he had between £500,000 and £600,000 in debts – around £58 million today[12]). He also had to oversee the huge interest payments

183 Private Lord Crawford was saddened by the officers' sense of entitlement, the inappropriate behaviour of the nurses and unpreparedness of the high command (1915).

184 As the only cabinet-level politician in the Lords to serve in the ranks, Bal felt he understood the men's plight more than any of his political colleagues (1915).

for the unpredictable and capital-hungry Wigan Coal and Iron Company, which was suffering due to increased production costs. His dividend dropped by half in 1913 while taxation doubled. Even though his enforced time at home brought him the happiest year he could recall, the 'attractions of Lancashire must be repellent to all except those brought up within its ambit ... Lovable it can scarcely become to the stranger.'

However, Bal was more concerned about shifts in European politics. On 27 July 1914 he noted that 'The Austro-Servian crisis is wrecking Bayreuth!'[13] On 4 August Great Britain declared war on Germany. Immediately, Constance, his wife, started adapting part of Haigh into a hospital. Within weeks it was being used to treat wounded Belgian officers.

Bal's keen sense of patriotism drove him to do his bit for the country. He had become a special constable and drilled as a private in the Inns of Court Reserve Corps and was a major in the Church Brigade but he still felt frustrated. Depressed with the direction events were taking, the forty-three-year-old peer enlisted in June 1915 and joined the Royal Army Medical Corps in which he served for fifteen months in Flanders – remarkably, the only cabinet-level politician in the Lords to serve 'in the ranks'.

As Private Crawford, he was established at the No. 12 Casualty Clearing Station at Hazebrouck, where he was later promoted to lance-corporal.[14] His experiences at Bethnal Green must have served him well – but he saw there was a self-entitled and arrogant attitude found alarmingly often in increasing numbers of ex-public schoolboy officers, sent out to replace more seasoned officers who had become casualties in the first waves of battle. As an experienced employer of servants, farmers and miners, he reacted strongly to those privileged officers and slovenly medics whose behaviour appalled him. He was saddened by the impression forced upon him by so many of his countrymen, both soldiers and nurses, for their alcohol abuse, malingering, 'nocturnal improprieties', corruption and self-inflicted wounds. The debilitating effects

of alcohol on his compatriots led him never to drink again.[15] However, he left his most scathing attacks for the military high command for their unpreparedness, and their failure to embrace new technologies or intelligent logistics command. But he marvelled at how he adapted and declared that he missed nothing except his family.

Even though too old to fight, he often found himself in danger and under immense pressure, handling many who had suffered the most appalling wounds. At one point over one thousand casualties a day were passing through his clearing station, many still untreated and bearing terrible life-changing disfigurement or suffering from shock. It is hard to see how these experiences could not have affected him in later years, while strengthening his moral compass in a way few of his contemporaries experienced.

In the meantime, he was offered many roles at parliament in an attempt to entice him back. This lowly lance-corporal of the RAMC was even put forward for Viceroy of India by Lord Curzon as well as Civil Lord of the Admiralty by Balfour. However, promoted to corporal in April 1916, he felt strongly that he was doing something more useful by remaining near the front. After fifteen months he was transferred to the Intelligence Corps in time to witness the start of the Battle of the Somme. He was finally offered a role in which he felt he could be useful and accepted Asquith's invitation to become president of the Board of Agriculture and Fisheries, in effect a cabinet-level position.

The country was in grave danger of starvation due to crop failures abroad combined with limited shipments because of German submarine activity and a shortage of farm labour. Indeed, he feared for the future of the empire. He was deeply disappointed by the inaction of the government and threw himself enthusiastically into his new cabinet role as chairman of the Royal Commission on Wheat Supplies (a position he held until 1925). One result of his appointment was the creation of the 'standard loaf', but more importantly, at a critical time he helped save the nation's food supplies, as well as other countries that relied on Great Britain. He brought clear and calm management to the department, reducing panic and alleviating the impending crisis. By the end of the war, the commission controlled almost all the world's exportable grain.[16]

His services were then called on to set up the 1926 commission that produced the Crawford Report, in effect the blueprint for the future of the then British Broadcasting Company, an entity nominally owned by the radio manufacturers. The result was a concise paper that gave constitutional form to a new public monopoly: the British Broadcasting Corporation. But he declined Baldwin's invitations to become the BBC's first chairman, considering himself quite unsuited for the task.[17] Nonetheless, he continued to sit on its committees.

His ability to grasp complex problems and find ready solutions to them earned him roles such as the chancellorship of the Duchy of Lancaster, minister of transport, trusteeships at the British Museum and chairman of the Board of Trustees of the National Gallery. He was instrumental in the creation of the Council for the Preservation of Rural England, set up to protect the future of the country's historic fabric. One of its first successes, in 1929, was to buy Stonehenge for the nation.

That he was never appointed to the highest offices may have been due to his quiet demeanour, while his other diverse interests, both financial and intellectual, may have lessened such ambitions. Much of his approach was driven by an urge to continue restoring the Lindsay name. Other than Edward, he felt his siblings were less interested in that mission, possibly because they recognized that he could do the job better. 'That is why I feel it my duty to get work.'[18] When the coalition fell in 1922, his work as a minister also came to an end. From then on, he immersed himself in the politics of culture, while presiding over the increasingly fraught prospects of the Lancashire businesses and the family estates and collections. He had hoped that those years would be spent in more leisurely activities.

The Wigan Coal and Iron Company was beginning to come under threat from radicals at home and cheap imports from abroad. By 1928 it had suffered its third successive year of losses and was forced to amalgamate with Pearson & Knowles Coal and Iron Co., creating what would become the highly successful Lancashire Steel Corporation along with the Wigan Coal Corporation. The steel mill eventually had an output of 400,000 tons of steel ingots per year and a cogging mill that was the first in Great Britain to roll out ingots up to five tons.[19] What had been a family business run on paternalistic lines was now destined to be nationalized, leaving no room for such patriarchal figureheads. Although he felt that he still had a contribution to make, he became resigned to the fact that such a considerable enterprise needed a different type of chairman, one more versed in international trade and adept at handling the unions. He was relieved to see that the company went on to prosper under its new chairman, John James.

A roll call of his other more important positions illustrates how 'Lord Balcarres more than fulfilled the model of an impressive peer who could achieve great things.'[20] Honorary doctorates were awarded by Cambridge, St Andrews, Manchester, Edinburgh and Liverpool. In front of 3,500 people, he was proudly installed as chancellor of Manchester University in 1923, where 'his unwavering support for the cause of education, combined with his own scholarly interests and personal qualities, made him an ideal Chancellor, and the pride of the University in him was unlimited.'[21] Just a few on the long list of appointments he accepted include the presidencies of the London Society, the Ancient Monuments Society and the Roxburghe Club. Then there were the chairmanships of the Royal Fine Art Commission, the North of England Institute for Electrical Engineers, the Manchester Geological and Mining Society, the Birmingham and Midlands Institute and even the vice-presidency of the British Drama League. He was also honorary colonel of the Manchester Territorial Battalion, a member of the council of the British School at Rome, the Royal Commission on Historical Manuscripts, and for some time was honorary secretary of the Society for the Protection of Ancient Buildings as well as being vice-chairman of the National Trust.

Indeed, there is scarcely a society of historical, antiquarian, literary or artistic interest of any importance which did not command his support – one must not overlook the fact that he became fellow of the Society of Antiquaries, the Royal Society and a Knight of the Thistle. For most people any one of these positions could be seen as the culmination for a life's work in serving others.

Bal had married Constance, 'Connie' (née Pelly), granddaughter of Lord Wemyss (1818–1914), after a bit of unnecessary drama. He had been rejected once and, in despair, had decided to escape to Siberia in 1899. But it had all been a misunderstanding due to a rival relation who had driven a wedge between them. Fortunately, the truth prevailed and they were able to walk down the aisle in 1900. It was happy marriage which produced eight children on whom he doted, clearly illustrated in the photographs that show his happiness when he was able to spend all too short periods with them. They are some of the warmest to be found in the albums. But too many other responsibilities would make those times precious and rare.

He was unimpressed by many of the influential figures of the time. He saw Curzon as inexpressibly common and a bore. Winston Churchill, meanwhile, was regarded as vain, priggish and nakedly ambitious, although he later accepted that he was the right man to lead the country in the Second World War. He rarely expressed any anti-Semitic feelings he may have had of his own,[22] but he did become increasingly concerned about the general anti-Semite movement, which he informed Churchill about, who was until that moment completely unaware of it.[23] But his underlying views, while less aggressive, could be harsh: 'A victory by the Axis would have one result which we have never thought about ... we should have to find homes in these islands for a million Jews from the continent of Europe – would not such an infliction preclude for ever the revival of Britain?'[24]

Somehow, in spite of such political concerns and the worries of running the estates and businesses, he had managed to complete a seminal study of

185 Bal was put forward by Lord Curzon to become Viceroy of India. However, he felt that he was doing more useful work at the front until, with Britain's food supplies in peril, he accepted the role as president of the Board of Agriculture and Fisheries (*c.* 1900).

186 Bal with his three eldest children (from left): Anne, David and Margaret (*c.* 1906).

Donatello,[25] the first English book on the artist. It brought him literary acclaim, encouraging him to write other pieces on sculpture, John Lyly and Dante among other works, papers and studies.

After becoming senior trustee of the John Rylands Library, he gave it over six thousand early manuscripts as well as twenty thousand French and European proclamations and broadsides from the sixteenth to nineteenth centuries. There had been nothing to approach the collection outside the National Archives of France. But he had felt that his vast library had possibly become too professional in its focus. The books appeared to have taken control of everything and the family were almost working for the librarians. Either it was going to remain static, which did not appeal, or it would have to keep growing to ensure it was complete in every area in which it claimed to be definitive. When Wigan became a Labour seat in the post-1918 era, little animosity remained between him and the men of the town, who still asked him to become permanent chairman of their own very fine library.

The death duties, land taxes and the decreasing returns from coal meant that selling part of the collection of artworks and literature was prudent. The greatest stamp collection ever assembled, a monument to his father, was less reluctantly let go of, though he appreciated its intellectual value. In 1923 a sale of fifty tons of books through Quaritch further alleviated some of the pressure. Though he regretted how it would ruin the careful catalogue created by his father, he realized that the collection had become unwieldly, with many books hidden away in dark corners and some still unclassified. But his timing was unknowingly prescient. A moment's prevarication in the days before the depression could have devastated the family's finances. Even with such a vast sale of books, the library remained one of the greatest in the country. Bal was happy to now realize that for the first time all the collections were finally 'worthily displayed'.

The financial crisis in 1930 eventually brought his chairmanship of the Lancashire Steel Corporation to a close. It did, however, allow him to focus on his

187 The extensive list of diverse presidencies and chairmanships that Bal accepted illustrate his extraordinary ability to gets things done (*c.* 1905).

own true interests, the British Museum, National Gallery, Manchester University and the Royal Art Commission. The 1930s were hard on everyone and, with the economic future looking ever bleaker, he tried to relieve the situation with the sale of some of the more treasured works, including Rembrandt's *Titus at his desk*.

The rise of the Nazis was viewed by all with increasing alarm. War was seen as inevitable as far back as 1935 and became a preoccupation, along with the scandal brewing over the King and Mrs Wallis Simpson's relationship.[26] He started to take necessary precautions. As early as September 1938, he arranged for pictures to be removed from 7 Audley Square, their London house, to Haigh for safety. He was still spending much of his time at the House of Lords or dining at his club, Grillions, often with the key political players. These included Winston Churchill who, in spite of his earlier reservations, Bal was growing to respect, while he was steadily distancing himself from those he saw as defeatist.

In June 1939 a short period of prosperity in the Lancashire Coal and Steel combine allowed Bal and Connie to have what turned out to be their last opportunity to demonstrate the family's patronage and gratitude by staging a large garden party at Haigh for 1,758 of the salaried staff of the pits. The impending upheavals, along with the likelihood of nationalization, meant the family's connections with Wigan that his great-great-grandfather Alexander had begun some hundred-and-fifty years before were now coming to an end.

Bal died suddenly on 8 March 1940 at Haigh. Six past and future prime ministers sent long hand-written letters of condolence to the family, while the Archbishop of Canterbury, his old friend Cosmo Lang, presided at the funeral.

He fulfilled his roles with the least amount of show in a manner that he saw not only as appropriate for an aristocrat but a gentleman. He led a disciplined life moulded by those earlier experiences and kept himself fit – he never drank and went for an early morning forty-five-minute run every day, though he never took part in any sport other than shooting.[27] His modesty remained intact; he was reported to have remarked that

188 Bal (left) with his daughter Margaret at the February 1922 opening of parliament, with Irish politician and philanthropist, Reginald, Earl of Meath.

he was publicly known as the premier Scots earl, whereas in reality he was a Lancashire coal merchant ... Here was a man who inherited from his father the wish to understand all aspects of a problem whether it concerned designs for public buildings, monuments, bridges, lamp standards or even a postage stamp. But he was not a domineering figure: his was not the role to dictate but to correlate differing opinions, in other words to secure results which could not be assailed.[28]

Further,

He sized up men and perhaps knew only too well those he liked or disliked. He was a born organiser and with a vast knowledge on many subjects, he was always ready to give excellent advice. He could not stand intrigue. He abhorred the self-advertising methods by which certain politicians without special ability sought to get into the limelight. His own views were based on facts and sound arguments. He could present his case with such good humour and expose that of his opponent with such ridicule that he carried conviction.[29]

Bal served under five monarchs and left an unblemished reputation and legacy that demonstrated a life of hard work, diligence and moral strength. His widow, Connie, lived for a further seven years and died in a nursing home in 1947, the same year her family had decided to finally move back up to Balcarres.

23

'Definitely not of common clay'

Constance Lilian, Countess of Crawford & Balcarres, 1872–1947

Constance Lilian Pelly, or Connie, was one of ten children descended from families who had distinguished themselves at home and at sea and in Great Britain's overseas territories. This tall, dark, attractive woman became a true matriarch and possessed a steeliness that enabled her to support probably the most industrious Lindsay of the century preceding the Second World War. She also raised a family in some of the most turbulent times of social upheaval the country had experienced since the civil war.

189 Connie was a highly accomplished embroiderer (*c.* 1915).

Her family had a notably adventurous history that included a period when Henry Pelly commanded the defence of the Thames with the Elder Brethren of Trinity House during the Napoleonic Wars. His son, one of Nelson's captains, became governor of the Hudson Bay Company in 1822, where he remained for thirty years, responsible for over three million square miles. He was later made governor of the Bank of England. His grandson and Connie's father, Sir Henry Carstairs Pelly,[1] married Lady Lilian Charteris, daughter of Francis, 10th Earl of Wemyss.[2]

The engagement between Connie and Bal was not straightforward. A rival kinswoman had successfully persuaded each of them that the other was only trying to placate their own family and did not truly wish the marriage to take place. Bal despondently set off across Siberia for a tour of the Far East before eventually, in 1900, truth and reconciliation triumphed and the wedding took place at St Margaret's in Westminster. It proved a successful and happy marriage. Bal rejoiced: 'I have crossed two oceans and three continents: and my beloved has become my wife. And while I am thus ten years older, I have grown twenty years younger.'[3]

As a young woman Connie needed to dovetail her life with his, which was already full and involved a broad range of passionate interests. Married life was a happy affair but hard for them too as, in addition to his other work, his duties as a whip entailed many late nights in the House. However, in the early days Connie showed fortitude and was described by John Vincent, who edited her husband's diaries, as a 'fastidious wife, religious, even mystical, in a way that

190 *below left* After an uncertain start due to a rival, Bal and Connie had a successful forty-year marriage, producing eight children (1910).

191 *right* Connie (*c.*1892).

192 *below right* Connie had many roles to fit in to as the wife of one whose life as a politician, soldier, estate and business owner figured centrally in cultural affairs (*c.*1915).

her husband was not, somewhat hypochondriacal, and definitely not of common clay.'[4]

Today it is impossible to truly understand the close relationship that many aristocratic families had with those who worked and lived on their estates. Even by the early twentieth century the patriarchal nature of their structured and interconnected worlds had dimmed little. If proof were needed that this nexus existed, Bal was elected, virtually unopposed, in the 1900 election for the third time. Connie spent much of her time carrying out visits to Wigan's elderly and infirm, while

she allowed Bal to flourish and even broaden his areas of expertise. She went on to raise eight children, became highly skilled at needlework and embroidery, and ran a number of large houses while playing her part in the family's pastoral responsibilities and as an MP's wife, support Bal readily acknowledged.[5]

She must have felt pangs of dread along with justified pride when in 1915 Bal joined the Royal Army Medical Corps. She did, however, have a brief experience of German aggression herself – her husband recounted how 'she went to Edinburgh on Sunday [2 April 1916] and ... the Zeppelins dropped a bomb into the very street where she slept! What a

193 Connie, left, with her sister Annie Pelly, who later married Thomas Bulkeley and became lady-in-waiting to HRH the Duchess of Connaught (*c.* 1874).

194 Bal and Connie with their children (from left) Anne, Elizabeth, David, Margaret and James, at Haigh, June 1911.

merciful escape. *Taube* bombs which have dropped all round our hospital are disagreeable enough, but from Zeppelins are ten times worse.'[6] Meanwhile, she regularly sent Bal, stationed at Hazebrouck, food hampers from Fortnum & Mason, which he shared with his colleagues. But more poignant was that they wrote to one another every day, with her on occasion sending him 'an expendable pocket handkerchief, a luxury unknown to men in the ranks'.[7] It was nine months before he got his first leave and was able to return to Balcarres to see her and their daughter, Barbara, born only a few days earlier, on 31 December 1915.

When the war was over, Connie returned to running the three houses as before: 7 Audley Square, Haigh Hall and Balcarres, but in less certain times. Her eight children spanned from the infant Barbara to David, who was by 1919 heading to Oxford. She outlived Bal by seven years, spending her final days in a London nursing home, and died in 1947, the same year that Haigh Hall was finally sold to the Wigan corporation.[8]

24

‘The Sensible Captain Lindsay’

The Hon. Walter Patrick Lindsay, 1873–1936

Walter, named after the first Lindsay to settle in Scotland, seemed to combine many of his more recent ancestors’ strong interests in literature, art and science. Haigh Hall looked out across a host of factories and engine houses connected to the mines, iron and cotton industries, all of which demanded a proliferation of workshops to support them. Regular visits to them subsequently drew him to a life in engineering. Of the seven children, only he and his youngest brother, Lionel, followed this path, so, after leaving Winchester College and serving his apprenticeship with Denny & Co., marine engineers in Dumbarton, he attended the University of Glasgow and University College London to become a qualified civil engineer.

INCORPORATED UNDER THE LAWS OF THE STATE OF COLORADO

No. 21 — 10,000 — Shares

The Davidson Flying Machine Company

CAPITAL STOCK, $1,000,000. 1,000,000 SHARES OF $1.00 EACH

ALL FULLY PAID AND NON-ASSESSABLE

This Certifies that The Right Honble The Earl of Crawford — is the owner of Ten thousand — Shares of the Capital Stock of The Davidson Flying Machine Company, Fully Paid and Non-Assessable transferable only on the books of the Corporation by the holder hereof in person or by Attorney, upon surrender of this Certificate properly endorsed.

In Witness Whereof, the said Corporation has caused this Certificate to be signed by its duly authorized officers and to be sealed with the Seal of the Corporation, at Denver, Colorado, this — fourth — day of August — A. D. 1908

SECRETARY

PRESIDENT

Walter’s father, Ludovic, the 26th Earl of Crawford, had a broad range of contacts in the field, one of whom was Michael Holroyd Smith, an inventor and engineer, who had been promoting the idea of manned flight since 1879, and gave Walter some useful early hands-on engineering experience.[1] Ludovic had already taken a brief interest in the Davidson Flying Machine Co., which was developing a highly improbable hydrogen-filled airship-type machine propelled by gyropter-like blades. It never saw the light of day.[2] From there he joined the flourishing family business, the London Electric Supply Corporation, by now one of the largest electricity suppliers in the world.[3]

195 *right* One of Walter’s first experiences in engineering was with a company that was developing a hydrogen-filled airship-type craft. It never took off.

196 *opposite* Walter at Haigh Hall. The local industries gave Walter and Lionel their first introduction to engineering (*c.*1894).

197 In 1905, only three months after the birth of their daughter, Walter informed his wife that he would be joining his father on his RYS *Valhalla* for a voyage around Africa (*c.* 1895).

198 Walter and Wa-Wa, the gibbon that his father brought home from Malacca on the RYS *Valhalla* (*c.* 1908).

After university in 1899 Walter joined his father and brothers, Eddie and Lionel, on a voyage on the family's beautiful three-masted RYS *Consuelo* that took them around the coast of France and Italy to Greece and back via Patmos, Rhodes, Crete and finally Naples. This was an expedition to hunt down rare manuscripts and books in every port and city they came to. His father wrote to his head librarian at Haigh that one day in Cairo 'I was accosted in the street by an Arab in a mysterious way saying his uncle had many papyri but I must go and see them. After much talking I did, and as a result Mr Walter and Edward and I have this morning swaddled in cotton wool and packed in tin 35 papyrus rolls, some very large and others smaller ... I feel now that the Egyptian Department is as well represented as any other private library.'[4]

Walter's brother-in-law, Jim Mason, who was married to Evelyn, had been working for the immensely profitable Messrs. Mason & Barry Ltd in Portugal, a firm set up by his father, James Mason. With Walter's family's mining background and his own engineering capabilities, it was an obvious place to find full-time employment. While there he became engaged in 1902 to Ruth Henderson, the daughter of Isaac Austin Henderson, a playwright and privy chamberlain to Pius X. They were married at the Dominican convent in Rome.[5] They had two children; their son, Kenneth, made his life in South Africa, married a South African, Kathleen Lovemore, and fought for the country in the Second World War. Their daughter, Margaret, married George Rawlings, with whom she lived much of her life in the Far East, but he was tragically killed in 1963 with one of his twin sons in a motoring accident in Afghanistan. Margaret died ten years later in a house fire, an equally dreadful circumstance.[6]

History does not relate Ruth's reaction when Walter announced he was joining Ludovic, just three months after Margaret's birth, on the largest private yacht in the world, the RYS *Valhalla*, for a voyage around Africa[7] in 'palatial accommodation, lit by electric light throughout, with freezer rooms and a number of stewards taking care of them' (they would take a crew of sixty-six).[8] This expedition took them down to Trinidade in the South Atlantic, around the Horn and up to the Comoro Islands to Suez and home. They were accompanied by a number of eminent scientists, who used the opportunity to find and record new and little-known species in remote locations. Walter, with his strong analytical and methodical mind, was able to assist the leading naturalist on board, Michael J. Nicoll, who later published a full account of his findings for the Zoological Society of London in *Voyages of a Naturalist*.[9] They were able to add further to the knowledge of many little-understood or -studied creatures and collected over five hundred bird-skins as well as other flora and fauna specimens for further research. They covered over nineteen thousand miles in seven months.

Transport engineering was going through revolutionary developments at this time, some of which inevitably attracted Walter's attention and briefly encouraged him to become a participant in motor sport. On 4 July 1908 he entered a 12.2hp Miniature Standard to be driven by C. E. Vialls into the first heat of the Third All Comers' Handicap Sweepstakes. It appears the car did not make it into the second heat.[10]

Walter was forty-one when the war broke out, which meant that he would not be enlisted but, like his brothers, he volunteered. There is a piece in the *Sketch* titled 'The Gallant 1st Kitcheners' that outlined much of Walter's wartime story and deserves to be recorded in full:

The name of the wounded, in a recent Roll of Honour, of the Captain the Hon. Walter Lindsay recalls what we are not likely to forget – the splendid record of the 1st Kitchener Army. Captain Lindsay, who is a brother of the Earl Crawford, was one of those who volunteered the moment war was declared; but as he was over forty, his services were declined. The day the age-limit was raised he went to Whitehall and enlisted, and for three months he served as a private in the Middlesex Regiment. He had been promoted to corporal before he was discovered and raised to captain, and then followed a long period in the trenches at a lively part of the Western Front. A winter there – one of those terrible winters that find out the weak spots in everyone – led to a dangerous illness due to exposure.

He had contracted nephritis, a dangerous kidney condition requiring urgent relief, and so he was invalided home.[11]

On partial recovery, Walter was posted to Cairo, where his brother Ronald was serving in the diplomatic service and where he was able to regain sufficient strength before being posted to 2nd/10th Battalion of his old regiment again, this time in Palestine. His men warmed to this professional but decent and good-humoured officer: 'Precise in his military duties, and strict as to their execution, his kindly understanding of the men under his command was soon appreciated. How he chuckled with delight when told of his discovery that he had been nicknamed "The Sensible Captain Lindsay".'[12] At the Khuwelfieh, north of Beersheba, strategically important for its wells, he was involved in heavy fighting and was wounded in the head. However, he remained on duty until the engagement ended and the M.O. 'absolutely insisted that he must go to hospital'.[13] The dangers of infection were well known; many more soldiers died from that than any other cause. This brought an end to his active service, though he was appointed to GHQ, where he served out the rest of the war.

After the war, Walter returned to his old profession and became a director of the Wigan Coal and Iron Co., as well as the British Aluminium Casting Co. He went through divorce in 1927 and died aged sixty-three in 1936, never having fully recovered from his wartime wounds and sickness from the trenches and Palestine. He was remembered by a fellow officer as 'quietly self-reliant, dignified, kindly in his criticisms, generous to us in our failings, but unhesitating in his condemnation of anything mean, petty or untrue. Truly a gallant, gentle man.'[14]

The Yachts and Their Stories

'A better "sea" ship has probably never been built'

The nineteenth century saw the first proliferation of rich private individuals looking seawards to pursue new leisure and intellectual activities and challenges. From royalty to industrialists and explorers to sportsmen, these gentlemen seafarers were able to use the new steam technology and lighter designs, commissioning the greatest and fastest private yachts the world had ever seen.

In 1874 the twenty-seven-year-old Ludovic,[1] a new member of the Royal Yacht Squadron, set out for Mauritius on his first major scientific expedition in the three-masted, 390-ton, Aberdeen-registered schooner *Venus*. He had already travelled to Cadiz for an earlier eclipse, but this was the first time he would take a large yacht; anything smaller would have limited the tremendous amount of equipment his team was going to need for the painstaking recording of every detail of the forthcoming transit of Venus, the most significant astronomical event of the century. The journey covered over fifteen thousand miles; although the Suez Canal had opened five years before, it was prohibitively expensive for a sailing vessel with no engine to take this shorter route, so he elected to sail south and around the Cape. Wind power would only cost him £2,000 while the coal for a steamer would have been £3,700.[2] Ludovic's assistant astronomer, David Gill, left weeks later and took that shorter course, arriving in August, some three months ahead. He was travelling with fewer large astronomical pieces, but did take fifty-two chronometers for longitudinal observations that necessitated a shorter interval from the moment the delicate timepieces had been synchronized at Greenwich.

Ludovic's party made its first call at the uninhabited four-square-mile, steep, rocky outcrop of Trinidade (not to be confused with the West Indian island) in the South Atlantic. Typical of his broad range of scientific interests, he arranged for other experts and specialists to join the yacht's company. They included Howard Saunders, whose findings to the Zoological Society of London, published in 1880, included details of both new bird species and rarely studied specimens.[3] His *Manual* became the standard for British ornithology into the next century. Meanwhile, Ludovic's chief astronomer, Dr Ralph Copeland, discovered a great tree fern high in the remotest reaches of the island which would later be named after him, *Cyaihea Copelandi*.[4] Coincidentally, they were following in the footsteps of Edmond Halley who, before becoming Astronomer Royal, had visited the island in the eighteenth century. It was Halley who in 1716 had put forward the idea that measuring a transit of Venus would enable accurate measurements of the distance to the planets and stars – exactly what this journey was ultimately focused on.

There was bad weather for much of the trip and they arrived in Mauritius with just days to spare before the great transit phenomenon. However, sickness on board struck an already asthmatic Ludovic, who came down with a tropical fever. While the expedition itself was a great success, it took a great deal out of him. On his return he was met in Naples by his wife Emmie, who hardly recognized the gaunt, wasted figure before her. It would be a while before he felt able to sail again.

His next yacht was the beautiful 546-ton steam yacht *Taurus II*, which he bought in 1898. He rechristened her *Consuelo*, the first of two to which he gave this name.[5] Ludovic's first voyage on her was a search for manuscripts. Sailing to Alexandria and then travelling inland to Cairo, the party collected hundreds of Greek, Coptic, Kufic and Arabic writings on papyri, vellum and paper, which would keep specialists busy for years.

The following year Ludovic took three of his sons, Walter, Edward and Lionel, on a voyage round Le Midi, down to Greece, across the Aegean and back via Patmos, Crete and Naples. Eddie was a keen photographer and much of the trip was recorded, including portraits of their officers and crew. Ludovic realized that he now felt a great deal better at sea and started

199 The *Valhalla*. The 245-foot, 1,490-ton yacht had been built in 1892 for Sir Joseph Laycock, who sold her to a descendant of Captain Bluebeard. The latter's heavy debts meant that Ludovic was able to buy her in 1900 (photograph by Bekin of Cowes).

200 *below* Ludovic bought the 546-ton steam yacht *Taurus II* in 1898 and renamed her *Consuelo.*

201 *opposite, top* *Consuelo* in Monaco harbour moored near Prince Albert I's yacht, *Princess Alice* (1899).

202 *opposite, bottom* *Consuelo* steaming carefully through the narrow Corinth Canal towards Athens (1898).

to use the yachts as a base from which he could concentrate on developing what he referred to as his 'historical method' of cataloguing the vast collections from the Bibliotheca Lindesiana.

His eye was taken by an even greater yacht and before long *Consuelo* was sold and replaced with what was then the largest and most lavish yacht ever built for private use.[6] The 185-foot, 708-ton *Wanderer*[7] was a three-masted, fully rigged schooner with eighteen thousand square feet of canvas. He renamed her *Consuelo II*. Piracy could be a problem so she was equipped with an armoury of small arms, bayonets and even two seven-pounders, along with a Nordenfelt multi-barrel organ gun capable of firing five hundred rounds a minute. All creature comforts were fitted, including baths concealed in the stateroom floors. Siemens electric lighting and Dr Normandy's ingenious distilling apparatus that could convert salt water into fresh at a rate of twenty gallons an hour were also installed. Ludovic also gave detailed instructions for a dark room, and a freezer room for both the provisions for lengthy passages and biological samples. Unsurprisingly, with his interest in technology, he had the latest Marconi wireless equipment.[8] There was an organ connected to a motor to power the bellows and a piano. But by 1900, having owned the yacht for less than a year, he had been distracted and set his sights on one of the greatest yachts the Solent had seen and the largest yacht in the Squadron, the 245-foot, 1,490-ton *Valhalla*.

Brigadier-General Sir Joseph 'Joe' Laycock, an Olympic sailor (and later a competitor in the last motorized power boat race of an Olympics in 1908) had Ramage & Ferguson of Leith build something on the lines of a smaller *Cutty Sark*. As with the Lindsays, his wealth derived principally from coal. The result was the three-masted *Valhalla*, designed by W. C. Storey, launched in 1892, at 245 feet just 20 feet shorter than the clipper and the only steam-powered yacht to carry a full ship rig. Her handling qualities were judged to be excellent.[9]

Like *Consuelo*, she had an impressive armoury: Hotchkiss cannons, as well as its two Holland & Holland signalling cannons,[10] rifles, pistols, pikes and swords were all added to the ship. In 1897, Laycock sold her to the Comte Boni de Castallane, who listed the pirate Captain Bluebeard as one of

203 *below left* *Consuelo's* head chef (1899).

204 *bottom left* The crew of the *Consuelo* on their return to Plymouth after Ludovic's first voyage in the yacht (1898).

205 *below right* Four of *Consuelo's* crew (1899).

206 *bottom right* Chief engineer Sutherland in *Consuelo*'s engine room (1899).

207 *opposite* For less than a year, Ludovic owned the 185-foot, 708-ton yacht the *Wanderer*, which he renamed *Consuelo II* (1900).

his ancestors, but turned out to be the type that would be less welcome at the Squadron. He married Anne Gould, daughter of the notorious robber baron and railroad millionaire Jay Gould. 'Our eyes met, our hands met, our lips met and then our lawyers met.'[11] She brought with her a healthy dowry of over $3 million[12] (approximately $90 million today). Restraint was far from their minds as they went on a wild spending spree which included buying the *Valhalla* for $500,000 (over $15 million today) and taking on the $100,000 annual running costs. Unfortunately for Anne, while her husband continued to sail through their money, racking up debts in excess of $4.4 million ($128 million), she found he was just as unreliable as a husband. And so ended their relationship with the *Valhalla*. Eventually, after being seized by the lawyers in 1900, the yacht was sold on to Ludovic.

As a technophile, he had to have the Brougham patent electrical steering-gear fitted. Additionally, in his charthouse

is an ingenious invention of his that shows by means of electric connections, the ships course by dead reckoning. When the course is set, by the use of pelorus,[13] *which is connected with a clock and the patent log,*[14] *the course of the ship is traced automatically and accurately on a slate.*[15]

There was also a pioneering depth-sounding device and the most up-to-date radio equipment.

Michael Nicoll, the naturalist who accompanied Ludovic on three of his longest voyages, recalled that:

A better 'sea' ship has probably never been built, and under the worst conditions it was rarely that she took water aboard. The way in which she rode out a cyclone off the coast of Mozambique was wonderful; the waves towered to a height beyond belief ... nor was any damage sustained. In fact, the only serious mishap experienced during my voyages occurred off Cape Guardafui, in 1903, when a sudden whirlwind snapped the jibboom, hurling it into the air like a straw.[16]

208 Ludovic's interests in the latest technological advances meant he had the *Valhalla* fitted with 'Brougham's patent electrical steering gear' as well as lighting, navigation, sounding and Marconi's latest telegraph equipment (*c.* 1900).

209 The *Valhalla's* deck included two steam launches, a cutter and several gigs (*c.* 1900).

On deck there were two steam launches, a Fife-built, six-oared gig and several cutters. There was a large new deckhouse amidships, which Ludovic called his workroom, fitted out like the most comfortable club drawing room. There was a pianola to one side and a large globe took centre place in a room lined with lockers for storing books and his stamp collection. Electric lighting was a great novelty at the time (even Balcarres, his Fife home, would not have it for another forty years). The six staterooms were mostly decorated in white, red and gold and fitted with every conceivable luxury. Ludovic's own bathroom was unusual in that he had to climb a short flight of steps as the bathtub was raised high up so that the space below could be reserved for more lockers.[17] Below there was a freezer room for the many tons of meat, sufficient for the longest cruises, which slowly would be replaced by the biological specimens.

Ludovic's first trial run took them to Ceylon (Sri Lanka) and on return he lent her to King Edward VII to take him north to Scotland.[18] The following year, 1902, while preparing for his first circumnavigation, he entered the Coronation Cup, a three-hundred-mile race for a trophy that he himself had put up to celebrate Edward VII coming to the throne. The experience would add to the crew's understanding of the yacht's abilities when they would later encounter less benign conditions. He came third, behind *Utowana* and *Czarina*.

Ludovic best summarized the endeavours that he and his crew undertook over the next few years:

We have had three voyages, in the course of which we have passed many southern seas, calling at various islands, and always adding to the store for the museum – thus sailing down the east coast of South America through the Straits of Magellan up to Valparaiso in Chili, we struck out west for an eight thousand mile run across the Southern Pacific Ocean, visiting islands new to us all, each more charming than the other, and so home after going round the world. Again we fitted out for a less ambitious cruise in the West Indies and the Gulf of Mexico ... we again set forth for the wilder and less known Southern Indian Ocean ... encountered two nice little cyclones on the Madagascar coast, and got into the group of practically unknown islands in the North, where man is so seldom seen that the birds take no heed of the visitor.[19]

Stopping at Pitcairn they were welcomed by a number of tall descendants from the mutiny of the HMS *Bounty* that had taken place 114 years previously. They all spoke perfect English to their guests (while using a dialect among themselves), and gave

210 Captain Caws remained Ludovic's chosen skipper on all his yachts and many voyages, including the 1905 Kaiser's Cup Transatlantic Race.

211 Ludovic had the *Valhalla* painted white after previous experiences of travelling in hot climates (*c.* 1903).

a rendition of the national anthem – 'I have rarely heard its equal,' Ludovic commented. Prior to his departure he was presented with a piece of iron ballast and some copper nails which had been saved from the *Bounty*.

On each voyage they were able to discover and name new species, including a fish, *Corvina crawfordi*, otherwise known as a drum or croaker, in Montevideo, and a moth in Tahiti named *Pyroderces crawfordi*. Their second expedition, which departed in December 1903, spent about five months exploring the Caribbean before proceeding to Florida 'where some excellent tarpon fishing was enjoyed' with sizes ranging from forty to ninety-five pounds in weight.[20] They succeeded in obtaining some four hundred birds, which included three new to science, one of which was the vitelline warbler, *Dendroeca vitellina crawfordi*, from Little Cayman.

There was to be a final hurrah for sail that showed the great yachts could still perform spectacularly. 'It was the final, privileged tournament of a gilded age: the last great race of princes, whether titled by birth in the Old World or minted by money in the New.'[21] In 1905, the German Kaiser, Wilhelm II, laid down a challenge: a 2,875 nautical mile race under sail from Sandy Hook, New Jersey to Cornwall's Lizard. His enthusiasm was triggered by an unhealthy sense of inferiority, stemming partly from his witnessing the Royal Navy's Spithead review in 1889. He had proudly brought the best of the imperial navy's twelve ships to the Solent, but they were dwarfed by the column of the British empire's seven fleets and squadrons that included over three hundred ships stretching twenty-three miles.

Offering an impressive solid gold trophy, the Kaiser announced the almost no-rule German Emperor's Cup Race for Yachts, also known as the Kaiser's Cup. It was akin to a maritime heavyweight duel and attracted entries from owners of eleven of the fastest yachts ever built, one of which was Ludovic's. The *Valhalla* arrived in New York a fortnight before the start with its fully prepared ship's company that had sailed her over 150,000 miles in the last few years. She had new sails bent and the hull was thoroughly cleaned in preparation. 'There has never been, in the history of yachting, an ocean race anything like the international importance of this one.'[22]

212 Ludovic with some of the live birds, including eight new species, from their six-month voyage around Africa ending in May 1906.

213 Inevitably, not all the animals made it back to Britain. Two young orangutans perished on the return voyage (1908).

After two days of fog, chaos and false starts, they got under way on 18 May 1905. Embarrassingly for Ludovic, *Valhalla* fouled the start line, necessitating a difficult return up-wind to start again, placing them almost last, two hours behind the field. But he caught up with his competitors within a couple of days. Scott Cookman, in his book *Atlantic: The Last Great Race of Princes*, evocatively described the start:

> *Lord Crawford, on the afterdeck of his* Valhalla, *watched the whole thing unfold with remarkable detachment. He was perched in the mizzen shrouds, dressed as he habitually was at sea: mis-shapen white commander's cap on his head, in his bright yellow oil-skin slicker with comfortable, threadbare carpet slippers on his feet. Captain Caws had the 1,490-ton, 245-foot-long square-rigger under twenty-two sails – far less than the fifty or more she could carry, but all that could be kept filled when essentially beating to windward in the gentle easterly breeze. Yet with her massive forward momentum building, she was moving toward the line like a juggernaut from the north.*[23]

Ice was a major worry for those taking the potentially faster northern route; the *Atlantic* reduced sail when it came across a half-mile-long iceberg in virtually the same place and season that that *Titanic* was to meet its end seven years later, though with a far smaller berg. But once they found themselves temporarily free from ice, the *Atlantic* got up to speed and managed the best distance for any single day of the race – 341 miles. The *Valhalla* was also in her element. Now carrying twice the sail, weight and freeboard, she was doing what she was built to do – taking on the great oceans. If this wind continued, she could win and break all records. As it was, she and the rest of the fleet were becalmed within 150 miles of the Lizard, an area normally known as a graveyard for its difficult and stormy approaches.

Eventually, the *Atlantic* crossed the line at a frustrating three knots, creating a record of twelve days and four hours – a speed that, to date, no monohulled sailing yacht has beaten while racing.[24] Those aboard the Kaiser's *Hamburg* were mightily disappointed to come in second over twenty-two hours later. The whole intention of the race had been to put Germany at the top of the rankings. A disappointed crew of the third-placed *Valhalla*,

214 The *Valhalla* having its hull cleaned in the floating dock at Pulau-We, North Sumatra, before returning home on Ludovic's last voyage (1908).

215 Ludovic with Mr Armour, one of his travelling companions aboard the *Valhalla*, sailing through the Red Sea (1908).

arriving twenty-four hours after the *Hamburg*, were cheered by Ludovic pointing out that despite starting next to last they were the first British entrant across the line and could be proud as their more southerly route was 150 miles longer.

In 1905 Ludovic embarked on the third and most successful of his major cruises to the Indian Ocean. The six-month voyage started in November and took them to Cape Town and up into the Indian Ocean, the Seychelles and back via Suez. Many specimens were collected, including nearly 600 bird species, eight of them new to science, among which were 'a lovely little tern' in South Trinidade named *Gygis crawfordyi*, a *Terpsiphone lindsayi* flycatcher from the Comoros Islands, and a *Butorides crawfordi* heron from Assumption Island.

It was while off the coast of Brazil that ornithologist Michael Nicoll recorded what became part of the *Valhalla*'s legend. He recounted to the Zoological Society of London in 1906:

At about 10.15 a.m., on Thursday, 7th December, 1905 ... Meade-Waldo and I saw a most extraordinary creature about 100 yards from the ship, and moving in the same direction, but very much slower than we were going. At first all that we could see was a dorsal fin, about four feet long, sticking up about 2 feet from the water; this fin was of a brownish-black colour, and much resembled a gigantic piece of ribbon-seaweed. Below the water we could indistinctly see a very large brownish-black patch, but could not make out the shape of the creature. Every now and then the fin entirely disappeared below the water. Suddenly an eel-like neck, about six feet long and of the thickness of a man's thigh, having a head shaped like that of a turtle, appeared in front of the fin. This head and neck, which were of the same colour above as the fin, but of a silvery-white below, lashed up the water with a curious wriggling movement. After this it was so far astern of us that we could make out nothing else ... They both [The first and third mates, Mr Simmonds and Mr Harley] *say most emphatically that it was not a whale, and that it was not blowing, nor have they ever seen anything like it before. After they had watched it for several minutes, it 'sounded' off the port bow, and they saw no more of it.*[25]

After such an eventful trip, they returned through the Suez Canal and were home by May 1906. Ludovic wrote to Min:

I have got home with a ship load full of birds dead and alive – nearly 600 dead, skinned, for the British Museum, and about 40 alive for the Zoo. They are most of them in my cabin on deck as I write – all shouting at the top of their voices so you would think you were in the Parrot House at the Zoo, except that there is not a Polly among them. I shall be quite sorry to lose some of them as I have got them almost all quite tame and can take them out, and when I catch a fly they come to my hand to eat it. But both they and I feel the cold here very much. How I wish this was a warm country and that I could be decently well in it.[26]

Ludovic's future expeditions were planned as much for his health and a chance to attend to his academic research undistracted. He put the *Valhalla* up for sale in 1906, though it would not be for another two years until she actually sold.[27] And so for a relatively short voyage he rented Alfred Edward Miller Mundy's 254-foot RYS *Narcissus*, built just a year earlier.[28] This yacht had similar proportions to his old *Consuelo* but was fitted with probably the first steam turbine engines, which enabled her to exceed her designed top speed of fourteen knots.

The opportunity to add to science was never far from his thoughts and so, joining *Valhalla* once more in 1907 in St Vincent off Cape Verde, he undertook his last great voyage to Borneo. Somewhat less glamorous than previous discoveries was a toad, new to science, that the expedition's accompanying ornithologist and conservationist, Edmund Meade-Waldo, named after the yacht *Duttaphrynus valhallae*.[29] It may now be extinct.[30]

A relaxed Ludovic was photographed in his favoured sarong as they cruised through the Suez Canal on 28 March 1908. But by now his health, in particular the chronic asthma that he struggled with to the end, meant this was to be the closing chapter on a remarkable series of adventures around the world. *Valhalla* was finally sold at the end of 1908. She now belonged to a bygone age and, like many such fine yachts, ended being used for less exotic cruises. She became a training ship for mercantile cadets before she was leased to the Royal Navy, who armed her with four twelve-pounders.[31] She was renamed *Valhalla II* as her name had already been allocated to HMS *Valhalla* and was last active during the Gallipoli campaign.[32] She was finally converted to a fruit carrier and foundered in a storm off Cape St Vincent while carrying a cargo of oranges and wine from Valencia to Dunkirk on 2 December 1921.[33]

25

Aide to the Tsar and Curzon

The Hon. Robert Hamilton Lindsay, 'Robin', 1874–1911

Perhaps the most stylish of the seven children of Ludovic, 26th Earl of Crawford, both in and out of uniform, was his fourth-born, Robert Hamilton Lindsay, known to his friends and family as Robin. Like all his brothers, he travelled extensively and served his country. From Australia to South Africa, Japan to Russia, he combined his skills as an excellent linguist, intelligence gatherer, courageous soldier, valued ADC and keen sportsman.

216 Robert was made ADC to Lord Curzon for the 1903 Delhi Durbar.

Robin joined the 2nd Dragoons (Royal Scots Greys) as a second lieutenant when he was twenty. He was always the most sporting of his family, an attribute that gave him the perfect credentials to make it as a successful officer in the Heavy Cavalry Brigade. He was popular with his men and played football for Sandhurst before joining his regiment in Edinburgh,[1] in time for his first major public duty when its honorary colonel, Tsar Nicholas II of Russia, and his wife, Tsarina Alexandra, visited Scotland. Arriving at Leith on 22 September 1896 on board the 400-foot imperial yacht, the *Standart*, they were welcomed by the Prince of Wales and Duke of Connaught (the Scots Greys' colonel) before taking the royal train north to Ballatar railway station, where they were met by Robin with his mounted escort, ready to accompany the couple with Queen Victoria, Alexandra's grandmother, to Balmoral. The next day he was asked to dine with them at the castle, where he was presented to the Tsarina.[2]

In April 1899 Robin was posted to Australia, where joined the staff as aide-de-camp of the new governor of New South Wales, Earl Beauchamp.[3] The latter was appointed honorary colonel-in-chief of the Australian Volunteer Horse, to which Robin was promoted to acting major and second in command.[4] However, as he was starting to engage with his new duties, he learnt that his regiment was being ordered to South Africa to take part in the First Boer War. With five years' preparation for such an eventuality, including a stint at the Hythe School of Musketry for training in weapon and marksmanship techniques but still without experiencing any action, he was

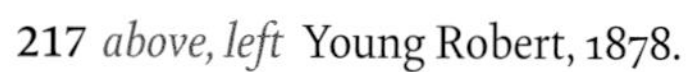

217 *above, left* Young Robert, 1878.

218 *above, right* A young cricket-playing Robert could not have known that his future mother-in-law would play a part in the history of the game.

219 *bottom, right* Robert visiting his mother at 2 Cavendish Square, when he was briefly stationed in London in 1896.

220 One of Robert's first assignments as a young officer in the Scots Greys was to escort its honorary colonel, Tsar Nicholas II, when he and the Tsarina visited Scotland from Ballater railway station to Balmoral (1896).

determined to get out to the Cape as soon as possible and share the trials and successes of his men. 'Just like a Lindsay, will say those who remember the distinguished services rendered to his country by his great-uncle, the once member for Wigan, General Sir James Lindsay', his home newspaper reported.[5]

He was given leave by Beauchamp and arrived at Cape Town on 7 December 1899 at the same time as the Greys on board the *Ranee*. With little time to spare, they were dispatched into the country, where they saw action almost immediately. His valour at Diamond Hill, Johannesburg, Driefontein, the battle of Paardeberg, Karee Siding, Sand River and the relief of Kimberley earned him the Queen's Medal with five bars. But within seven months, on 10 July, the night before the battle of Nitral's Nek near Pretoria, he broke his ankle badly while relieving Baden-Powell's small force. It was enough to have him sent to the rear and confined to hospital, but it may have saved his life. The following day his comrades were outgunned three to one by the Boers under General De La Rey, who killed almost all of the Scots Grey troopers, gunners and half its officers.[6] His entire squadron was forced to surrender. Robin was invalided home on the *Kildonan Castle* just nine months after he had arrived.

On account of his injury and a subsequent illness he was put on half pay and, while still recovering, was promoted to captain and received the fortuitous invitation by Lord Curzon, Viceroy of India, to become his ADC until he was well enough to rejoin his regiment. Robin was more than just a battle-tested officer with a clear understanding of protocol; he was a fine linguist with a quick grasp of languages that included French, German, Italian, Russian and Dutch, and for this posting he made sure he learnt

221 Janet Clarke, Robert's mother-in-law, presented a small terracotta urn she had bought in an Egyptian bazaar, believed to have been a perfume bottle, as a prize for a friendly cricket match she hosted between England and Australia. It was filled with ashes from the bales they had burnt following the match. It is still known as the Ashes.

CONTAINING THE "ASHES" OF ENGLISH CRICKET: AN URN IN THE POSSESSION OF LORD DARNLEY.

Hindustani. The timing of the posting coincided with the extraordinary 1903 Delhi Durbar held on 1 January to celebrate the coronation of King Edward VII, Emperor of India. With Curzon in charge of the meticulous planning of two weeks of events, it was inevitable that Robin would be at the heart of the proceedings.

The festivities started with a dazzling parade in which the young officer, seated high up on the second elephant's howdah, arrived in the centre parade ground of the elaborate and vast tented city that had sprung up in the few months prior on what had previously been a dusty plain. The gathering brought more bejewelled Indian princes together than ever before, accompanied by the massed ranks of the Indian army under Lord Kitchener. It set off a series of dinners and balls, military reviews and displays, polo matches and a host of other sporting competitions. The consequences of that broken ankle were both life-saving and life-changing – during this timely and propitious appointment he met a young Australian lady, Miss Mary Clarke.

Mary was 'one of the best known and best liked girls in Melbourne Society'[7] and so their wedding later in 1903 became a high point of the state's season. Robin's father, aboard the RYS *Valhalla*, was due to attend, but bad weather prevented him from arriving in time. Nonetheless, it was a grand affair as the Clarkes were pillars of local society. Her late father, Sir William, a highly successful businessman, agriculturist and generous philanthropist, had been the largest landowner in the colony and was a household name in Victoria. He had been central to organizing the Melbourne International Exhibition in 1880, the first World's Fair in the southern hemisphere, for which he was knighted[8] – the first person from the State of Victoria to be granted a hereditary title.[9] The Rupertswood Battery of horse artillery that he had raised lined each side of the aisle while her mother, Janet, Lady Clarke, gave Mary away.[10] Janet had once worked as governess for Sir William and married him after his first wife's death.

The family entered cricketing folklore thanks to his presidency of the Melbourne Cricket Club. While the England team were on their 1882–3 tour of Australia they were asked to spend Christmas at the family's great country house, Rupertswood (they had a similarly large townhouse called Cliveden). There they had an informal match with the Australia team organized by the family's music teacher, Florence Murphy (who later married the England captain, Ivo Bligh, later Lord Darnley) and beat them. Earlier that year there had been a mock obituary in *The Sporting Times* that proclaimed that English cricket had died, having been beaten by the Australians; it suggested 'the body will be cremated and the ashes taken to Australia.'[11] Janet, meanwhile, had a small terracotta urn, believed to be a perfume bottle she had bought in an Egyptian bazaar, which was hurriedly filled with the ashes from the bales burnt after the match and presented it for fun to Bligh. After his death Florence gave it to the Marylebone Cricket Club. This seemingly insignificant object became the symbolic trophy for the test series that forever after has been known as the Ashes.[12]

Meanwhile, when the wedding was over and Robin fit once more, he needed to return home to rejoin his regiment. His father offered the couple

222 Dorchester, 1908. On return from duties abroad, Robert was stationed for exercises in the south of England before moving to York.

passage home on the *Valhalla*, but Robin declined as he realized that the Russo-Japanese War was imminent and felt that travelling to Japan might serve as a useful intelligence-gathering mission. He had been expected to join his regiment but as he was in that part of the world he saw this as an opportunity as well as potentially useful to his career. Over the course of Robin and Mary's travels through the country in 1903, he compiled ten large volumes 'of every-day accounts from the chief Japanese, English, French, German and Italian newspapers, covering the period from the first talk of war until the conclusion of peace; and in the first volume, among the cuttings, he stated his opinion emphatically.'[13] He had long felt that Japan would be victorious whereas most Western powers were stunned when the Russians suffered multiple defeats, the first time in the modern era that a European power had been defeated by an Asian country. Its failure was to have profound effects on Russia's future.

On returning home, he gained his majority on account of his thirteen years in the army and was made major. The couple were quartered variously in Norwich, Edinburgh, Dorchester, Salisbury Plain and finally York. But his death at the age of thirty-seven from pneumonia came suddenly. It was thought that he had caught a chill on a recent staff ride with the Northern Command, but only survived for two days before succumbing. He was buried in the Ardington cemetery near his great-uncle Robert, Lord Wantage, VC, who had been laid to rest there ten years previously. The funeral was presided over by his brother, the Revd Edward, known as Eddie, an ex-soldier himself and recipient of the Military Medal. Among those who sent wreaths were the tsar and HRH Prince Arthur of Connaught, a fellow officer and friend of Robin's in the Greys.[14] The effigy of him lying in his uniform with his head held by an angel was made even more poignant by the three small figures of his children kneeling at his feet: Robert, Joyce and Rosemary, who were aged seven, six and three.

The Revd J. A. Melville made the eulogy during a crowded special service: 'He was the most lovable man I ever met. He lived in a perpetual atmosphere of nobility. Chivalrous and charitable, reverent and

223 The Lanchester Motor Co. produced some of the most successful cars of its time. Robert had a 1906 Tourer, while his mother had the grander Double Landaulet (1907).

224 Mary Lindsay (*née* Clarke) with baby Robert in her mother-in-law's 1907 28 h.p. Lanchester Double Landaulet.

225 Robert in his tiller-steered 28 h.p. Lanchester Landaulet at Balcarres in 1907.

226 Horses played a large part in Robert's life, both in work and play. Here he is playing on Merlin at Balcarres (*c.* 1885).

generous, high principled and unselfish, he had that mind which inspires every word and deed with grace.'[15] His name lived on when, at the outbreak of the First World War, his widow Mary converted her Mayfair home, 7 Charles Street, into the Robert Lindsay Officers Hospital as a memorial to him. She remained in London until 1926, when she finally returned to Australia and bought over fifty thousand acres of property in Western Australia, which she personally managed until she died in 1960, aged eighty-four. She renamed one of her estates Yasdnil – Lindsay spelt backwards.

The eldest of their three children, Joyce, married a distant kinsman, Martin Lindsay,[16] later to become baronet, who went from winning Nigeria's Grand National horse race to leading one of the first expeditions from West to East Africa through the Ituri forest in what was then known as the Belgian Congo. He then turned his attention to the Arctic, where he completed several expeditions, earning him the King's Polar Medal, and set a new world record after sledging and mapping over 1,050 miles, mostly through unexplored territory on the first successful Trans-Greenland expedition in 1934. The intelligence he and Peter Fleming gathered from their mission to Norway at the start of the Second World War was highly influential and altered the course of events both there, militarily, and at home politically, helping to precipitate the collapse of the Chamberlain administration.[17]

26

Serving God and Country

The Revd Hon. Edward Reginald Lindsay, MM, 'Eddie', 1876–1951

Eddie's family had been fervent supporters of the Anglican Church, so it is not surprising that at least one member of the family would develop some deep form of spiritual leaning; along with influences from the surrounding religious iconography in family collections, there were libraries and corridors filled with books on theology and religious manuscripts.

Eddie's childhood was spent mostly at Haigh Hall, where he built up his collection of fossils and shells in 'Noah's Ark', the bungalow-like building on the roof where he and his brothers lived a fairly feral existence. As well as summers at Dunecht, there were expeditions abroad – mainly to Villa Palmieri, where he was exposed to even more Christian symbolism.

In 1898 he joined his father and Walter on a voyage aboard the RYS *Consuelo* around the Mediterranean to visit the sights and seek out new material.[1] Ancient writings on fragments, rolls, books and sheets of papyri, vellum and paper, including Korans and Bibles and many works with hieroglyphics, were collected. In the end they accumulated hundreds of items which would keep specialists busy for years. A few months later Eddie and his father, this time accompanied by Lionel, were back on board the *Consuelo* for another expedition, round the coast of Greece, across the Aegean and back via Patmos, Rhodes, Crete and Naples.

Eddie had no immediate calling for the church and was destined to go into law. After leaving Charterhouse and Magdalen College, Oxford, he

227 *right* The Lindsay family was based most of the time at Haigh Hall in Lancashire, but it was at Dunecht and later Balcarres that they most looked forward to spending time. Eddie with his brothers Robert and Ronald (*c.*1882).

228 *opposite* The Revd Eddie, *c.*1920.

229 *below* Eddie joined his father and brothers Walter and Lionel on two extensive voyages around the Mediterranean aboard the beautiful RYS *Consuelo* (1899).

230 *top, right* Lakota couple from Wood Mountain.

231 *centre, right* Eddie standing outside the Railway Mission in Regina, Saskatchewan, where he worked for five years. Here he oversaw the building of a number of churches for farming communities and local Lakota converts (*c.* 1912).

232 *bottom, right* 'Melly's Indian motorcycle invention'. Melly was one of a small number of other priests whom Eddie lived with (*c.* 1915).

was called to the bar in 1902. *The Wigan Observer* announced that 'The Hon. Edward is twenty-three years of age and gives promise of superior abilities which may carry him far if he determines to practice.'[2] But he was changing direction. His eldest brother, Bal, who had gone to the same college, had maintained his relationship with the Oxford House in Bethnal Green, the first 'settlement house' where students and graduates could volunteer to spend time learning first-hand about the realities of urban poverty. It was less than half a mile from there, at the Anglican St Matthews Church, that Eddie became a curate in 1903.[3]

In 1910 the Archbishop of York, Cosmo Lang, a close friend of Bal, had set up, along with the Archbishop of Canterbury, Randall Davidson,[4] the Archbishops' Western Canada Fund to finance a venture known as the Railway Mission based

233 Eddie left the mission to join the ranks in 1917, seeing action throughout and earning the Military Medal. When peace came, he became a Catholic priest (*c.* 1915).

at Regina, Saskatchewan. (Coincidentally, this town was only fifty miles from the settlement of Balcarres, named after its first postmaster, Balcarres Crawford.)[5] Eddie headed this project in 1912, which involved assigning priests to various areas in this remote, sparsely populated state. By the time he had finished, he had built a number of churches that mostly served the farming communities and some local Lakota converts.[6] He remained there until 1917, when he set off for England to volunteer for the war effort.[7]

On 23 March 1917 he arrived in England, enlisted on the 25th and by 28 May found himself assigned to the Royal Garrison Artillery (RGA),[8] which he joined as a gunner aged forty-one.[9] Shortly after, he was posted to France, where he saw out the rest of the war and earned the Military Medal. This was awarded to personnel below commissioned rank for acts of gallantry and devotion to duty under fire. Had he served as an officer or even chaplain this would have been the Military Cross.[10]

He finally left the army in January 1919 and put his new address on his discharge notice as Birdsall, near Malton in Yorkshire, where he was made vicar. However, in a move that would have shocked his grandparents, who had been ardent Anglicans, he took himself to Oscott College, one of the three Roman Catholic seminaries in England and Wales. From there he travelled to Beda College in Rome, where he was received into the Catholic Church and ordained in 1930.[11] On his return to England he was sent to the Church of St Joseph and St Etheldreda at Rugely, Staffordshire. When he was transferred fifteen miles away to the Church of the Immaculate Conception and St Dominic in Stone, a testimonial from Rugeley lamented:

The Catholic colony feel that Fr. Lindsay did so much valuable and hard work in the parish, and conducted all the church services with such efficiency and dignity, that they ought to make some recognition of this and the manner in which he endeared himself to all. Fr. Lindsay associated himself with many movements in the town, and was a popular friend of all classes and denominations, and it is felt that many of these friends – other than those of his new flock – would like to make some small contribution as a token of the respect and esteem in which Rugeley held him.[12]

Edward remained at Stone until 1951 when he died, aged seventy-five. He may have been slight in stature, but he played a large part in the lives of those he worked with, was well received, respected and loved in all the places he was assigned to. He may not have made a great impact in the Lindsay annals but those around him, particularly the less fortunate, felt his influence and the benefit of his efforts. Sadly, such was the bitterness felt at his conversion to Catholicism that his nephews and nieces were never allowed to see him again.

27

'An immensely dignified diplomat'

The Hon. Sir Ronald Charles Lindsay, 1877–1945

There must have been something about the statesmanlike, 'moose tall'[1] bearing of Ronald Charles Lindsay that generated immediate and universal respect. This six-foot seven-inch giant seemed naturally able to quickly grasp complex situations, calm them down and confidently offer intelligent solutions that had not hitherto been apparent.

As the sixth child he felt a certain intimidating atmosphere at home on occasions and in his memoirs he described how his father could be cantankerous, even explosive. But in his later years Ronald knew his father had grown to feel a great deal of affection towards his sons and daughter. His mother, meanwhile, was 'unfailing with passive affection'. But at that boyhood age, he was less enamoured with his elder brothers, Bal, Walter and Robin, whom he described as 'very ominous to me'. He and Eddie were made to beat for them when out shooting and young Lionel was very persecuted, particularly by Robin, who he felt was 'a terrible bully.' His boyhood years with Lionel were strained, maybe out of a sense of jealousy of the youngest, who claimed more of their mother's time, but they all later became and remained the best of friends. For their sister, Evelyn and her husband Jim Mason, all the brothers had the deepest affection.

234 Ronald's steady climb saw him stationed in Russia and Persia and serve as ambassador in France, Egypt, Turkey, Germany and the USA (*c.*1905).

Ronald entered Winchester in 1890 and appeared to enjoy the lifestyle, but did not particularly shine in an atmosphere he called 'boisterous barbarism'.[2] Deciding that university would be a waste of time and having had a long-standing interest in a career in diplomacy, he spent the next three studying at Scoone's crammer in Garrick Street for his Foreign Office exams and travelling extensively to learn foreign languages. His efforts paid off: he came first in the entrance exam and immediately started in the Western Department. He found it an intoxicating experience and was fascinated by the machinations of diplomacy and geopolitics. Each day there was something new and intriguing; he was always amazed to see the secret telegrams that arrived every week with information about, for example, the Spanish plans to recover Gibraltar. The office still worked in the early Victorian way; there were no new-fangled typewriters or even telephones. Everything was written out long-hand. After the initial novelty wore off, he found the work stifling, but his request for leave to join the Imperial Yeomanry at the outbreak of the Boer War was turned down by Lord Lansdowne.[3]

Ronald's first foreign posting was in 1900, when he was dispatched to St Petersburg. While fending off the unwanted interests of a daughter of ambassador Sir Charles Scott, he became fully engaged as a junior officer in the embassy, learning Russian and building crucial long-term relationships with

235 Ronald (*c.* 1880)

236 Ronald described his relationship with his older brothers as 'very ominous to me'. However, they became close in later years (1891).

his senior colleagues, especially the Anglo-Irish diplomat Cecil 'Springy' Spring-Rice. Springy felt Ronald was far better looking than he, so when asked by the press for an engagement photograph, he sent one of Ronald instead. Meanwhile, there were plenty of attractions for the young energetic trainee. While there he took up polo on Krestofsky Island, where Prince Serge Belosselsky ran a polo club.

In each of his postings Ronald appeared to have been parachuted into the heart of some of the most defining and critical crises of the age. None more so than in Russia, where he witnessed the last scenes of the tsar's reign. Before the latter retired to the 'gloomy seclusion' of Tsarskoe Selo and Peterhof, Ronald attended what was probably the last great court ball at the Winter Palace.[4] The country's war with Japan was imminent, while riots and the stirrings of revolution were apparent; such occasions were brief moments of glittering peace before the maelstrom.

Ronald's description of the dazzling ball was somewhat surprising:

It was not as brilliant a spectacle as a Court Ball at Buckingham Palace. Russian Society was very limited in numbers compared with that of London, there was less fine jewellery, and the colour range of the uniforms was less varied, but the scale was tremendous! Four thousand guests would assemble. To attend them, every respectable servant in town would be pressed into service for the evening. His moustache would be cut off, he would be put into a gold laced livery coat and paid five roubles before being sent home in the small hours of the morning. And at the appointed hour the orchestra would strike up a polonaise and, led by the Emperor and Empress, each of the four thousand guests found his way to some place at a table in one of the vast halls, and to each, from the highest to the lowest, and simultaneously, a good hot supper was served on silver plates, while the Emperor walked round his party to see that they were all enjoying themselves.[5]

From the cold Baltic winds, he was sent to the dry heat of cholera-infested Tehran in 1903. This was his introduction to Middle Eastern politics and,

237 Ronald's first posting was to St Petersburg, where he attended probably the last great ball at the Winter Palace. 'It was not as brilliant a spectacle as a Court Ball at Buckingham Palace,' he observed (*c.* 1903).

238 In his sixteen months in Russia he travelled extensively on horseback, learning the dialects, customs and politics (1904).

239 'Leaning over backwards for my country.' Ronald's sense of independence and self-confidence led him to avoid university, but he travelled widely in the course of a career in diplomacy that took him to the highest positions in the Foreign Office (*c.* 1900).

as there was a shortage of staff, he virtually ran the legation, rising to second secretary and travelling extensively through the region, often on horseback, learning about the people and politics. But within sixteen months he was on his way again, this time westwards.

Ronald's first American adventure came about in 1905 because Britain's ambassador, Sir Mortimer Durand, was not getting on well with Theodore Roosevelt. The president's and Ronald's mutual good friend Springy Spring-Rice, who would later himself become ambassador to the USA, suggested that Ronald, with his good looks, affable personality and love of polo, would fit in well, while his role as secretary to the embassy would give his candidate a chance to 'humbug' with the president. This feather in the young diplomat's cap marked him out for future advancement.

While in Washington he met his future wife, Martha Cameron, the youngest daughter of the former Republican senator from Pennsylvania, James Cameron. She was the only child of the latter's second wife, Elizabeth Sherman Cameron, regarded as one of the most beautiful and brightest women in Washington at the time. But in 1907 Ronald was transferred to the British embassy in Paris's rue du Faubourg Saint-Honoré just as things were starting to get serious between them. He spent sixteen months there, which included accompanying King Edward VII to Biarritz. His role – fending off pestering letters from the French – did not take up too much time and so he was able to spend it mainly playing golf. His efforts, such as they were, earned him the MVO[6] before he was eventually moved back to London to become assistant private secretary to the foreign secretary, Sir Edward Grey. Meanwhile, his steady entreaties to Martha continued. She finally accepted the proposal from the 'tall blue eyed extremely handsome' man[7] and they married in 1909, whereupon Ronald felt obliged to offer his resignation from his position due to an unwritten understanding that diplomats marrying foreign women was frowned upon.

Ronald was fortunate in that one of his greatest friends was his superior, Robert Tyrrell (later knighted), private secretary to Sir Edward Grey. Tyrell was less bothered by such traditions and appointed Ronald to the Eastern Department of the

240 The great art historian Bernard Berenson declared that though Ronald's Stepleton had but one bathroom and was poorly lit, he would 'love a house so beautiful and so secluded'. Ronald standing beside his new Ford V8 (1933).

Foreign Office to focus on Russia. Within a year he was moved to the Hague, where he was appointed first secretary. His varied duties included being secretary to the British contingent at the International Opium Conference.[8] He returned briefly that year for the coronation of King George V as one of the Gold Staff Officers, for which he received the Coronation Medal.

His biggest challenge yet came in 1913, when he was made under-secretary of state for finance for the Egyptian Government. Back in 1873 mismanagement and corruption had forced the Khedive, Isma'il Pasha, to sell Egypt's shares in the Suez Canal to the United Kingdom. The country's finances were weighted so much by the canal's influence that it led to British and French financial controllers being installed in the Egyptian cabinet to protect their investment. This led to Britain declaring the country a protectorate in 1914, mainly in reaction to the threat from the Turks joining the Central Powers. The next six years' catastrophic events internationally, with the country's pivotal geopolitical position and the critical need for the United Kingdom to maintain such an important Middle Eastern foothold, meant that Ronald gained the most valuable of groundings. These included tackling particularly complex negotiations, developing financial and administrative skills, and becoming fully bilingual in French, in which all written business was conducted. His experiences would set him up for the highest offices on the diplomatic circuit.

While Ronald and Martha remained in Cairo during much of the war, her mother, by now estranged from her husband, and her companion Henry Adams,[9] having made it out of Paris just in time, found refuge at a house in Dorset called Stepleton. Initially they leased it in 1910 and then, with Mrs Cameron's money, bought it from its owner, Randolf Baker, in 1923. 'It was an escape from what verged on Hell.'[10] Adams tried to give some money to Ronald in thanks for providing refuge, but it was suggested that a donation to Martha's nursing fund for injured soldiers would be more welcome. On one occasion while in Dorset, Adams had the great art historian Bernard Berenson to stay. Berenson, also avoiding the Continent, wrote to his wife Mary from the 'fair haven' of Stepleton, admitting that though the house had but one bathroom and was poorly lit, he would 'love a house so beautiful and so secluded'.[11]

Tragedy struck the couple just nine years in to their marriage when in 1918 Martha contracted typhoid in Cairo. She returned home to Stepleton but failed to recover and died shortly after, aged just thirty-one. A fine 'Donatellesque' white marble relief of her by François Sicard was installed by Ronald and his mother-in-law in the small Norman church beside the house where she was buried.[12]

In the year after Martha's death, Ronald moved back to Washington, where he was to fill in as counsellor and act as chargé d'affaires while David Lloyd George sought a suitable ambassador to replace Lord Reading. It was during this period that Ronald became thoroughly disillusioned with American politics while witnessing the 'wooden pedagogue' Woodrow Wilson's problems over the ratification of the Treaty of Versailles.[13] However, the transient nature of appointments in diplomatic careers and the need to drop experts in one particular field into another region, meant that within a year he was packing his bags and back at the British embassy in Paris. He was now at the heart of the process of balancing war debts, disarmament and the development of the League of Nations, while dealing with the biggest threats to the status quo – the rise of fascism in Italy and communist rule in Soviet Russia – but his main focus remained the complexities of the Middle East.

In 1923 he was brought in by the Marquess of Curzon to work on one of the big issues of the day – the formation of the Treaty of Lausanne, which would define Turkey's borders as it renounced the remainder of the former Ottoman empire. The combination of his language skills and knowledge of the region's dynamics made him especially well qualified for the job. Initially there was no role for an ambassador, so he was made Her Majesty's Representative, but he would be appointed to that

senior position for the first time in 1925. He was now in charge of the most complex negotiations, including the reshaping of borders, particularly those near Mosul between Turkey and Iraq, the results of which would have an effect on the region's stability for the next hundred years. He later recalled: 'I don't think that I have enjoyed any of my posts as much'.[14]

Ronald's happiness had been further brightened in 1924 when he married his late wife's cousin Elizabeth Sherman Hoyt at Stepleton. She was the daughter of Colgate Hoyt, head of the New York stock exchange and prominent railway financier. Her mother, Lida Sherman, was the niece of the Civil War general William Tecumseh Sherman, after whom the battle tank was named. Elizabeth became a respected landscape architect at a time when formal training for such work was not open to women. Unperturbed, after studying botany and horticulture at the Arnold Arboretum, she proceeded to build up a successful business until the outbreak of the First World War, when she joined the Red Cross. The administrative skills she had learnt stood her in good stead when she was sent to France in 1917 to help standardize garments and dressings. On Elizabeth's return she became the first head of the United States Women's Bureau before joining the executive staff of the Red Cross. Between them, the couple would become quite a force.

Ronald's next assignment was as ambassador to Berlin in 1926. The country was seemingly going through a short period of relative prosperity, political stability and some international harmony (Germany had just joined the League of Nations as permanent member of the Security Council) – but it was an illusion. In the meantime, he would strive to cement what he saw as the imperative Anglo-French relationship, which would help ensure Germany would comply with the Treaties of Versailles and Locarno. Ronald's principal dealings were with Gustav Stresemann, the German minister of foreign affairs, with whom he had an affable relationship. While Stresemann was trying to strengthen Germany's trading position with both the East and West, he was also intent on both reducing the reparation payments and also keeping open his country's claim on Poland and other territories lost after Versailles. These he hoped to annex through economic war. However, while foreign secretary Austin Chamberlain was relaxed about the peaceful reshaping of Germany's Eastern borders, he became uneasy with Ronald and Stresemann's mutual affinity and

241 Ronald's first wife, Martha, died from typhoid at thirty-one. Six years later he married her cousin Elizabeth, seen here. It was a happy marriage, but just prior to the outbreak of war illness prevented her from travelling with him to the UK. They were never able to see one another again. He died in 1945.

242 After Ronald was appointed ambassador to the USA, the *Spectator* noted approvingly that 'Anglo-American relations require now not so much a great public figure ... as a well-disposed man of ability who has a complete knowledge of the intricate discussions' (1930).

decided to bring him back from Berlin in 1928, but he promoted Ronald to permanent under-secretary at the FO.[15]

In 1930, when the MacDonald administration came in, this role came to an end and Ronald was sent to Washington to take up the post of ambassador to the United States. This was in spite of Ronald's discomfort and personality clashes with some of the new socialist politicians at home, especially over their antipathy towards what they saw as an aristocratic cabal in the Foreign Office. But the prime minister rated him above all others. The *Spectator* summed up the appointment:

It is interesting that the Labour Government have not gone outside the diplomatic profession for an Ambassador at what is now by far the most important post. We believe that they are right. Anglo-American relations require now not so much a great public figure ... as a well-disposed man of ability who has a complete knowledge of the intricate discussions.[16]

Ronald was delighted at the prospect: his preference for working in diplomacy rather than the constraints of the FO, being on his wife's home soil, in the new Sir Edwin Lutyens-designed embassy made it the perfect, and, as it happened, final assignment. This was regardless of the fact that he had come 'to the uncomfortable point of actively disliking America!'[17]

Unfortunately, shortly after their arrival, Elizabeth experienced a coronary thrombosis, which meant that she spent much of the first year away from her husband and embassy seeking treatment while he was supported by his niece, Lady Elizabeth Lindsay,[18] who stood in to act as hostess at numerous functions. When his wife was able to return, her professional gardening expertise once again flourished and at 3100 Massachusetts Avenue she was able to create what became one of the most celebrated gardens in Washington. In 1938 the American Rose Society had named a variety in her honour, the 'Honourable Lady Lindsay'.

Ronald's duties, meanwhile, included briefing and hosting Sir Winston Churchill who, at one point, was recovering from a near fatal car accident that took place while he was crossing Fifth Avenue in New York. 'These two made the oddest contrast,' Churchill's secretary Phyllis Moir later wrote. 'The immensely dignified diplomat standing extremely ill at ease at the foot of Churchill's old-fashioned four poster bed, with the Peter Pan of British politics sitting up, a cigar in his mouth, his tufts of red hair as yet uncombed, scanning the morning newspapers.'[19]

The behaviour of the Duke of Windsor was a worry for most British diplomats. He was desperate to find a role and was seen as a menace to security through his relationship with Nazi Germany. In 1937 Ronald wrote to his wife that the duke was 'trying to stage a comeback, and his friends and advisers were semi-Nazis'. A month or two later, Lindsay wrote, officially:

The active supporters of the Duke of Windsor within England are those elements known to have inclinations towards Fascist dictatorships, and the recent tour of Germany by the Duke of Windsor and his ostentatious reception by Hitler and his regime can only be construed as a willingness on the part of the Duke of Windsor to lend himself to these tendencies.[20]

While the duke travelled through the United States, he tried desperately to get invited to stay at the embassy, which he saw as his right. A great deal of correspondence went back and forth to London and eventually a tacit agreement was reached whereby a small reception was laid on for the duke instead.

Ronald's tenure as ambassador lasted nine years, one of the lengthiest periods held at that most important of posts. As he was then the longest-serving ambassador to the USA from any country he was made dean of the diplomatic corps from 1934 to 1939. All the missions were being forced to adjust to a new America emerging from its depression years but sensitive to any outside influences that could upset its recovery. It brought on an isolationist approach, which hampered the support the British needed as they looked at the alarming trends in Germany in the

243 Ronald's position as representative of his government or sovereign in the USA brought him into contact with every significant figure who passed through Washington. Here in 1931 he is seen with (shortly after Sir) Malcolm Campbell after the latter's land-speed record run of over 245 mph at Daytona Beach, Florida.

Rhineland and Spain's civil war. Added to this, the strong Irish contingent were opposed to any form of alliance with the UK, so it fell to Ronald to bridge the gaps, maintain the relationship and strengthen what ties there were.

The Neutrality Bills that the United States debated throughout the 1930s would have the most important direct effect on US–British relations. Ronald saw that it was vital that legislation passed which would allow the USA to sell arms and allow loans and credits to England and France while withholding the same to Germany, Japan and Italy. The first versions of the act would have prevented any nation from gaining such benefits. Then the law changed so that any country could benefit on a strictly cash-and-carry basis (whether belligerent or otherwise) but eventually, with the obvious mounting aggression of the Axis countries and the gentle but firm pressure from Ronald on behalf of the European allies, the isolationists lost out and Franklin D. Roosevelt succeeded in passing the final version of the act in 1939 that allowed for shipments, loans and credits only to Britain and France, but now on a Lend-Lease basis. The quid pro quo was that the USA would continue to have a hold on those countries, ensuring their democratic values and would strengthen long-term relationships as they repaid their loans.

While ambassadors would continue to come and go, Ronald was effectively the last in a line of eminent diplomats who represented their countries at the very highest level. In time, improved communications would allow presidents and prime ministers to speak directly, so while these high-ranking diplomats continued with their plenipotentiary powers (full authority to represent their government or sovereign) they, nonetheless, would lose some of their standing in the public's eyes. In the run-up to the Second World War, most Americans' interests in foreign affairs became ever more focused as they watched with unease the developments in Europe. Ronald thus became the most recognized face and voice of the United Kingdom. As Alistair Cook recorded in his *Letters from America*, 'it was front page news if the British Ambassador appeared before the president and so much as hinted that His Majesty's Government took a dim view of such and such'.[21] Until this time, countries' leaders rarely met their foreign counterparts, so the ambassador's performance was both scrutinized by all and crucial to any outcome.

By 1938 Ronald was finally ready to retire, but he was encouraged to remain in place for what should have been a straightforward and enjoyable occasion but turned out to be a minefield that even this most experienced diplomat found more than onerous. The state visit of King George VI and Queen Elizabeth to Washington in 1939, the first ever to the United States by a reigning monarch, caused almost as many fissures as it healed in its attempt to foster good relations. It was to be the social event of the year and, needless to say, the clamour for invitations was overwhelming. When asked about the list, Ronald said, 'You know, the garden party is like heaven – few get to go.'[22] There was some irony in that many in the United States were pressing for isolationism and attempting to divorce themselves from worrying trends in Europe. But sometimes the needs of people's social standing can override even the most fervent political beliefs. Forced to call a press conference about the control the British appeared to have over the guest list, Ronald was asked why more '*average* Americans' were not invited. 'There's such an awful lot of them,' he replied.[23] The visit carried

244 Ronald on a voyage home in 1933. Until communications improved, countries' leaders would rarely meet their foreign counterparts, so the ambassador's ability was both scrutinized by all and pivotal to any outcome.

great significance as it marked the dawn of new era in British and American cooperation that would turn out to be vital over the following few years. The King and Queen changed the perception of the American people, which encouraged them to do more for Great Britain when war eventually broke out.

When the time came for Ronald to return home in August 1939, he had to leave Elizabeth behind while she attended to family business. They had planned for her to follow as soon as possible, but strict new travel restrictions meant it was not to be. With the onset of the battle of the Atlantic, she was unable to join her husband.

Ronald's career path and character meant that he was far from effusive or even particularly animated. A friend of his mother-in-law, George Caspar Homans, would, over the years, occasionally come to stay at Stepleton as her guest. Maybe Ronald was tired after a life of travel and being at the forefront of world affairs. Or perhaps he was just uninterested in small talk. And much of his demeanour must have been due to the sad oceanic divide between him and his wife. Either way, George found the retired diplomat extremely hard work if not intimidating, rarely getting even a 'good morning' from his less than hospitable host. 'His defining characteristic seemed to be that he would not make the slightest effort about anything, certainly not about me. His superiority, if he had it, was the most effortless I have known.'[24] Ronald's nephew, David, later the 28th Earl of Crawford, may have touched on another characteristic that could explain some of the old diplomat's reserve. Reminiscing in a letter to his sons in 1944, he noted that Ronald thought he had never done enough with his life. He had nothing tangible to show for it and no children from either marriage. Such a misguided view demonstrates some lack of self-esteem, which clearly was wholly unwarranted. David also knew that Ronald's father showed complete indifference when he was young and apparently wrote him only two letters in all his life. With one failed marriage and a long-distance one forced upon him by the war, it is perhaps not surprising that he became less congenial.

Ronald and Elizabeth were never to see one another again. He spent his last years at Stepleton, often in the company of his wife's aunt, who was also his first wife's mother, Elizabeth Sherman Cameron. His mother-in-law died in 1944 and was followed a year later by Ronald, aged sixty-eight. Ronald was buried with his first wife, Martha, and her mother at Stepleton. But back in America, Elizabeth continued working for the various charities on behalf of the war effort from her newly built home, Lime House, on her family's 173-acre estate on Centre Island, NY. Her own health gradually declined again and, aged sixty-nine, she died in 1954.

28

'An example of determination and heroism'

The Hon. Lionel Lindsay, MC, 1879–1965 and Kathleen 'Yone', 1880–1970

Lionel's citation for his Military Cross sums up the underlying strengths of the youngest of the Crawfords' seven children: 'He took charge of the whole front line and organized the position. Later he advanced forward and established a new position. He set a splendid example of coolness and courage throughout.'[1] There was perhaps something inescapable in this soldier's conduct, being the last born into what was a robust but not the warmest of childhoods.[2] It was probably that toughening experience that led him to follow hardier paths when he set out into the world.

At Haigh Hall, he and his five brothers led an undisturbed, semi-wild existence high up on the roof of the house in their 'Noah's Ark'. Few cleaners ever dared to venture there – and Lionel was certainly never allowed into its Mess Room, the inner sanctum. There was an aviary along with the boys' collections of fossils and antiquities and even a rabbit farm run to raise money for fireworks.[3] Lionel had his own collection of shells, something that became a lifelong interest.[4] However, it must have been a worrying place to be with only one's larger brothers as company. Although he eventually became extremely close to his immediate older brother, Ronald, their early years were less harmonious. Ronald had felt that his sibling was spoilt and indulged by their mother; Lionel was deemed to be her favourite and Ronald described him as 'a rather odious little boy of whom

245 *right* Before Lionel's father returned Balcarres to the senior line of the Lindsay family, most of their summers was spent at Dunecht in Aberdeenshire. Here with his mother, Emily, Countess of Crawford (*c.*1886).

246 *opposite* 'In our tent', Lionel, June 1904.

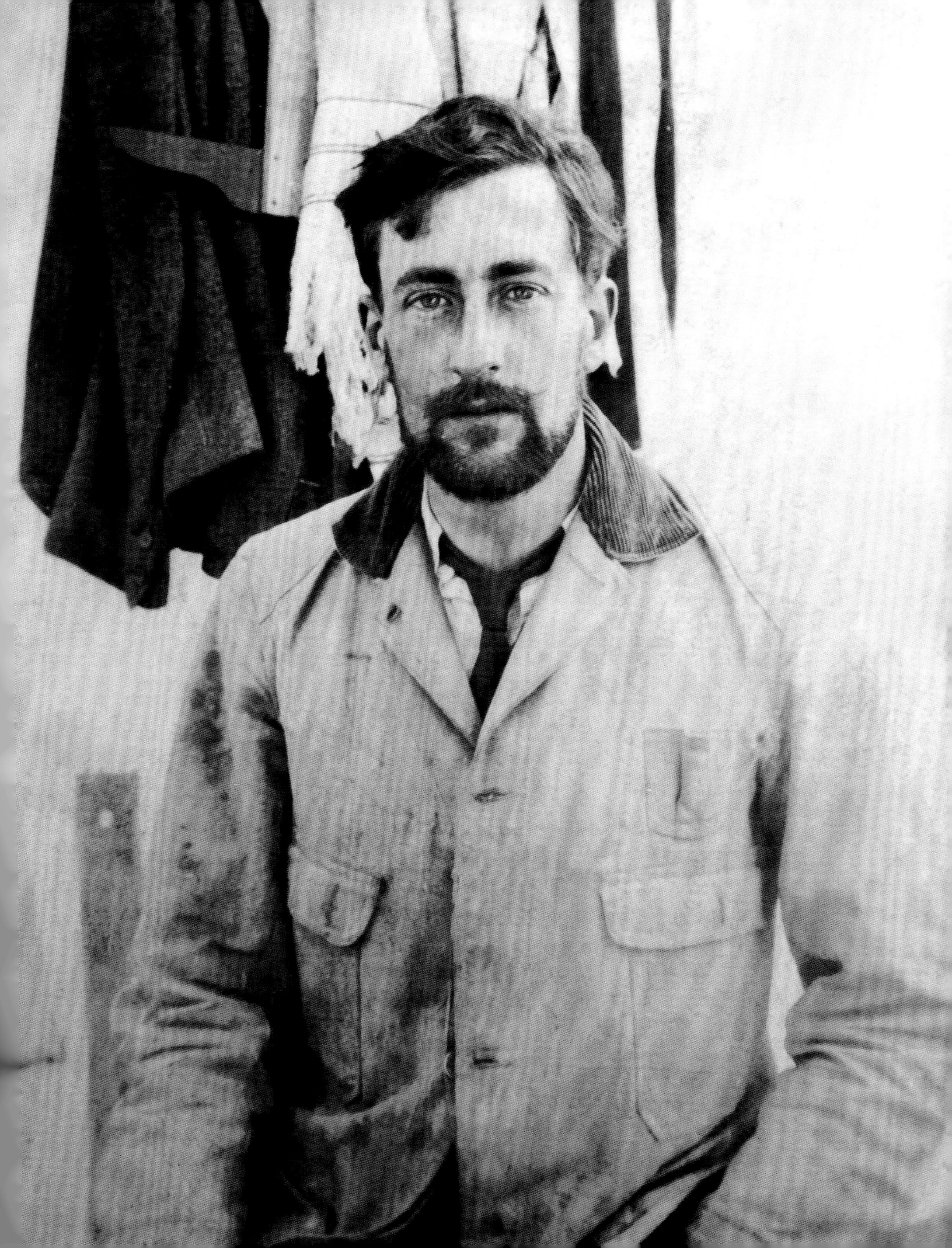

247 The entry in Eddie's album reads: 'We had just been to a funeral'. Haigh Hall (*c.*1907).

248 As children, Lionel had a difficult time with Robert, seen here when on leave. But in time all the siblings grew close. Haigh Hall, Christmas 1907, less than three years before Robert died of pneumonia.

249 In 1899, after finishing at Charterhouse and Cambridge, Lionel joined his father and Eddie on a Mediterranean voyage aboard the RYS *Consuelo.*

I was always rather jealous'. The next eldest was Edward (Eddie),[5] who treated him and Ronald with great severity – perhaps a harbinger of the life of strict religious vows he would later lead. On the other hand, his sister, Evelyn, and her husband Jim Mason, were much adored and would have them to stay at their Cotswold home, Eynsham Hall, where Jim had a pack of harriers and would take them hunting with the Heythrop.[6] Lionel remained a keen horseman and, along with his brother Walter, kept a string of polo ponies at Hurlingham between school and university.[7]

After Charterhouse and gaining his BSc at Trinity College, Cambridge, in 1897 he joined his father and Eddie in 1899 on a voyage around the Mediterranean aboard the RYS *Consuelo.* Eddie was a keen photographer and subsequently a rare record of their trip was made as they set out from Tangier to Pompeii, Athens, Bodrum, Crete, Monte Carlo and Malaga, among many other ports.

Lionel travelled to the United States in 1904 to enrol in the University of California's Mining School. Coincidentally, at the same time his first cousin,

250 Mining and engineering played a significant part in the Lindsay family throughout the nineteenth century. After Cambridge, Lionel carried this on, studying mining at Columbia University before working throughout North America from 1904 until the war in various mining concerns.

Gelasio Caetani,[8] had also begun studying mining, in his case at the Columbia University School of Mines. He later established his own company, Caetani, Burch & Hershey in San Francisco.[9] As reported in *The Mining and Scientific Press* (of which Lionel was a sometime assistant editor) and the monthly bulletins of the American Institute of Mining Engineers, it appears he travelled extensively throughout these years: in 1905 he was living in Berkeley, California, then in 1907 in El Oro and Sonora in Mexico and by 1909 he was in Denver, Colorado.

Many of the mining settlements were in some of the most remote and rugged regions of the Rockies. One such concern was Tomboy in the San Juan Mountains of Colorado, now one of the highest of all the ghost towns in the United States.[10] Originally called Savage Basin Camp and mined for gold, by the time Lionel reached this isolated settlement, miners had turned to the easier and hence more profitable zinc seams. Arriving after traipsing for hours up through mountain tracks, he ran into George Backus, an old friend from the University of California, who invited him to his family's Thanksgiving supper. George's wife recorded in her colourful reminiscences that

He was a charming and appreciative guest at our frugal table. I well remember his appetite. He ate three large baked potatoes, three servings of turkey, an equal amount of tomatoes, several slices of my home-made bread, and topped all with dishes of ice cream and many cups of tea.[11]

He probably did not understand how hospitable the family really were: these were true frontier towns where food could run perilously low, as was the case with the Backus family.

In July 1910 *The Mining and Scientific Press* announced that Lionel was leaving Mexico to sail for England by way of Tehuantepec and Cuba, but he later returned, this time taking in a journey across Canada, where he was able to visit his brother Eddie, who had moved out to start the Railway Mission in the remote town of Regina, Saskatchewan.

At the outbreak of the First World War Lionel quickly signed up and was initially assigned as a private, before being gazetted as a lieutenant in the original establishment of the 16th King's Royal Rifles, linked to the Church Lads' Brigade.[12] The battalion was raised by Field Marshal Francis Lord Grenfell, who was married to Margaret Aline, daughter of Lionel's aunt Margaret 'Minnie' Majendie (née Lindsay).[13]

He was then made a temporary captain as of February 1915[14] before becoming a full captain as he shipped out for France under orders of the 100th Brigade in the 33rd Division in November of that year. Almost immediately he encountered the horrors of war and was mentioned by name for his part in the action against Hazy Trench near Les Boeufs on

251 Yone in the Romanian national dress for a ball in Austria. She spent some of her childhood in Bucharest, where her father was ambassador.

252 Lionel signed up as a private but within a year he was made full captain and led his men into battle. His 'determination and heroism' earned him the Military Cross and Légion d'honneur (*c.* 1918).

5 November. The attack was to use a rolling barrage on the ridge with the platoons attacking in echelon. It began at 11:00 hours and progressed well, though the 16th's right flank was left perilously exposed due to the adjacent 1st Queen's Battalion not attacking their intended objective. This was due partly to confusion about orders and partly to getting lost en route to their start position. However, his 16th were able to make contact with 2nd Worcesters, who were to the right of the Queen's. 'This was mainly due to the example of determination and heroism exhibited by Captain Hon. L. Lindsay, who re-organized and consolidated the line'.[15] Between them, Lionel's force and the Worcesters were able to plug the gap in the newly captured position until reinforcements arrived.[16] The attack was not only successful but casualties were comparatively few. In addition to his MC, he was later awarded the Légion d'honneur (fifth class). In the latter stages of the war, relief came when he was stationed in Paris with the special duty embassy staff.[17]

Kathleen Yone Kennedy[18] was the attractive daughter of Sir John Kennedy, a distinguished officer of the diplomatic service who had served in St Petersburg, Santiago, Edo (Tokyo) and eventually Bucharest, where he was appointed Envoy Extraordinary and Minister Plenipotentiary to the Court of the King of Romania.[19] Her mother was Evelyn Bootle-Wilbraham, a sister of Emmie,[20] Lionel's mother, making them first cousins. Yone's parents had experienced a particularly tragic war, losing three of their four sons, all killed in action. Prior to that, Yone had seen much of the world and would have known Lionel for much of their childhood – indeed, photographs show them spending holidays together at Balcarres and Haigh Hall in their teens. But it took the old friends until they were in their early forties before they finally tied the knot in 1921.

They made their home at Hambrook House in Sussex, where they brought up their only child, Colin, born in 1922. Here Lionel immersed himself in the local council while maintaining his lifelong interest in science (especially molluscs) that saw him elected to the Malacological Society. He was also made a fellow of the Zoological Society. He lived until 1965, outliving his siblings by many years. Yone died just over four years later.

253 Haigh Hall, Christmas 1907. From top left: Robert, Ronald, Eddie, Walter, Jim Mason, Lionel and Bal. Front row (from left): Mary (Robert's wife), Emily, Evelyn and Connie.

The Haigh Colliery & Foundry and the Wigan Coal & Iron Company

'Collier lads get gowd and silver, Factory lads get brass'

Alexander, the 6th Earl of Balcarres, who married Elizabeth 'Bessie' Bradshaigh Dalrymple in 1780, inherited a dilapidated estate in need of considerable investment. Fortunes created abroad were key to maximizing investment in the relatively nascent industries of iron and coal.[1] Of course, in today's more reflective approach to history, one might be reminded that the industrial revolution came about partly on the backs of the more ruthless mercantile approaches of European nations, while the owners, workforce and cities across the Continent profited from that colonial booty. Indeed, however unpalatable the source was, the investments were vital for developing the Lancashire concerns.

When Alexander took over the mines, there were almost no maps of the pits or records of their workings. He was equally ignorant about the coal itself and so he compared the shells found in the strata of different pits and conducted experiments in calorific values in his bedroom grate.[2] Spurred on by his dislike of farming, he channelled all his energy into these new industries. His low regard for the plough and distrust of the landed estate led him to write to his grandson: 'Colliers we are and colliers we must ever remain.'

The Haigh estate and its lands down to Wigan lie over some of the richest and highest-quality seams in Britain. The earliest accounts of 'cannel' mining in the district, as distinct from ordinary bituminous coal, go back to the mid-fourteenth century.[3] This prized fuel has the highest calorific value, a brilliant flame, so clean it can be held in white gloves without marking, and is virtually ashless. There was even a toilet seat made from it at Haigh Hall. As Alexander's great-grandson, David, 'Bal', the 27th Earl of Crawford, said in an address to the Manchester Statistical Society in 1933: 'Cannel is the greatest, indeed the noblest fuel in the world.'[4] There was a legend in Wigan that one of the earls and his guests ate a meal off plates made of cannel – and then added them to the fire.[5] It has also been used in jewellery and can be turned on a lathe. The Haigh Hall summer house was built of the glossy material; its benches were clean enough to allow the ladies to sit on. Safe, lacking in the explosive nature of less dense types of coal, it can, nonetheless, be lit with a match.

Cannel's high hydrogen content made it a principal source for producing domestic gas for lighting and it was used extensively for the manufacture of paraffin and kerosene. While more expensive than coal, ton for ton, it was far more efficient. It was found that the illuminating power of twenty sperm whale candles for ten hours would cost 6s 8d, coal would only be 4½d, while cannel was just 3d and produced far fewer pollutants and less smoke or smell. Cannel was in high demand and was shipped internationally; one delivery arrived in Paris on 14 July 1789, the day the Bastille fell, though the collapse of the regime temporarily halted demand for this more exclusive product.

As smaller pits became available, Alexander would try to acquire them. Part of his strategy was to buy up parcels that could then connect with one another and prevent rival operators from linking up with the canals, the essential arteries that provided transport to their main markets. If the agricultural land above held no interest for the coal business, then he would promptly resell those acres, reserving the mineral rights below. He was, though, acutely aware that his commodity could not last forever, but he kept a long-term vision that seems extraordinary by today's standards: 'Allow me to suppose that our collieries would last for one hundred years. That long term may not be satisfactory for those who look to the endurance of their family for three hundred years.'[6] This family obsession to build up the business into

254 Prospect Pit at Standish was one of the Wigan Coal and Iron Co.'s many pits (*c.* 1905).

255 The only image, albeit a composite photograph, of the Haigh Foundry's *Walking Horse*, the world's third locomotive, built by Robert Dalgleish (*c.* 1812).

256 The locomotive *Crawford* having a refit in the Haigh foundry's workshops.

a permanent structure reached a milestone in 1865 when his eldest son, Lord Bal, merged the Haigh Colliery company with the equally large Kirkless Coal and Iron Company and others, forming the vast Wigan Coal & Iron Company Limited. At that time this was both the largest coal-producing firm and joint stock company in the country.[7] Its size was later superseded by the railway companies, but it always remained the most significant coal and iron business in Lancashire. Eventually, aided by two of the country's most able mining engineers and directors, William Peace and his successor Alfred Hewlett, the company were able to pay out a dividend most years.

James, known as Lord Bal, was popular with his workforce and kept a close eye on both their efficiency and welfare. He had strongly held religious views and a firm belief that it was industry that would be the saviour and drink the downfall of his workforce. His son commented that

a few years ago the Sunday was always spent in drinking, the Monday generally and the Tuesday frequently. We consequently introduced a rule that unless the collier appeared on Monday sober and did a fair amount of work he should not be employed during the remainder of the week. The effect of this rule on this ground alone is excellent.[8]

By the time of the merger of the Haigh and Kirkless concerns, the collieries were producing over a million tons of coal per year,[9] while the Kirkless ironworks' great blast furnaces, each eighty feet high, which lit up the night sky for miles, were producing almost 60,000 tons. These rapidly growing

257–9 The Haigh Foundry manufactured some of the country's largest pumping engines and most powerful factory engines. By the middle of the nineteenth century they had produced over one hundred locomotives. Lord Lindsay's interests in the classics led him to christen many of the locomotives with names such as *Ajax*, *Jupiter* and *Venus*, but others had a family connection: *Minnie*, *Ludovic*, *Wantage*, *Balniel* and *Lindsay*.

operations covered a vast estate twelve miles by two miles with over thirty pits and there were others in neighbouring areas.[10] By 1869, 75 per cent of the shares of the corporation were owned by the family, including Lord Wantage, Lord Overstone, Sir Coutts Lindsay, General James Lindsay and the Hon. Colin Lindsay.

The changing shape of industry and the materials needed for the great manufacturing and urban growth of the period encouraged the company to broaden its supply lines. High-quality coke was needed for steel, while tar, pitch and an array of chemicals produced from them had an ever-expanding market. Even the blast furnace slag did not go to waste and was used for concrete flagstones. Meanwhile the company invested further afield and mined haematite in Furness, other iron ores in Co. Fermanagh and Algeria and, until the 1917 Russian Revolution, manganese on the Black Sea.

The ever-deepening and lengthening pits demanded ingenious solutions to ensure their viability, as much for safety as expansion, hence the ready use of technology and the latest in engineering capabilities. On the death of his father in 1880, Ludovic carried on as chairman of the company and, due to his scientific interests, was instrumental in putting some of the first electric system into the mines, and the iron- and steelworks. Poor lighting in the industry had brought on thousands of cases of nystagmus, a debilitating disease that caused involuntarily eye movements, hence its common name, 'dancing eyes'. The early introduction of lighting in the decade before the First World War was a help, but miners still had to wait until the electric cap lamps of the 1930s for a significant improvement. The power station built at Kirkless in 1908, one of the first in the industry, was fired by waste gas from their own coke ovens and supplied five thousand volts to the Haigh and Aspull collieries, the iron- and steelworks, the tarmacadam works, engineering works, offices and washery.[11]

Sir Roger Bradshaigh started digging 'the Great Sough' in 1650 and within twenty years, without benefitting from the use of explosives,

260 In 1865 the Haigh Foundry was amalgamated with others to form the Wigan Coal and Iron Co., creating one of the largest such entities in the country. It included fifteen blast furnaces up to 80-ft high.

this tunnelling marvel was over 1,121 yards long. By 1870 it had grown to over two-and-a-half miles, connecting the Park and Aspull pumping pits. It is still operational today. Such engineering competence was essential for both the running of the mines and to protect them from neighbouring concerns, which might divert their own drainage systems into their competitor's. The build-up of water in old, sometimes inaccurately mapped, workings could, if breached accidentally, cause devastating floods, so efforts were constantly made to find ways to channel or pump the water away from the pits. New technology and better pumping equipment enabled these mines to cope with one-and-a-half million gallons of water every week. Nevertheless, there were always going to be dangers as the shafts and workings got longer and further from the pit head.

During the mid-nineteenth century, the company had started building their own steam cutters and by the 1930s the largest pits had entirely machine mining. Innovations extended to their own private telegraph system, with lines running to all the collieries, on which orders were tapped out in the latest communication system, Morse code.

As the pits got deeper, mine ventilation became more of an issue, resulting in a number of devastating ignitions of what the Wigan miners once described as 'fiery damp', or methane. Each day a fireman, covered in wet sackcloth, would enter the shaft and crawl towards where small gaseous accumulations were likely to form along the tops of tunnels and hold out a long pole with a lit candle attached. Depending on the quantity of gas, an explosion of flame would run along the roof while he lay flat until it passed. Only then would the next shift move in, which in turn would prevent the accumulation of gas while their movements stirred up the air.[12] Company-built steam engines were increasingly used, essential tools both for pumping fresh air in and water out. This also helped reduce the prevalence of respiratory diseases.

Perils, both below and above the workings, were never far away. Each mine recorded its own share of often multiple fatalities each year. Invariably, these were violent incidents, such as being crushed by wagons, roof falls, explosions, falls and even drownings. Between 1836 and 1940 the records show that there were almost six hundred deaths from such accidents in the business. William Peace, who later became the company's secretary, remarked in 1856 that 'this rate of 11 in 200 is normal' for the Haigh

Colllieries. The Maypole Pit in 1908, shortly before it came into the company, had suffered a major catastrophe when an explosion killed seventy-six miners. There are no accurate records showing the mortality rate from respiratory illnesses.

The Haigh Foundry was created in order to produce the steam engines and other equipment for the company's mines and railways. Robert Dalglish, who became one of the century's greatest railway engineers, was employed by Alexander in 1804 to manage the foundry. While there he built a range of pumping, winding and blast engines, including the world's third commercially successful locomotive. He had seen the locomotives that

261 The foundry's reputation for high-quality castings and forgings drew orders from around the world including, in 1854, a commission from the Isle of Man for the 72-foot *Lady Isabella* water wheel.

John Blenkinsop had designed for the Middleton Railway near Leeds in 1812, and so, under licence, he built the *Walking Horse* to a similar, but improved, design to Blenkinsop's *Salamanca* for John Clarke, a Liverpool banker and owner of the Winstanley and Orrell colliery and railway.[13] First operational in January 1813, it was the first in the world that could haul loaded wagons up a 4 per cent incline and was in continuous use for over forty years. This development was timely as the Napoleonic Wars had increased the cost of horses and horse feed. The high quality and effective designs of the company's later engines meant they were sought after by engineering and mining concerns internationally. In 1838 the ironworks, by now leased out for twenty-one years, supplied another two, *Snake* and *Viper*, to Isambard Kingdom Brunel for the Great Western Railway[14] and over the next twenty years there were a further 114 locomotives.[15]

The foundry gradually developed its own extensive railway network using its own trains and wagons, which massively reduced their transportation costs and times. The earliest rails were made of ash, beech or oak, often with strips of wrought iron nailed to the upper surface, with sleepers and gravel from the estate's quarries. As the technology improved, so did the capacity and size of the fleet. By 1850 there were seven locomotives and 270 wagons, which could each carry three-and-a-half tons. By the 1920s this had increased to 11,000 twelve-ton wagons. Ludovic, with his keen interest in astronomy and the classics, christened many of the locomotives with names such as *Ajax*, *Jove*, *Jupiter*, *Venus*, *Saturn*, *Hector* and *Achilles* as well as some with closer connection to the family, such as Crawford, Ludovic, Minnie, Wantage, Balniel and Lindsay, the last of which still runs today on the Carnforth Railway. At weekends the boilers would be washed out by their drivers, who took great pride polishing and burnishing their machines. They would often seek to ensure that their sons or relatives could succeed them in the coveted roles as locomotive drivers.

The Isle of Man had no coal of its own to run pumps, so Robert Casey designed a system using a water wheel above the village of Laxey. In 1854 the 72-foot diameter Lady Isabella (named after wife of the island's Governor, Charles Hope) using castings from the Haigh Foundry started its three-revolutions-a-minute cycle to pump water from the Glen Mooar part of the Great Laxey Mines industrial complex. Today an image of what is still the largest water wheel in the world appears on the back of the Isle of Man £20 note.

To further profit from foreign markets, a number of sea-going steam ships were built for the company, including the SSs *Lady Lindsay*, *Lindsay* and *Balniel*, mostly for trade between the Liverpool Garston Docks and Belfast and Dublin. In 1877 the 250-foot *Balcarres* was launched from Barrow. In 1871 Edward Binney, addressing the Manchester Geological Society (which he founded), said: 'It is singular to think that ... in this district thousands of women were employed in such work and the greater part of the coal wrought in Lancashire was conveyed along the bottom of the mines by women on all fours.'[16] In 1842 James felt that women should no longer have to spend so much time below ground, so he reduced their hours from their usual ten per day, but this was met with stiff protest from families who relied on that extra income. In the same year it was recorded that there were 836 boys and girls, some as young as six, working night and day down in the pits in the wider Wigan district.[17] However, such matters were taken out of their hands when legislation passed later in the year ruling that all females under the age of eighteen were excluded from working underground. Many unscrupulous mine owners ignored this, undercutting the Haigh Colliery business, so losses mounted quickly. It was not until two years later that a workable system came into force that ensured proper mine inspections. Women and children continued to work for the company, and became known as the Pit Brow Girls, or to some the 'broo wenches'.

The business had its share of sometimes violent industrial disputes, though often these shadowed more widespread regional disputes. The rise in food costs in the 1830s brought great hardship for many

whose wages failed to keep up, while the advent of the Chartist movement encouraged even greater discord among the workforce. Wigan witnessed heated scenes like those taking place in Bolton and Manchester. On 12 August 1842 an angry mob of over ten thousand from surrounding areas descended on the local industries and closed operations down while demanding higher wages. The following day about three thousand Wiganers appeared on the lawns of Haigh Hall. A sympathetic but wise James gave them food, drink and even money, calming matters down. Lord Derby, the Lord Lieutenant of Lancashire, was appalled at this and queried why James, as a magistrate and Deputy Lieutenant, had not dispersed the mob using the detachment of the 72nd Highlanders stationed nearby. Offended, James immediately resigned from his judicial and ceremonial positions. This stand must have endeared him to his workers for when in 1848 another sizeable body of Chartists were reported to be on their way from Bolton to cause mischief, a large group of colliers came to his support and stood guard around the Hall so that 't' Lord could drink his port wine i' peace'. Casks of a strong ale called 'Tommy Thumpers' from

262 One of the family's last duties before nationalization was opening the company's futuristic Clock Face Colliery's baths. Workers could go to and from the pits in all weathers; it also included a canteen, rescue station and cycle sheds.

Haigh Brewery were circulated to those on guard and found to work wonders.[18]

The largest strike took place in February 1912 with nearly a million miners out across the country accounting for most of the nation's mining workforce. The shutdown brought about the Coal Mines (Minimum Wage) Act, which guaranteed 6/6 per day for a collier. This reduced workers to eight hours a day, but caused a reduction in output and revenue; miners' incomes and finance for reinvestment both suffered. National output briefly peaked in 1913 at 287 million tons, but this figure was never repeated. The dissatisfaction brought about by the reduced incomes lingered on to bring about the two great coal strikes of 1921 and 1926, followed by the Great Depression of 1929–31. The Wigan Coal and Iron Co. was impacted as much as any. With mounting losses, no dividends were paid from 1924 to 1935.[19] Demand was down, but capacity was up; investment was needed, but profits were down and a constant clamour for higher wages brought repeated strikes and a growing demand for nationalization.

In an attempt to stimulate and protect their various concerns, an amalgamation was eventually formed in 1930, principally between the Wigan Coal & Iron Co., Pearson & Knowles Coal & Iron Co. and Partington Steel & Iron Works. Two new corporations – the Wigan Coal Corporation and the Lancashire Steel Corporation – were created, with David, Bal, 27th Earl of Crawford, as chairman. By

263 Patrick (left) and Robin Lindsay with their father David. They were the last of Lindsays to visit the mines before the Coal Industry Nationalization Act of 1946.

the time of the Coal Act in 1938, when the government took over all the country's coal seams, the company was employing over fourteen thousand in the collieries alone, the largest colliery owner in Lancashire. Later, when Attlee nationalized the mines in 1946, the company was producing almost three-and-a-half million tons a year, while their pit at Leigh was the deepest in Great Britain. The steel business had an even larger workforce, employing almost twenty thousand.[20]

Bal felt keenly that the paternalistic approach that had always existed between the family and workers was essential to the well-being of that community along with the venture's success and survival. While it cannot be said that the workforce lived in anything other than cramped and uncomfortable conditions by today's standards, the company made continued efforts to improve their lot by building decent houses and even whole villages – many of which have not altered much since.[21] The farm adjoining the newly built Crawford Village in the mid-nineteenth century was renamed Balcarres Farm, while close by there was a Crawford Arms pub. In each village they added amenities, including a nine-hole golf course, tennis courts, football fields and cricket clubs. Schools were built, some still in existence today, and efforts were made to improve older workers' education through talks and courses. Pithead baths were built at the mines including the Clock Face Colliery baths, a fresh and contemporarily designed building for the miners, who could now also have their clothes cleaned after work at no charge – a much needed change for the hygiene at home and less of a burden on their wives' purses.

The family, like other liberal Tory employers of the time, remained proud of their business and maintained a close eye on the workers' health and wellbeing. Even years after nationalization, the relationship with miners remained strong and many still referred to 'th' Lord's pits'. There was a pride in working for the company, and Bal strove hard to protect a connection which had lasted so long. The last garden party was held in 1938, when more than seventeen hundred people from both steel and coal corporations were invited to the Hall. This was to be the swansong before the war and eventual nationalization in 1946. It must have been sad and frustrating for Bal, to say nothing of the loss of income to the family, that even while he was president of the Mining Association of Great Britain, he had to hand over to the state one of the greatest firms in the industry. By the time the mines were eventually closed in the 1990s, it was estimated that the Manton pit, the largest in the company, still held reserves of over thirty million tons of coal.

29

The Art Historian's Art Historian

David Lindsay, 28th Earl of Crawford & 11th Earl of Balcarres, 1900–75

David Alexander Robert, Master of Lindsay,[1] was born at 49 Moray Place, Edinburgh, in 1900 into a family that was at the height of its influence, with three estates in Scotland and England, houses in London and Florence, some of the greatest coal and iron operations in the country, and one of the world's most important libraries. His future seemed bright – in the same month as his birth his grandfather completed the purchase of the largest private yacht in the world. But two world wars and the gradual near-revolutionary social changes were going to challenge all his abilities to steer the family's dwindling prospects as well as help guide some of the country's most significant art institutions through the most turbulent of times.

He was happy to play the role of the eldest, although it did create distance between him and his siblings that would remain for the rest of their lives: 'They were "fagged" mercilessly for me all through the holidays, as I was always supposed to come back from my private school from Eton so exhausted (by hard work) that I needed a rest: and so my sisters were told to work for me.'[2] However, Margaret, the oldest of them, dominated their world as far as the stables were concerned. It appears she took her authority on all matters equestrian rather too energetically for his liking and thus he was never a keen rider. He had an especial distaste for hunting, having been revolted by the sight of his first kill. Thereafter, on the rare occasions he did hunt, he would always avoid that final moment. His lack of enthusiasm was not helped by his belief that the Fife hounds were probably the worst in the country. He was, indeed, far more taken with academia than any country pursuit.

Much of the childhood was spent in that world high up on the nursery floor, a kingdom ruled over by Nanny, in David's case the fearsome but kind Mrs Purves, supported by her two nursery maids:

She would fight like a tiger for anything to do with the children: and there were constant rows between the Nursery and the rest of the household: the rows were all the more tremendous when ours was not the only Nursery and when cousins were also staying for their holidays in the house. Then the rival Nurseries and Nannies set an internecine strife of the greatest magnitude: and we children received the backwash of it all.[3]

When he was ten, David was asked to act as page to his grandfather, Ludovic, who, as Great Steward of Scotland, played an important part in the coronation of George V. It was a proud moment entering the

264 In 1924 David became member of parliament for Londsale, the former constituency of his future father-in-law, Lord Richard Cavendish.

265 David, Master of Lindsay, with his mother, Connie. In the previous half-century the family had experienced its greatest ascendancy in influence and fortunes but due to wars, economic and social changes over the next fifty years much of that progress would be reversed (1901).

266 Margaret, Anne and David on a walk with a nursery maid and the indominable Mrs Purves. He recalled how 'She would fight like a tiger for anything to do with the children.'

267 David, Anne and Margaret being taken on a morning drive at Haigh (*c.* 1906).

268 Although enthusiastic as a child, David admitted that he later lost all interest in farming (*c.* 1906).

269 David acted as one of the pages to his grandfather, James Ludovic, 26th Earl of Crawford, in his role as great Steward of Scotland at George V's coronation (1911).

abbey dressed in the family's dark blue velvet livery, highlighted in red, holding up the heavy coronation robes for his strikingly tall, red-bearded chief, who seemed to have come from a distant century. Ludovic was widely commended as the greatest spectacle of the already spectacular pageant. Dressed in full Lindsay tartan, velvet doublet with its Cairngorm-mounted silver buttons, dirk and *sgian dubh*, with the longest and most spectacular sporran, while carrying the great silver and enamelled staff, he attracted everyone's attention. That continued after the ceremony as they escaped, making a hasty dash through the crowds, escorted by policemen 'into a dense crowd who uttered a moan of joy, catching their breath, and parting in front of us and closing behind without any crushing'.[4] David remained fond of his grandfather: 'He was the most impressive person I had ever seen: but we were never in any way frightened of him.'[5]

Most of his early years were spent at their London house at 74 Bruton Street when his father was working with the museums or carrying out parliamentary business. He enjoyed returning to Haigh, where most of the family's business concerns were centred. David's first introduction to the mines was when he was taken down the Alexandria pit aged nine. 'Haigh was very black then with black smoke and dust in the air, grass and flowers ... the grapes were nothing compared to those of Balcarres.' Any fresh snow would rapidly turn to dark slush before the day was out. It had become so bad at one point that the laundry was regularly sent by train to Balcarres.

Each summer they would pack everything up and head north, taking everything including cots, bedding, baths and rugs. A series of hansom cabs or a 'station bus' would take all this to King's Cross. It was not the most comfortable journey; there would be draughts coming through the rattling windows, hampers were needed as there was no restaurant car, the seats were hard, and it could be cold enough for Lindsay tartan rugs to be spread out over him and his siblings. On arrival at Kilconquhar station one of the foresters would raise the Lindsay flag, decorated with the colours of the coat of arms, red with a blue and white chequered band, or more correctly 'gules a fess chequy azure and argent' up on the Craig tower, visible for miles around. He and his siblings were now in heaven. As with previous and later generations, they would frequent the nearby seaside, progressing, as they grew, from the Elie sandy beaches to the challenging rock climbing around Kincraig; or there would be trips by pony trap to the local fishing villages, for church in Pittenweem or to see the fish being unloaded from the myriad painted fishing boats and auctioned in that noisy covered market. During the First World War they could hear the heavy guns from the house when the Royal Navy was engaged in North Sea battles. His sister Margaret recalled witnessing the German fleet surrendering in nearby Largo Bay.

With the responsibilities of an inheritance, a childhood surrounded by the greatest accumulation of art and books along with guidance from his father and grandfather, his path was preordained. Ironically, he claimed that he and his siblings did not get to read many of the books as they were frightened of the librarians.[6] Fortunately, those interests were strengthened at Eton by the influence of the

270 Anthony Eden founded the Uffizi Society at Oxford as a forum for friends to discuss fine art: 'a club so exclusive that it withered away because eventually nobody was considered worthy of election.' David (second from left) seen here with Richard Dutton, Anthony Eden and Lord David Cecil to his left (*c.* 1920).

classical scholar A. S. F. Gow (who was to teach and inspire the writers Anthony Powell and Eric Arthur Blair, better known as George Orwell). Anthony Blunt later wrote of Gow:

he was almost the only don to take a positive interest in the art of the past and his rooms were the one place where one could find a good library of books about the Italian Renaissance, a fine collection of photographs of paintings and above all stimulating conversation about the arts in general. Though his influence in this field only spread to a relatively small circle of undergraduates it had a vitally important effect on them and through them on others in Cambridge and eventually elsewhere.[7]

Gow would join David after the war as a trustee of the National Gallery.

David, now Lord Balniel after the death of his grandfather in 1913, went up to Magdalen College, Oxford, as his father had and where his son, Patrick, would follow. There he rowed for the college and studied French, gaining a second-class degree.[8] In joining the Uffizi Club, started by Anthony Eden, he found likeminded undergraduate friends. Here they could discuss painters and painting, past and present. Efforts were made to induce leading critics and painters to address the society. The future prime minister Sir Anthony Eden gave what was regarded as a masterly talk on Cézanne. However, John Rothenstein, later director of the Tate Gallery, wrote that it was 'a club so exclusive that it withered away because eventually nobody was considered worthy of election.'[9]

David carried on a family tradition that saw him spend part of his young career in politics. After Oxford he became the honourable attaché in Rome, drawn to the position, no doubt, by the city's artistic attractions. In 1924, aged just twenty-three, he entered the House of Commons as the Conservative member for the Lancaster seat of Londsale. This was the constituency that his future father-in-law, Lord Richard Cavendish, had held between 1895 and 1906. His abilities were quickly noticed and from 1924 to 1929 he acted as parliamentary private secretary to the minister of agriculture and fisheries and was given the same position at the ministry of health from 1931 to 1940.

Lonsdale was not far from Holker Hall, the home of Lord Richard, brother of Victor, 9th Duke of

271 David won the Lonsdale seat for the Unionist and Conservatives in 1924 and held it until 1940, when he moved to the House of Lords on the death of his father.

272 Mary and David with Robin and Patrick at the Cartmel Races near Holker (*c.* 1936).

Devonshire and grandson of William, 10th Duke of St Albans. It was there that he would visit Mary Katherine Cavendish, the third eldest, whom he married in 1925. By then, the thread of politics ran widely through the extended family: two of his brothers-in-law were Conservative members, as was his wife's brother-in-law, and an ex-husband of another of her sisters, along with three husbands of her first cousins.[10]

His father was always supportive in his political exploits, though sometimes with his tongue firmly in his cheek:

Spoke for David at Carnforth and Ulverston. At the former meeting David gave an answer to a question about poultry and the price of lard which I thought was masterly. I am sorry that at a crisis with such great issues before ourselves and the world, so much should pivot on the price of lard, but at any rate I'm glad David is master of the subject.[11]

Alongside his parliamentary duties he had to make time for the family's coal and iron concerns, of which he was a director. These were some of the toughest periods for the business – for ten years from 1924 no dividends were paid. Strikes and the great depression brought serious hardship for such companies as well as those who were reliant on them, although the unfortunate need for re-armament in the mid-1930s started to make a difference. He was actively involved in the running of the mining operations and by the late 1930s he was vice-chairman and would succeed his father as chairman in 1940.

David, however, was most at home and made his greatest contributions to public life in the art world. He had already started to add to the collection, including Winifred Knight's *Flight into Egypt*. She wrote in 1927: 'My beautiful David, Lord Balniel, wants anything I like to do.' His first significant role came when, at the age of twenty-nine, he jointly organized with Kenneth Clark (later Lord Clark) an exhibition at the Royal Academy of some of the greatest Italian masterpieces, including works by Titian, Botticelli, Giorgione and Piero della Francesca, most of which had never been seen

273 David inspecting the troops in Wigan. He volunteered for the Home Guard at the outbreak of the war, but it was his services in safeguarding the nation's art collections that became his greatest contribution to the war effort (*c.* 1940).

outside Italy. Opening on New Year's Day 1930, this was a critically acclaimed event, although there were some who felt that it played too much into Mussolini's hands by enabling him to use the event for propaganda. Nonetheless, it was an extraordinary opportunity for the young duo to catalogue some of the world's greatest masterpieces.

The two would complement each other over the years, David being the more scholarly of the pair with a keen interest in museum administration. His father, though, was less enamoured of Clark: 'a very arrogant little chap, but clever as a monkey.' Clark, by then director of the National Gallery, recalled that David 'knew more about Italian art than I did. Heir to a long line of cultivated and scholarly ancestors ... he was brought up surrounded by such books, and by a collection of pictures from Duccio to Rembrandt; they had entered his bloodstream.'[12] (Sadly, though timely due to the financial strictures brought on by the impending crises, in 1939, David and his father agreed to sell Rembrandt's portrait of Titus at his desk to the Boijmans Van Beuningen Museum in Rotterdam.) The pairing remained strong, with David joining the gallery as a trustee in 1935 and becoming chairman of the trustees in 1937. Clark dedicated his 1939 book, *Leonardo da Vinci: An Account of his Development as an Artist*, to David and always maintained that the best thing to come out of the Italian exhibition was their friendship.

David became chairman of the National Trust in 1945 and his work on behalf of the country's greatest galleries continued long after the war, where we leave him for now. His lengthy entry in the *Dictionary of National Biography* adds that

his prolonged tenures of these and other appointments made him uniquely influential, and he applied himself energetically to each with wide-ranging knowledge, unobtrusive forcefulness, and a charm of manner that communicated itself to junior officials as well as to the senior directing staff. He was unsparing of himself, conducted a vast correspondence in a minute and idiosyncratic hand.

He was awarded the Order of the Thistle as his father had been and as one day his eldest son would be.

The year 1940 was a monumental one for both him and his family. All the museums closed and he had to manage the depressing evacuation of the treasures to safe havens far from London. His father died, and now with a family, heavy death duties, war and the progressive nationalization of the mines, he saw that the future of Haigh Hall was untenable. The rapid contraction of their financial freedoms brought uncertainties about their future. The family retired to Scotland and Balcarres once again became permanent home of the clan Lindsay chief. But they were no longer living with the comforts they had got used to, fine house though it was: 'What a tragedy it is that Electricity was not brought to Balcarres when the "going was good"! For who knows if now we will ever be able to afford it? ... it is unlikely that we will ever again be able to afford to live in the big rooms upstairs.'[13] But the photographs reveal that they rediscovered life's simpler pleasures, while making a refuge for the family, happy to re-engage with its Scottish roots.

30

The Countess Rode a Donkey

Mary Katherine Lindsay, Countess of Crawford & Balcarres, 1903–94

Mary Crawford introduced David Balniel[1] to a more relaxed world, an atmosphere absent from the scholarly confines of Haigh and the political comings and goings in London. Balcarres had been used more for relatively short summer retreats than a full-time home, but at Holker the pace of life was slower, and the neighbours had fewer preoccupations about the outside world and lacked pretentions to grandiosity.

Holker had long been known for the great house parties that Mary's parents had held, with picnics on the nearby shoreline and walks out on to the estuary to catch shrimps or swimming in the returning tides, warmed as they flowed back over miles of the sun-soaked sands of Morecambe Bay. It was the perfect escape for the couple to ride out with her sisters and younger brother, Richard, up into the steep hills behind that marked the southern tip of the Lake District fells.

Queen Mary, preferring to avoid Balmoral, visited in 1938. Like so many before and since, she was attracted by Holker's rare mix of a pastoral paradise combined with all the comforts of a grand house and an informality that appealed to a wide range of talented, successful or just amusing friends and cousins of all generations. However, the honour of welcoming such a guest was often balanced by the efforts that had to go into catering to all their whims and accommodating their staff. On this occasion Queen Mary was accompanied by a 'reduced entourage' of nine servants: two dressers, a footman and page, a lady-in-waiting (with her own maid), two chauffeurs and a detective. Fresh barley water was to be placed in her room every two hours, ice in the bedroom at 11.30 p.m., six clean towels every day – but she brought her own linen.[2]

Mary's siblings were born over a period of twenty years, meaning that there was rarely just one generation staying. Holker had a vibrancy that other such houses with smaller families could never equal. But for all their geographical remoteness and apparently informal atmosphere, the children still had a footman on hand on the nursery floor while their ponies would travel by train to London for the season from the local station at Cark.[3]

Mary was the most creative of the sisters. She combined drawing and watercolour skills with an ever-present sense of humour and recorded much of what was happening about her. As a child she discovered a love of archaeology and the endless possibilities of uncovering remnants from earlier civilizations. Although she never studied formally, she later took the opportunity to learn through her husband's involvement with the British Museum, of which he later became its chairman of the trustees. She was at her most comfortable in the outdoors, taking her divining rods or pendulums on (often successful) searches across muddy fields for evidence of Stone Age remains. She was equally happy being out with her horses, numerous donkeys and dogs. She certainly preferred learning about wild flowers to taking an interest in formal gardening. That lack of grandeur combined with a distaste for extravagance and pretentiousness chimed well with David, whom she married in a winter wedding in London in 1925. One characteristic that any of her frequent house guests would recognize was that she was never interested in food and David did not notice. Her nephew, Hugh (later Lord Cavendish of Furness), described how her 'own meals ranged from the inadequate to the downright dangerous. In this as in much else, Mary was intensely frugal.'[4]

She was third child of seven though her first brother, John, died when only seven months old. All of Mary's siblings had strong characteristics that endeared them to many with an intelligent but always-present mischievous edge that added to their appeal. The eldest was Elizabeth, known as Betty, an indominable figure, a useful trait when she became the chatelaine of two of England's greatest houses, Hatfield and Cranborne, and as the wife of the 5th Marquess of Salisbury, better known as Bobbety, the grandson of the prime minister. The next was Alix, tall, elegant and popular in the grandest circles that included friendships with Albert, Duke of York (later King George VI), and his brother, Prince Henry, Duke of Gloucester. But she contracted tuberculosis and died when only twenty-four, just six months before Mary's wedding.

Six years younger was Diana. Original, sharp yet warm, often seen with a large cigar, she built up a wide cosmopolitan circle of friends from Nancy, Lady Astor, to John Betjeman and Cyril Connolly. Her first of three marriages was to the colourful politician, author and broadcaster, Robert 'Bob' (later Lord) Boothby in 1935. But it was an unfortunate mistake and lasted only two years though she was spared his many years of indiscretions. Her two further marriages were far happier.

The youngest sister, who came some twelve years after Mary, was Sybil. Although the least intellectual, she was the most down to earth and went on to lead the most uncomplicated life of them all, marrying Laurence Dykes, the parson from nearby Cartmel. In later life all three younger sisters would return to Holker, where their nephew, Hugh, lent them houses.

274 *opposite, top* Alix (far left), Betty holding baby Richard, Diana and Mary with Sybil seated (*c.* 1917/18).

275 *opposite, centre* Mary's home, Holker Hall, introduced David to a world less steeped in academia and business but one that appealed to the great and good for its comforts, regular outdoor excursions to the Lake District and riding, swimming or picnicking on the nearby Leven Estuary.

276 *opposite, bottom* A large contingent of family and relations was on hand to support Moyra and Richard Cavendish when they had Queen Mary to stay at Holker in 1937. Including Mary (second from left), David (far right) and their young sons, Robin and Patrick.

277 *right* Although Mary Cavendish was niece of the 9th Duke of Devonshire and granddaughter of the 10th Duke of St Albans, she abhorred grandiosity and maintained a life of simplicity (*c.* 1921).

278 *left* A portrait of Mary in the modern manner (*c.* 1930).

279 *opposite, top* Of the sisters, Mary enjoyed the outdoors most, especially sailing, riding, skiing and walking. Here she is at the helm of the *Pinta* in Sweden (1934).

280 *opposite, centre* Mary's greatest interests were her horses, donkeys and dogs, as well as archaeology and wild flowers (*c.* 1925).

281 *opposite, bottom* Mary opening the women's section of the Wigan Coal & Iron Co. Clock Face Colliery Bath House (1939).

They were collectively and affectionally known by him as the 'Aunt Heap'.

Like Sybil, her youngest brother, Richard, was born during the First World War; their father was away fighting much of the time and eventually returned wounded. As a child Richard, like his sister Alix, contracted tuberculosis and this, along with rheumatic fever, steadily weakened him and contributed to his early death at fifty-five. In 1940 he had joined the Sherwood Foresters before making captain in the Royal Horse Guards. After his father died, he worked relentlessly to save Holker from punitive taxation and lack of income and eventually opened it to the public in 1950, only the second home owners to do so after Lord Bath admitted visitors to Longleat.[5]

David and Mary travelled extensively throughout Europe, visiting museums, music festivals and hiking and skiing in the Alps and Dolomites. In Norway one year they took their two eldest sons, Robin and Patrick, for their first skiing holiday. Even less developed than the Alpine ski resorts, they stayed in a remote mountain village that the train struggled to reach through the deep snow. Unperturbed, the small group of early ski tourists clung on to a long rope with a horse at one end and a sleigh with their luggage at the other and were pulled on their skis for the last ten miles.

Mary was never proud and always happiest dressing down; she often joined the Fife hunt on one of her donkeys.[6] But she embraced her husband's activities in supporting the workforce's welfare at a crucial time leading up to the war. She would then seamlessly step into the London scene to support her husband's increasing responsibilities heading some the country's greatest cultural establishments. Long after the war and her husband's death she continued to live at Balcarres, before eventually returning for her last years at Holker, remaining the matriarch of the Lindsay family.

31

'Supreme self-possession that was disconcerting at first'

Lady Margaret Cynthia, 1902–97, and Lt-Col. Henry Cyril Harker Illingworth, MC, 1896–1979

Margaret Lindsay was named after her parents' friend, Princess Louise Margaret of Prussia, Duchess of Connaught.[1] The eldest daughter, she had a manner and bearing that led one impressionable young lady to describe her as 'tall and regal and beautiful, with supreme self-possession that was disconcerting at first.'[2]

They spent their summers at Balcarres, where she and her siblings seemed to have their happiest times, riding up over the surrounding hills and visiting friends on neighbouring estates. In autumn she returned for the hunting season. Her older brother, David, ruefully looked back on how she dominated their world as far as the horses were concerned. It was a safe and almost perfect little world with its woods and dens, wide rolling fields and dairy farms or busy sawmills, cut off from the outside by the mile-long drives in all directions, free from the pollution of their industrial Lancashire home. This was their escape, where they had more contact with their parents, who were less tied up with industrial activities, parliamentary responsibilities, museum roles and challenges that came with her father's university positions.

That sense of security, however, must have come under strain when she had to wave farewell to her father, who enlisted in the Royal Army Medical Corps in 1915 to do his bit in France. She would not see him for another nine months, when he was finally given his first, brief leave. The closest that Margaret came to experiencing the war was listening to the heavy guns of the rival navies engaged in battle on the North Sea.

Later she recalled witnessing the defeated Imperial German Navy amass for its surrender – within sight of Balcarres. Operation ZZ saw 150 cruisers and destroyers of the Royal Navy's Grand Fleet, the largest gathering of warships ever off British shores, appear, still ready for action, to meet Germany's mighty dreadnoughts. On 11 November 1918, the day all hostilities ceased, celebrations were to be had throughout the nation, but none more so than on those British ships gathered in Largo Bay, just four miles from the house. As it got dark Margaret watched the extraordinary sight of all the ships' searchlights lighting up the sky while the supporting supply, merchantmen and hospital ships fired their green, red and white signalling rockets, accompanied by a continual cacophony of sirens, whistles and fog horns in celebration.[3] The German navy was instructed to gather off the Isle of May before being escorted up the Forth to Largo Bay. From there, on 21 November, Admiral Beatty sent his humiliating signal to the German admiral in command, ordering all their ships to haul down their flags, ending the Kaiser's dream of domination of the seas, before they finally signed the terms of surrender off the island of Inchkeith, near the Forth Bridge.

In her early twenties Margaret was frequently asked to take on duties on behalf of her mother, Connie, who was often unwell. She continued to lead a conventional life by her background's standards and found herself at the heart of a social scene. In 1924,

282 The strong-minded Margaret was described as 'regal and beautiful' (*c.*1927).

283 A portrait of Cyril Illingworth, most likely posed in profile due to the injuries to his right eye he sustained while fighting in France.

284 Margaret helping out in the Haigh stable yard.

285 Margaret with Haigh's head gardener, Mr Johnson.

along with HRH the Prince of Wales, later the Duke of Windsor, she was made godparent to Patricia Edwina Victoria Mountbatten, later the 2nd Viscountess Mountbatten of Burma.[4] One of the local newspapers reported that 'Lady Margaret possesses that quiet and unassuming manner that puts one at ease immediately and coupled with her charming smile this has secured for her a circle of devoted friends.'[5] Additionally, she was seen as 'a young lady of much charm and strong personality, and is endowed with considerable physical attractions.'[6] An unusual skill was whistling; she was good enough at this to perform in public at Red Cross gatherings.

That self-confidence served her well when she decided to go to India, where she met her future husband, Cyril Illingworth. In 1927 she ventured across Canada, at one point reaching the remote settlement of Regina, Saskatchewan, the same town where her uncle the Revd Hon. Edward Lindsay[7] had set up his mission before the war. A strange short article appeared in its local newspaper, written by an Evelyn Bevan (aged eighteen), that described the trials and tribulations of a young woman going about her life, including an occasion when she had been introduced to various guests 'whose names were promptly forgotten, with one exception – Lady Margaret Lindsay.' This was the same girl who had described her as 'regal and beautiful.' 'The daughter of a peer!' Evelyn whispered thrillingly afterwards. She did not know who the peer was – 'Not a very important one perhaps,' she added. 'But a peer's a peer for a' that.'[8]

Henry Cyril Harker Illingworth[9] was from a family whose fortune came from the wool industry. His great-grandfather had established Daniel Illingworth & Sons at the Whetley Mills, one of the largest factories in Bradford. But before Cyril had a chance to join the company after Eton, war broke out and instead he found his vocation in the army. He saw action with the King's Royal Rifle Corps (KRRC) on the western front and was awarded the Military Cross soon after on 1 January 1915. His commanding officer wrote: 'During the time he was my adjutant he was invaluable to me. His keenness was wonderful,

286 Margaret in her mother's 1906 Lanchester in the Balcarres stable yard (1907).

and his efforts largely contributed to the successes we had last September.'[10] In 1916 he was both injured and taken prisoner.[11] For at least six weeks from 28 February 1917 the twenty-one-year-old was posted as 'Missing, believed killed.'[12] News finally came through that he was a prisoner of war. While the relief was enormous for his friends and family, it must have been tinged with sadness when they discovered that he had lost his right eye and, for the time being at least, the use of his right arm.[13] It was not until December 1918 that he managed to get home to his parents at Wydale Hall in Yorkshire.[14]

He was desperate to return to duties, even with one eye. Margaret's niece, Francesca Wall, recorded that she had heard that 'When being examined to see if he was fit and able to take an active part in the second World War he simply covered his bad eye twice and was declared fit and with perfect eyesight! Imagine how inefficient the person examining him must have been!'[15] Having returned to the KRRC, he rose through the ranks, serving as ADC to Frederick Thesiger, Viscount Chelmsford, Viceroy and Governor General of India. On his return home in 1928 he and Margaret married. Now a captain, he became ADC to General Sir Percy Radcliffe, GOC-in-Chief of the Scottish Command in 1932,[16] and then assistant military secretary in 1935.[17]

When the Second World War broke out, Cyril was appointed as personal assistant to General Viscount Gort, Commander-in-Chief, GHQ British Expeditionary Force. Eventually he rose to lieutenant-colonel. Margaret, meanwhile, was still and remained long into her nineties the indefatigable force and indomitable figure she had been when young. At the outbreak of war, she joined the Red Cross, headed the Yorkshire branch and was later awarded the Associate Royal Red Cross (ARRC) medal for exceptional service.[18]

287 One of Margaret's father's first successes with the newly formed National Art Collection Fund was the raising of funds to allow the portrait of Christina, Duchess of Milan, by Hans Holbein to be saved for the nation. In celebration, Margaret dressed in the same manner for a fancy-dress ball.

32

At Home But a Refugee

Lady Cynthia Anne, 1904–97, Folke Arnander, 1899–1933, and Giovanni Fummi, 1886–1970

Anne Lindsay felt the full effects of the upheavals of the first half of the twentieth century. She went from the security of the sheltered world at home to immersion in an unpredictable one abroad that led to tragedy, then temporary relief, before the rush to escape the Nazis with her children.

As with her namesake and collateral ancestor, the writer and artist, Lady Anne Barnard, she had an adventurous spirit and yearned to travel. When still young women, she and her elder sister, Margaret, were often asked to stand in for their mother, Connie, whose health was wavering. Throughout Anne's season she carried out these engagements, while fitting in some travel, including a few months in Bermuda.[1] It was apparent that she could fulfil these assignments efficiently and at twenty-one[2] was appointed maid of honour for the Edinburgh Lord High Commissioner to the General Assembly of the Church of Scotland.[3]

In 1926 Anne met a young Swede, Per Erik Folke Arnander, while he was on a trip to England. He was a diplomat with a brilliant career ahead of him. However, it was only in 1930 when she was staying with her father's cousins Prince and Princess Bassiano in Rome that romance blossomed.[4] Arnander was born in 1899, had entered the Swedish diplomatic service aged twenty-two and had already been posted to Riga, Prague and Berlin before eventually landing the position of first secretary of the Swedish legation in Rome. He was seen as one of the

288 Anne with her brother David and sister Margaret in the Renaissance manner (*c.* 1911)

289 Nino and Anne with their Fiat 1500 (*c.* 1938).

290 Folke Arnander had already been posted to Riga, Prague and Berlin before he was made Sweden's First Secretary in Rome, aged twenty-seven.

291 Anne aged twenty-two.

most promising younger members of the service and took a special interest in economics and history.[5] He and Anne were married in November 1931. This was the third time her father had given away a daughter at St Margaret's Church, Westminster, in a service officiated by his old friend, Cosmo Gordon Lang, the Archbishop of Canterbury. Anne insisted on the wedding being a simple affair while the country was going through such straitened times.

In December 1932 they had their only son, Christopher James Folke. He would never know his father. One day, only six weeks after her son's birth, Anne was told her young husband had had an accident. He had left their flat in Via di Porta Pinciana for a short drive, but a student trying out his car for the first time collided with his.[6] Anne arrived at the Polyclinic hospital, accompanied by her sister Margaret, where she was given the horrific news that she needed to go instead to the morgue.[7] It later transpired that the other driver was Benito Mussolini's nephew. After the funeral, held at the English Church in Via Babuino, with the Swedish flag draped over the coffin, and the burial in the historic Non-Catholic Cemetery for Foreigners, better known as the English Cemetery, in Testaccio, the sadness must have been profound. Anne's bright future had suddenly become wretchedly uncertain.

Anne had the support of friends and family, but Giovanni 'Nino' Fummi, a leading figure in Rome's banking world, became especially close and supportive. Nino's first wife, an American, had died of cancer, bereaving him and their fifteen-year-old daughter, Luisa. They took Anne and her son into their lives and in April 1934 the widowed couple married, this time at St James's, Spanish Place in London. Anne was twenty-nine, and Nino, forty-seven. The service was officiated by her uncle, the Revd Hon. Edward Lindsay. There was no reception; the couple left almost immediately for their honeymoon abroad, then returned to Rome and moved in to his house on the Via Appia Antica.[8] Less than a year later, they rented the magnificent house in Via di Porta Latina that belonged to Dino

292 Anne with her second husband, Giovanni 'Nino' Fummi, attempting to appear relaxed in an uncomfortable setting in Munich, 1936. As J. P. Morgan's Italian representative, he was at the heart of loan negotiations between Italy, Germany, the USA and UK.

293 Anne with her daughter Francesca Fummi and son Christopher Arnander (*c.* 1935).

Grandi,[9] who was then serving as ambassador to the United Kingdom (and would later be deemed a traitor to Italy by the Fascists for not supporting Mussolini). There, Anne gave birth to a daughter, Francesca Giovanna Maria, in January 1935.

Those brief pre-war years together were something of an Indian summer during which they could enjoy the pleasures of Italian life, travel through Europe, including to Germany in 1936, or visit Chesa Lodisa, the large house he had built in St Moritz, Switzerland.[10] The first tangible experience, as far as Christopher and Francesca felt, of the changing political scenes came in 1938 when, back in Italy, the children, against their parents' strict instructions, went to the end of the garden and witnessed Mussolini and Hitler's cavalcade passing by, in emulation of the returning Roman victors of the first and second century. Francesca recalled:

> *I suspect there was an almighty row that evening when my parents returned from their lunch and doubtless innocently my brother related the story of our afternoon watching Mussolini and Hitler processing past our front gate.*[11]

Nino was the highly respected representative in Italy of the leading US bank, J. P. Morgan, and had already acted on behalf of Count Giovanni Volpi, the country's former finance minister, and most of Italy's aristocracy. Nino helped Morgan become Italy's prime foreign bank, arranging financing for the state and top private companies, resulting in him holding directorships at Fiat, Pirelli and Edison. He also forged a close relationship with the Vatican, which had, in the Lateran Treaty of 1929, given up the Papal States in return for financial compensation and sovereign recognition.[12] He had been enthusiastic about Mussolini's plans to make Italy a great Mediterranean power but Nino, the 'funny, charming, and sentimental' man, was 'less of a Fascist than a conformist willing to sacrifice his principles for *la dolce vita*.'[13] He did his best to secure loans for Italy from the House of Morgan but, with Mussolini's Abyssinia campaign and eventually locking arms with Hitler, the bank proposed what Mussolini felt was an overly onerous contract.

Relations between the bank and the regime deteriorated and on 20 September 1940 Mussolini had Nino abducted and held incommunicado at the Regina Coeli prison. His marriage to a British subject as well as his declarations about how anglicized he had become must have got Il Duce's antennae nervously twitching. He further believed it was Nino's machinations that prevented Morgan from offering more favourable terms. But that anger and punishment was misplaced – Nino had done his best to seek loans from Morgan and later argued that, had they been agreed, Italy may not have sided with Germany.[14] He was released only ten

294 Christopher and Anne in St Moritz (*c.* 1939).

295 Refugees at Balcarres. Christopher and Francesca spent the war staying with cousins throughout the UK (*c.* 1945).

days later through Morgan's intervention (Italy and America were not yet at war) and immediately left for Switzerland.

At the outbreak of the Second World War, Nino started to make plans for his family to go to Britain. Just in time. In May 1940 Anne, Christopher, Francesca and Luisa took what turned out to be the last train through Europe before Paris was occupied. They arrived safely and stayed first at Anne's uncle Lionel's home, Hambrook in Sussex, but as refugees they had to move to the British Camp Hotel[15] in the Malvern Hills for some months with no home of their own. However, affidavits from her brother, David, now the Earl of Crawford, and her brother-in-law, Reginald Manningham-Buller, enabled them to move freely within the UK and stay with their various relatives. For rest of the war Anne became deeply involved in supporting the Red Cross.

In July 1943, Nino managed to get a visa through the Vatican to travel to London in order to safeguard the Vatican's gold that was secretly shipped to the Federal Reserve Bank of New York. His role was pivotal in saving bullion worth over $9.2 million (about £82 million today) from the Nazis.[16] Such was his reputation that he was also entrusted with a delicate mission to make a separate peace with the Allies after the deposition of Mussolini. The British media simply could not understand why this Italian gentleman was allowed to travel to the United Kingdom from an enemy country. He even made it up to Balcarres to visit Anne and the children. The press only learnt why he was given safe passage long after the war.

Nino and Anne had not been particularly happy in their marriage in the late 1930s. Indeed, it must have been a stressful time, with the combination of each living under the shadow of lost loved ones, sharing the responsibilities of their children and stepchildren, a wide age gap and the distancing brought upon them by the war. The marriage did not survive, despite efforts at reconciliation in 1946, and Anne remained with her children in Britain thereafter, while Anne's stepdaughter Luisa returned to Italy to marry an Italian diplomat, Nello Cozzi.

33

The Most Creative Lindsay of His Generation

Major the Hon. James Louis Lindsay, 1906–97, and the Hon. Bronwen Mary, 1912–2003

If a large family is brought up surrounded by a great collection of art and antiques, much of which was amassed over generations and of the highest quality, it would be surprising if none of them developed some vestige of creativity themselves. James, Lord Bal's second son,[1] certainly did, inheriting many of his great-aunt Jane's artistic talents along with a curiosity and passion for the family story from his grandfather, Lord Lindsay. He could have settled down to a life of a craft – painting and drawing, woodcutting and engraving, silversmithing – all of which he excelled at. However, they remained pastimes while he concentrated on farming, and his sense of duty drove him to serve in the military, the diplomatic service and parliament.

After Eton and Magdalen College, Oxford, an interest in dairy farming took James to Africa in 1930. He returned in 1935 to join the army, initially the Royal Tank Corps,[2] before his transfer to the 22nd (London) Armoured Car Company and then the Scouts as part of the Scottish Horse.[3] From

296 James followed a tradition of many of his forebears into farming, fine art, the military, politics and diplomacy (*c.*1920).

297 James, tongue in cheek, with his sisters and nanny, about to leave for the christening of their first cousin, Robert Rivers-Bulkeley (1914).

298 Fire drill at Haigh Hall, with Margaret, James, Anne and Elizabeth on the estate Merryweather & Sons fire engine. Note the Lindsay crests and coat of arms painted on the side (*c.* 1915).

there, in 1938, he transferred to Queen Victoria's Rifles. His father was amused by his initial posting at the outbreak of war when he learnt that he was 'stationed at some school in Holloway scheduled for civilian duty to keep order in case of riots after an air raid or incendiary attack, when it is expected there will be an outbreak of looting!'[4] As a captain he fought in Europe, some of it with the Commandos, but was wounded in 1944, forcing him to relinquish his commission and end his service. He was subsequently granted the honorary rank of major and joined the Dominions Office.

In 1933 he had married the Hon. Bronwen Scott-Ellis in great style – she had fifteen bridesmaids.[5] By 1941 they had had three sons – all of whom later joined the army, two of whom went into the Black Watch, a regiment founded by a Lindsay ancestor – and a daughter.[6] Bronwen was the vivacious daughter, a twin with her brother John, born in 1912 to the immensely rich and eccentric polymath, Thomas, 'Tommy', 8th Lord Howard de Walden and Margherita (née Van Raalte), who had trained as an opera singer. His was an extraordinarily full life. As a young officer in the 10th Hussars he had served in the Boer War. A great sportsman, he fenced, sailed, was skilled in falconry and had a passion for horse racing. New technology fascinated him, too; he attempted to design an aircraft but enjoyed more

299 Bronwen Scott-Ellis arriving for her marriage to James with her father, the great polymath Thomas, Lord Howard de Walden (1933).

successful with powerboats, in which he represented Great Britain in the 1908 Olympics.[7]

Tommy was the most generous patron of the arts, particularly in his adopted Wales, a country that he loved and he long dreamt of it gaining independence. He was both a supporter of its performing artists and an author of plays and operas himself. His fascination with genealogy drove him to write extensively on the subject and he co-authored *The Complete Peerage*. He had been abandoned as a small child by his dysfunctional parents and escaped into the romance of chivalric stories and theatre. In 1899 he had inherited two vast fortunes when his grandmother, Lady Lucy Cavendish-Bentinck (sister of the 4th Duke of Portland) and his father died in the same year, enabling him to indulge in any passion, including arranging great gatherings from the world of art and literature and an annual medieval-style tournament at his Welsh home, Chirk Castle. He volunteered at the outbreak of war and served in the trenches Passchendaele and Gallipoli. But war took much of his earlier zest for life out of him. In a letter to his son John in 1921 he wrote: 'The one that writes to you now is no more than the husk living out a life that he finds infinitely wearisome.'[8] Nonetheless, he travelled widely, including in Africa. And it was there that James and Tommy's lives, through their shared interest in agriculture, crossed.

James served through the war and later became MP for North Devon. But he never lost his creative passions and retained his long-held interest in the family's genealogy, perhaps encouraged by his father-in-law's similar passions. He eventually distilled his great-grandfather's[9] substantive three-volume *Lives of the Lindsays* into his own version and went on to privately publish the more condensed, and readable, *More Lives of the Lindsays*.[10] This book gave great pleasure to his immediate family and, twenty years after his death, it was republished as *A Lindsay Family Story* with the addition of many illustrations.

300 James and Bronwen leaving their wedding, 26 April 1933.

34

Such Potential Cut Short

Lady Elizabeth Patricia Lindsay, 1908–37

The 'Popular Fife girl', Elizabeth, the third of the 27th earl's six daughters, initially followed a path expected of anyone of her background. She came out in 1927, but as her mother now found the London season too great a strain on her health, she asked the Duchess of Devonshire[1] to chaperone her for the court presentation.

The Dundee Courier, perhaps proud of one of 'their own', recorded that the debutante 'has frequently been singled out as one of the most attractive of the interesting group. Lady Elizabeth, on her appearance at the first Court on Tuesday night, justified the flattering things which have been said of her. She attended, gowned in beautiful white silk lace, embroidered with silver thread, with bows of white satin on the shoulders. Her train was also of white satin.'[2] As with most of her contemporaries, she went on to enjoy the colourful array of the usual events of the season, including Goodwood and shooting parties, twenty-first birthdays and coming out dances, weekends and weddings.[3]

301 Elizabeth was frequently asked to host functions for her uncle Ronald during his time as British ambassador in Washington (1932).

Elizabeth frequently stood in for her mother at garden fêtes, charity sales and gymkhanas, all part of the fabric that still held so much of country life together. She must have impressed and endeared herself to her uncle Sir Ronald Lindsay, who had been the Britain's ambassador in Washington since 1930. He was in need of some support as his wife, also Elizabeth, had experienced a coronary thrombosis, which meant that she spent much of the first year of his posting seeking treatment.

Ronald was a kindly man but he was not going to ask anyone to step into his wife's shoes unless he was convinced that that person could support him by engaging with the most important figures in government and commerce. Between 1932 and 1936 Elizabeth travelled out regularly to act as hostess for various functions. There was no diplomatic mission more important or scrutinized by those at home and the people of North America. Ronald's position was held in the highest regard while her contribution must have been invaluable. Great Britain's sometimes understandably confusing rules for hereditary and courtesy titles meant that Ronald's silver-haired wife was often mistakenly referred to as Lady Elizabeth Lindsay (rather than the correct form, Lady Lindsay). It must have baffled some observers when they were then introduced to a much younger, dark-haired lady of the same name who seemed to share the same role.

Elizabeth had travelled extensively before her voyages to the United States, including to Rome. When making a return visit there over the winter of 1936–7 she contracted a virulent strain of influenza

302 Elizabeth Lindsay by Alexander Bassano (*c.* 1923).

303 Elizabeth with her nephew, Robin (1929).

that was sweeping through the country. She had only been there for a week, staying with her sister, Anne Fummi. Her condition worsened, so she was moved to Lady Berkeley's villa, where she could be better cared for by the nurses from the nearby Anglo-American Nursing Home. It quickly developed into double pneumonia. However, recovery looked possible and all were convinced that she was going to get well. Unfortunately, she took a turn for the worse and died a few days later at the age of just twenty-eight.[4] She was given a small funeral and laid to rest at the same Protestant Cemetery as her sister Anne's first husband, Per Folke Arnander, whose burial she had attended four years previously.[5] Their families' grief can only have been heightened by the knowledge of how young both of them were and that their potential was never truly realized.

304 Elizabeth making her way across on the Kincraig rocks near Balcarres, a favourite activity for generations of Lindsays (*c.* 1925).

35

A Remedy for a Bullying Manner

Lady Mary Lilian, 1910–2004, and Reginald Edward Manningham-Buller, 1st Viscount Dilhorne, 1905–80

Mary always described herself as completely uneducated. That she was brought up in the most academic of surroundings, had a governess who taught her to speak French fluently and then spent time in Florence studying the Renaissance meant that she was, in fact, both intellectually aware and well informed – the perfect complement for a husband who would one day hold one the highest offices of state.[1]

Mary, like her siblings, was certainly not one of the period's 'bright young things', having been carefully chaperoned and brought up in a more sheltered environment by a deeply religious mother, Connie, Countess of Crawford and Balcarres, who would have severely censured any wayward, bohemian behaviour. That stricter approach, and her own form of enriching education, gave Mary attributes that established her as one of the more popular and striking debutantes. She soon fell for the tall Reginald Manningham-Buller,[2] who, though possessing little in the way of financial prospects at the time, was marked out as a rising star in both the legal and political world. In December 1930 'the tall bonny girl with beautiful dark hair and lovely eyes'[3] was given away by her father[4] and married by his friend, Cosmo Lang, the Archbishop of Canterbury, just as her sisters had been.[5] The couple went on to have a son, John, and three daughters, Marion, Elizabeth and Anne.[6]

Politics was in their blood – her father had served as a government minister and president of the Board of Agriculture and Fisheries, while Reginald was the son of Sir Mervyn Manningham-Buller, formerly MP for Kettering and then Northampton until 1940, and although Reginald had been called to the bar by the Inner Temple in 1927, his intention was to one day

305 On 18 December 1930 Anne was married to Reginald Manningham-Buller, later 1st Viscount Dilhorne, by Cosmo Lang, Archbishop of Canterbury.

306 *opposite* Mary, second from left, at the wedding of her brother David to Mary Cavendish (1925).

307 *above* Mary always felt she was uneducated but an upbringing in the most cultured surroundings meant she was actually well prepared for the roles she would one day fill (*c.* 1914).

enter parliament. Mary made the ideal companion for a man who became known as particularly formidable by both his political and legal opponents as well as his own colleagues, so much so that he was later referred to as 'Bullying-Manner'.[7] Her own father had been described as stern, so she was able to rise above her husband's behaviour and be equally disarming herself when confronted with pretension or pomposity, though with kindness and humour.

She was one of the members of the committee that organized the 1938 England Ball to raise funds for the Council for the Protection of Rural England, an event that was clearly taken seriously at the highest levels: its last committee meeting was held at 11 Downing Street.[8] Up to the point at which we leave them in 1940, their lives had followed a steadily rising path as Reginald rose through chambers. Thereafter things would change during and after the war. Mary was involved in training carrier pigeons that were used to communicate with resistance members in occupied Europe while, after the conflict, he went on to become attorney-general and eventually was appointed lord high chancellor of Great Britain by the Queen.

308 *right* Mary's husband Reginald Manningham-Buller, who later became lord chancellor, ensured through his affidavits that Anne Fummi and her children could travel freely throughout the UK during wartime in spite of her being married to an Italian (*c.* 1935).

36

The Daughter, Wife, Sister and Mother to Four MPs

Lady Katharine Constance, 1912–72, and Sir Godfrey Nicholson, 1st Bt, 1901–91

Katharine's family had provided politicians from every generation, so when she fell in love with the young Godfrey Nicholson MP, she was not entering uncharted territory. She was more prepared to live the life of a politician's wife than most, accepting her husband needed to put his constituency first. In spite of this, she successfully brought up a young family and made her own indelible mark.

Katharine, like her siblings, was encouraged to become involved in local charitable and civic causes as so many of them were connected to the family's estates. The nearby towns and villages, both in Fife and Lancashire, were tight communities closely linked to the family farms and businesses in which the Lindsays took their duties of care seriously. The work was not always onerous, but they contributed where they could. At one of its meetings in Colinsburgh, the small village just a mile to the south of Balcarres, Katharine followed a Mrs Fulton's demonstration 'on net making – fishermen's nets, garden nets and those of a finer mesh' with a contrasting talk on the life and works of Anthony Trollope.[1]

309 *right* Katharine at Haigh Hall (1925).

310 *opposite* Katharine and her siblings were all encouraged to become involved in local charity events that gave them the confidence for more serious roles in later life.

She was twenty-three when she became engaged to Godfrey Nicholson in 1936 and married at St Paul's, Knightsbridge, an occasion that was described as 'one of the most brilliant weddings of the London season'.[2] Godfrey had grown up in Hampshire on a large farming estate. From a young age he had wished to go into politics but his father had insisted he concentrate on the family gin business.[3] At that time politicians did not earn a salary, nor did they have their expenses paid, so it was felt that he needed to earn a living.[4] Eventually, he got his way and in 1931 was given permission by his father to have one attempt at standing for parliament.

Morpeth was a tough mining community but his reforming instinct (that later led to life-changing legislation that provided support to mineworkers and their families) enabled him to overturn a 16,500 Labour majority.[5] His knowledge of business and demands for welfare improvements broke down barriers that allowed him to become lifelong friends with Ebby Edwards, the president of the National Union of Mineworkers. Equally, it must have endeared him to his future father-in-law, Bal, who was similarly involved in the mining industry. Godfrey was deeply saddened to lose the seat in the next election, but he and Katharine returned repeatedly as he had made many friends in the constituency. For the next election he was selected to stand in Farnham, which he represented until 1966.[6]

At the outbreak of the Second World War they moved out of London to a house near Newbury and he joined the Royal Fusiliers. In 1940 he was sent to the Isle of Arran to help raise No. 8 Commandos in November[7] before being given a captaincy in the Home Guard. While Katharine was able to support her husband and bring up the children,[8] she had her own missions and became chairman of the local NSPCC. In later life she was vice-chairman of Dr Barnardo's.[9]

311 A British Red Cross surgical works party in the South Library at Balcarres (1915).

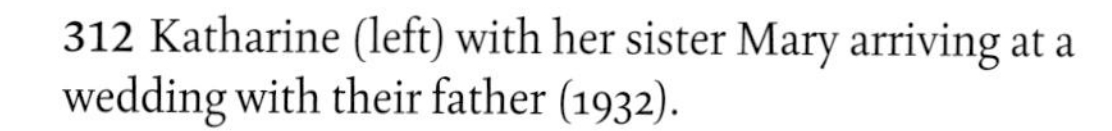

312 Katharine (left) with her sister Mary arriving at a wedding with their father (1932).

37

Lady Omega

Lady Barbara, 1915–2001, and Col. Richard Lumley Hurst, 1904–62

Bal's diary entry for New Year's Day 1916 reads: 'The news has reached me this morning that Lady Omega [his baby daughter Barbara] has arrived at Balcarres. God bless her and her mother, too. I hope to get leave on Monday morning.'[1] He was thus relieved, at fairly late notice, to learn that he could return to spend a precious eight days at Balcarres to see his newborn child and family, his first leave from his posting with the RAMC in France in nine months.

After the war much of Barbara's time was spent at 7 Audley Square, though when her engagement was announced, it was Haigh Hall that was deemed to be her residence. She spent much of her infancy during the First World War in the safety of their Fife home, Balcarres, but in peacetime that favourite escape became, once again, their summer retreat. Evidence of where they spent much of their time comes not just from the family papers but from the local newspapers as it was still a time when the public took an interest in the comings and goings of their aristocratic neighbours and landowners. So, for instance, when Barbara and her mother left Balcarres on the 9.27 p.m. train from nearby Cupar railway station at the end of the summer in October 1934, it was reported in *The Dundee Courier.*

313 Barbara painting (*c.* 1935).

314 Connie gave birth to Barbara in December 1915 while Bal was serving with the Royal Army Medical Corps in France.

315 Barbara was able to join her sister Anne Fummi for a final skiing holiday in St Moritz before the Second World War broke out later that year (1939).

316 Barbara holding her nephew Robin, later 28th Earl of Crawford, in the Rose Garden at Balcarres (1927).

Barbara became a gifted artist. Surrounded by a great art collection, encouraged by a mother who was herself a highly regarded as an expert in embroidery and with an older brother, James, who was a true craftsman, she became equally skilled. At the age of sixteen she was awarded the Royal Drawing Society's James Linton Memorial Prize in the Children's Royal Academy at the London Guildhall.[2]

After coming out, she spent some time in 1937 travelling through Europe. She was in Rome with her sister Anne Fummi,[3] when her twenty-eight-year-old sister Elizabeth[4] succumbed to influenza, which brought on double pneumonia. It must have been a terrible time for them all seeing her decline, rally briefly, and then tragically die soon after.

Early in 1939 Barbara joined her sister Anne in St Moritz for a final winter holiday as the world lurched towards war. With ideal conditions up on the Corviglia Heights they joined other skiers including Rose Kennedy, wife of US ambassador to the UK, and her children.[5] Before her trip Barbara had met a 'noted lawyer', Mr Richard Hurst,[6] and by spring they were engaged. His father, Sir Cecil Hurst, was the judge and president of the Permanent Court of International Justice in the Hague and was instrumental in the drawing up of the Treaty of Versailles and the Covenant of the League of Nations. They would make their home at the medieval priory Rusper Nunnery near Horsham, a house which had been in the family since 1839 and which he had bought from his brother.[7]

At the time of the wedding, Richard was a practising barrister, but after the outbreak of the war he changed direction and made the army his chosen career. He rose to the rank of colonel in the Royal Sussex Regiment. Their wedding service was conducted by Cosmo Lang, the Archbishop of Canterbury, her father's old friend, assisted by George Bell, the Bishop of Chichester at St Paul's, Knightsbridge. Although married life was put somewhat on hold during the war, they did manage to have three children during it.[8]

38

Three Sons of Balcarres

Robert Alexander Lindsay, 29th Earl of Crawford & 12th Earl of Balcarres, 'Robin', b. 1927, the Hon. Patrick Lindsay, 1928–86, and the Hon. Thomas Richard Lindsay, 1937–2021

The approach of the Second World War coincided with the childhood of the last three Lindsay boys to be brought up at Haigh Hall. They were still able to inhabit a rare, sheltered world that only such large estates could provide and benefit from the inspirational surroundings and unique influences that helped shaped their future paths. Because this family chronicle set out to cover only the first century of photography up until 1940, it is not possible to follow all of Robin, Patrick and Tom's many achievements, rich lives and experiences that would help shape their legacy for the following generations.

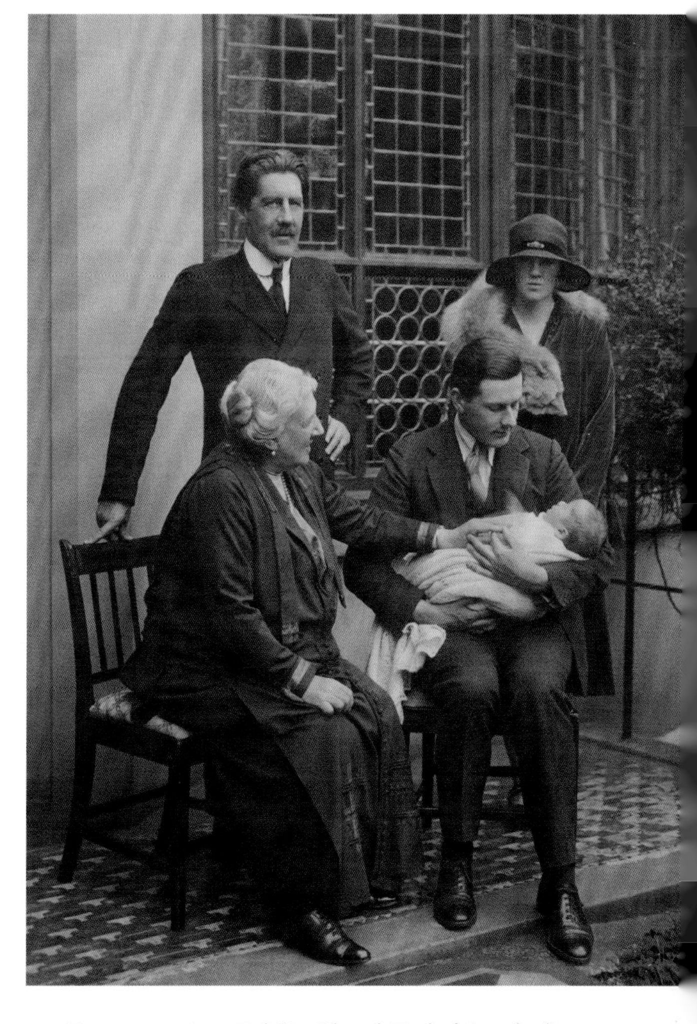

317 Four generations: Bal (David, 27th Earl of Crawford); his mother Emily, dowager Countess of Crawford; Mary and David (then Balniel) with their baby, Robin, after his christening (1927).

A stern group portrait taken in the courtyard at 7 Audley Square for Robin's christening shows him in the arms of his father, David, then still Lord Balniel, looking stiffly down. Around him are his mother, Mary, and grandfather, David, the 27th Earl of Crawford, beside his great-grandmother Emmie, widow of the collector, astronomer and yachtsman, James Ludovic, the 26th Earl.

Robin and Patrick were between nine and ten years older than their younger brother, Tom, and so during the long summers at Balcarres they spent much of their time together enjoying the outdoors, shooting rabbits and pigeons or exploring the farms and dairies, woodlands and sawmills. Then there

318 *below, right* Summers were always spent at Balcarres. Patrick (left) and Robin with their mother, Mary, in the stable yard (*c.* 1931).

319 *bottom, right* Robin (left) and Patrick helping their young brother Tom (1939).

320 *opposite, top left* Robin and Patrick on a day out in Edinburgh (1935).

321 *opposite, bottom left* Tom on his tricycle at Haigh (1939).

were the holidays at the home of their mother, Mary – the Cavendishes' Holker Hall near Cartmel, set in its rolling deer park, between the Lake District and Morecambe Bay. Here, shrimping and picnics down at the estuary or riding up into the fells played more of a part. Haigh Hall also had its attractions, with exciting visits down the mines or to the great ironworks. Inside this great house, built by their three-times great-grandfather, it was inevitable that their knowledge of the classics, art and history would be constantly strengthened, surrounded as they were by one of the world's greatest libraries. Added to this rich cultural environment they would often meet leading figures from the art world and politics, literature or industry, who came to see their father or to visit the collections.

After Cothill and Eton, Robin went straight into the Grenadiers and was posted to Palestine for a period that he found fascinating. From there he went on to Trinity College, Cambridge, where he read history. Meanwhile, by now his parents had decided to sell Haigh Hall, which meant that Balcarres once again became the family's principal home. Once he had left the army he concentrated on his own career, taking on several roles in parliamentary committees, entering politics full time in 1955, and serving for the next nineteen years as MP for Welwyn and Hatfield.

In 1970 he was appointed minister of state for defence and two years later minister of foreign and commonwealth affairs in the Heath government. At one point he was touted as a possible leader of the Conservative Party. However, he retired from full-time politics when, in 1975, he was created a life peer as Baron Balniel of Pitcorthie, after the house and lands on the eastern fringe of the Balcarres estate. His wife, Ruth (née Meyer), had come from a Swiss family who were heavily involved in contemporary art, so it was in keeping that in the mid-1960s the couple chose Trevor Dannatt to design their modernist house to be built over the foundations of the original Georgian neo-classical Pitcorthie House that had been demolished after an earlier fire.

Robin was highly regarded in all the fields he worked in and it was little surprise that the Queen

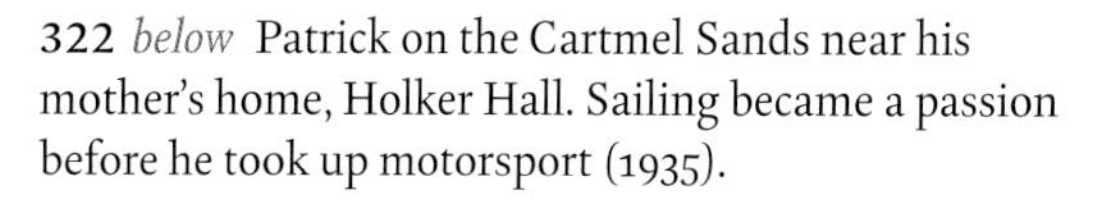

322 *below* Patrick on the Cartmel Sands near his mother's home, Holker Hall. Sailing became a passion before he took up motorsport (1935).

323 *bottom* Tom with his mother, Mary, Balcarres (1940).

324 *left* Robin succeeded as chief of clan Lindsay in 1975. After nineteen years as an MP, five at ministerial level, he held the office of lord chamberlain to HM Queen Elizabeth, the Queen Mother. In 1996 he was appointed Knight of the Thistle (1945).

325 *centre* Patrick became head of the old masters picture department at Christie's while pursuing a passion for historic aircraft and cars (1946).

326 *right* Tom went on to become one of the UK's leading picture restorers and took on restoring Hedingham Castle, left to him by his cousin Musette Majendie (1955).

made him a Knight of the Thistle, as his father, grandfather and great-grandfather had been. The last senior roles he took on at the time of writing were as commissioner of the Crown Estates and last lord chamberlain to Queen Elizabeth, the Queen Mother. It was a position he held for ten years until her death in 2002, requiring him to play a pivotal role in the planning of her state funeral.

After Robin's father's death in 1975, he became more involved in the running of the Balcarres estate and immersed himself in the family's collections, about which he became knowledgeable. As well as adding to the library he commissioned leading restorers to repair and safeguard the considerable number of rare and delicate incunabula, papal bulls, manuscripts and books for posterity. The library and vast family archives (much of which make up the second-largest collection at the National Library of Scotland with about forty-five thousand items[1]) remain a destination for serious bibliophiles and historians.

Patrick followed Robin through school but his education was likewise interrupted when he joined the 2nd Battalion, Scots Guards, and was sent to the Far East to tackle the Communist pro-independence fighters in the Malayan emergency.[2] On return, he went up to Magdalen College, Oxford, but could not complete his degree due to breaking his neck skiing in Davos. Sport, nonetheless, remained one of his life's passions. Whether it was in sailing, motorsport or flying, he was attracted to historic machines as he loved the art of the engineer although he had little mechanical aptitude himself. Similarly, he had long been captivated by the old masters and so, after coming down from Oxford, he started working in Florence under the great art historian, Bernard Berenson, before joining Christie's the auctioneers. By the early 1960s he was heading its old masters picture department, and in the early 1970s he started the first regular historic car auctions.

Patrick always held a love for Balcarres and the fondest memories of Haigh, but he and his wife

Amabel (née Yorke, daughter of Philip, 9th Earl of Hardwicke), having both lived in such large houses when young, agreed that they only ever wanted to have smaller, more manageable properties. His father had been left Stepleton in 1945, the beautiful Queen Anne house near Blandford in Dorset, by David's childless uncle, Sir Ronald Lindsay, ex-ambassador to the United States and he, in turn, gave it to Patrick. However, Amabel and he never lived there, although she decorated it for her cousin Robert Fermor-Hesketh, who rented it from them for a few years. In the early 1980s they decided to sell the house as they felt happier at their more practical weekend retreat, Folly Farm near Hungerford.[3]

As well as being a keen shot, an ornamental wood turner, a successful historic racing driver and a collector of steam engines, it was flying that became Patrick's most consuming passion. He joined up a number of fields at Folly Farm to create a runway so each weekend on his way down from London he could pick up one of his aircraft from High Wycombe and fly home. He put together one of the finest historic aircraft collections in private hands and restored an array of aircraft that included a Spitfire. He still had plenty of plans and ideas to fulfil but his life was cut short by cancer at the age of fifty-eight.

Tom was only ten when the family moved up to Balcarres, so Haigh played far less of a part of his youth. While still at Eton, he was asked to act as page to his father at Queen Elizabeth II's coronation in London.[4] The extraordinary pageant took place on 2 June 1953, and was the first such occasion to be televised and broadcast live around the world. His father, David, was asked to stand in for HRH the Duke of Rothesay as the Great Steward of Scotland. With David dressed in the family's coronation robes, Lindsay tartan kilt and plaid with its doublet, adorned in silver-mounted cairngorm stones, Tom's role as page included carrying his coronet and train.

Three weeks later, on 24 June, they arrived at Edinburgh for the National Service of Thanksgiving and Dedication that was held at the High Kirk of St Giles. This was a less glittering and majestic event, with the Queen dressed more informally since Winston Churchill wanted to downplay the Scottish monarchy element. Nonetheless, it was as significant and important to Scotland and its subjects as the coronation had been to the English and one in which was treated in Edinburgh with as much reverence. David was given the privilege, as Premier Earl of Scotland, of bearing the sceptre, one of the Honours of Scotland, as the Scottish crown jewels are known.

After Eton Tom, like Patrick, joined the Scots Guards for his national service. Thereafter, he went to Canada with a friend to travel and find work. A period attempting to sell encyclopaedias resulted in absolutely no sales but he was not particularly bothered as he knew that his future lay in his first love, art.

Tom's mother and his uncle James were both talented craftspeople. He inherited their skills, along with an appreciation of the old masters, that led him to study under Helmut Ruhmann, one of the leading art conservators of his day. After two years studying drawing at the Slade, he started his own restoration business from his Cadogan Gardens flat and over the following years became one of the country's leading picture restorers. His brother, Patrick, in his role as head of the old masters painting department at Christie's had little hesitation in recommending him. His father, not one to risk damaging any works in the collection, asked him to investigate his full-length portrait of Alexander, 6th Earl of Balcarres's sister, Lady Margaret Fordyce (née Lindsay) by Thomas Gainsborough. She was dressed in black, but Tom was able to reveal her original, and far more attractive, pink silk dress once the top paint surface was removed.

Another Lady Margaret Lindsay, the daughter of Alexander, Lord Lindsay, 25th Earl of Crawford, had married Lewis Majendie in 1870. He had inherited Hedingham Castle in Essex, a fine Queen Anne house that stood near one the best-preserved Norman keeps in Britain. They had left it to a son, James, who, although he had two sons himself, left the whole property to his daughter, Musette, Tom's second cousin once removed.[5] She never had children but became close to Tom and on her death in 1981 she left Hedingham to him.[6] This was not solely due to a special relationship – he was also able to trace his own lineage back to Aubrey de Vere, who had originally constructed the keep in the twelfth century. Tom and his wife, Virginia, 'Ginnie' (née Capel Cure), split their time between there and the Old Rectory, Ashmore in Wiltshire, before eventually handing it on to their second son, Jason.

When Robin and Ruth moved into Balcarres in the 1970s, they brought new life to a home that had once witnessed great house parties and endless activity; by then much had been shut up with cold, darkened rooms filled with furniture covered in dust sheets, and was, except during the summer holidays, bereft of the sounds of children. The stable yard was no longer busy with horses being groomed nor the house filled with the comings and goings of a young family. But through their efforts at Balcarres and enterprises elsewhere, the Crawfords made it the principal home for the head of the Lindsays with a large family once again – the first time Balcarres had played such a role in one hundred years. The next generation, too, headed by Anthony and Minnie Balniel, has continued to build on this and has given this house beloved by the wider clan an added sense of vitality, belonging and permanence for generations to come.

327 Robin, 29th Earl of Crawford, celebrating his ninety-fourth birthday on 5 March 2021, holding his great-grandson Ludovic James Lindsay, with Alexander, Master of Lindsay, and Anthony, Lord Balniel (standing). Photographed by Anthony's brother, Alexander Lindsay, in the drawing room at Balcarres.

Notes

Abbreviations have been used in these notes as follows for frequently cited works:

BL Nicolas Barker, *Bibliotheca Lindesiana: The Lives and Collections of Alexander William, 25th Earl of Crawford and 8th Earl of Balcarres, and Ludovic, 26th Earl of Crawford and 9th Earl of Balcarres* (Bernard Quaritch, 1977)

CP John Vincent, ed., *The Crawford Papers: The Journals of David Lindsay twenty-seventh Earl of Crawford and tenth Earl of Balcarres, 1871–1940, during the years 1892–1940* (Manchester University Press, 1984)

LL i–iii Alexander Crawford Lindsay, Earl of Crawford, *Lives of the Lindsays: or, A memoir of the Houses of Crawford and Balcarres* (three volumes, John Murray, 1858)

MLL James Lindsay, *More Lives of the Lindsays* (private publication, 1970)

1 · 'The Grand Project' *pages 14–16*

1 *MLL*, p. 91.

2 Letter from Dame Dorothy Bradshaigh to Charles Dalrymple, Haigh, 21 May 1780, quoted in Donald Anderson, *Life and Times at Haigh Hall* (Smiths Books, 1991), p. 69.

3 *MLL*, p. 93.

4 *MLL*, p. 113.

5 Maria Nugent, *Lady Nugent's Journal: Jamaica One Hundred Years Ago* (A. & C. Black, 1907, reissued Cambridge University Press, 2010), p. 18.

6 https://www.historyofparliamentonline.org/volume/1820–1832/member/lindsay-james-1783–1869

7 *MLL*, p. 93.

2 · A Vicereine of Ireland *page 17*

1 *LL* ii, p. 201.

2 Stephen Taylor, *Defiance: The Life and Choices of Lady Anne Barnard* (Faber & Faber, 2016) p. 26.

3 Francis Peter Plowden, *The History of Ireland, from its Union with Great Britain* (J. Boyce, 1811), vol. i, p. 171.

4 Rosemary Richey, 'Yorke, Philip', *Dictionary of Irish Biography* (Royal Irish Academy, 2020).

5 Charles O'Mahony, *The Viceroys of Ireland* (J. Long, 1912), p. 211.

6 Revd Henry Pepys, *The Remains of the Late Lord Viscount Royston: with a memoir of his life* (John Murray, 1838), p. 176.

3 · 'Colliers we are and colliers we must ever remain' *pages 18–23*

1 School of Art History, University of St Andrews.

2 Sergeant Major Patrick Gould (d. 1815) of the Royal Edinburgh Volunteers. During his twenty-one years, the drill sergeant trained upwards of two thousand men.

3 *MLL*, p. 160.

4 https://www.ucl.ac.uk/lbs/person/view/21571

5 *MLL*, p. 164.

6 *BL*, p. 66.

7 *MLL*, p. 174.

8 *BL*, p. 126.

9 Lady Jane Lindsay, Second Writing of Memories (manuscript, 1935).

10 *BL*, p. 138.

11 Lady Jane Lindsay, Second Writing of Memories (manuscript, 1935).

12 Lady Mabel Lindsay, handwritten reminiscences (1912).

4 · 'In appearance very well but no beauty' *pages 24–26*

1 *MLL*, p. 160.

2 *MLL*, p. 174.

3 *BL*, p. 67.

4 *MLL*, p. 175.

HAIGH HALL *pages 27–36*

1 The Lancaster Canal is now part of the Leeds and Liverpool Canal.

2 See chapter 3: James, 7th Earl of Balcarres.

3 See chapter 22: David, 27th Earl of Crawford & 10th Earl of Balcarres.

4 *Ancient Monuments Society Yearbook*, 1926.

5 James Ludovic, 26th Earl of Crawford & 9th Earl of Balcarres.

6 Donald Anderson, *Life and Times at Haigh Hall* (Smiths Books, 1991), p. 142.

7 Lady Mary Meynell, *Sunshine and Shadows over a Long Life* (John Murray, 1933), p. 38.

8 Lady Jane Lindsay, Earliest Written Memories, begun in 1928.

9 Ibid.

10 Alexander, 25th Earl of Crawford & 8th Earl of Balcarres.

11 Lady Jane Lindsay, Earliest Written Memories, begun in 1928.

12 Lord Lindsay had originally been interred at Dunecht but his body was stolen. It was retrieved a year later and moved to Wigan.

13 Lady Jane Lindsay wrote that by the end of the century much of the laundry was sent by train to Balcarres to clean as the soot and pollution around Wigan had got so bad.

14 Anderson, *Life and Times*, p. 163.

15 Ibid., p. 177.

16 Ibid., p. 179.

17 Giles Worsley, 'Country Houses: The lost legacy' *Daily Telegraph*, 15 June 2002.

5 · 'My first master in Italian art' *pages 37–49*

1 Lady Mary Meynell, *Sunshine and Shadows over a Long Life* (John Murray, 1933), p. 25.

2 Lady Mabel Lindsay, handwritten reminiscences (1912).

3 *BL*, p. 11.

4 The 2nd Earl of Caledon was married to Lady Catherine Yorke, daughter of Alexander's aunt, Lady Elizabeth Hardwicke (née Lindsay).

5 *Val d'Arno: Ten lectures on the Tuscan art directly antecedent to the Florentine year of victories. Given before the University of Oxford in Michaelmas term, 1873* (George Allen, 1891).

6 *BL*, p. 29.

7 Ibid., p. 31.

8 Lady Mabel Lindsay, handwritten reminiscences.

9 Early printed books, especially those printed before 1500.

10 *BL*, p. 12.

11 Lady Mabel Lindsay, handwritten reminiscences.

12 Ibid.

13 Ibid.

14 *BL*, p. 128.

15 Lady Mabel Lindsay, handwritten reminiscences.

16 See chapter 12: Lord Wantage.

17 *BL*, p. 270.

18 Meynell, *Sunshine and Shadows*, p. 28.

19 Lady Mabel Lindsay, handwritten reminiscences.

20 *Wigan Observer and District Advertiser*, 18 Dec. 1880.

21 Raymond W. Blanchard, 'Gardens of the Villa Palmieri at Florence', *Landscape Architecture Magazine*, July 1923, vol. 13, no. 4.

22 Salvatore Cortesi, 'An Historic Italian-American Villa', *Independent of New York*, 16 June 1910.

23 Ibid.

24 Giovanni Boccaccio, *The Decameron*, Introduction to the Third Day.

25 Alexander was now 25th Earl of Crawford but was commonly called Lord Lindsay for the rest of his life.

26 Lady Mabel Lindsay, handwritten reminiscences.

27 Ibid.

28 Lady Mary Meynell, *Sunshine and Shadows over a Long Life* (John Murray, 1933), p. 238.

29 *Wigan Observer and District Advertiser*, 18 Dec. 1880.

30 *BL*, p. 271.

31 *Reports before High Court and Circuit Courts of Justiciary*, May 1882–Dec. 1885, vol. v, p. 66, 1887.

32 'Mystery of Body Snatching', *Scotsman*, 31 Oct. 2016

33 Lady Jane Lindsay, Reminiscences.

34 Paul Brown, *Messages from the Sea: Letters and Notes from a Lost Era Found in Bottles and on Beaches Around the World* (Superelastic, 2016), p. 69.

35 Meynell, *Sunshine and Shadows*, p. 22.

6 · 'A soldier in every sense' *pages 50–53*

1 Sir Garnet Joseph Wolseley, 1st Viscount Wolseley, *The Story of a Soldier's Life* (1903).

2 *BL*, p. 65.

3 James's second cousin Charles, 5th Earl of Hardwicke, was married to Sophie Wellesley, niece of the Duke of Wellington.

4 *MLL*, p. 222.

5 *MLL*, p. 223.

6 Sarah's mother, Anne, Countess of Mexborough, was the daughter of Elizabeth, Countess of Hardwicke, sister to Alexander, 23rd Earl of Crawford.

7 Mabel (d. 1928) married Lt-Col. William Ramsden; Mary (1851–1911) married John Coutts Antrobus.

8 *BL*, p. 137.

9 'Lindsay, Sir James Alexander', *Dictionary of Canadian Biography* (online ed.), (University of Toronto Press, 1979–2016).

10 *Manchester Courier*, 17 Aug. 1874.

7 · 'So manly bold and uncompromising' *pages 54–59*

1 *MLL*, p. 228.

2 *The Christian Remembrancer*, vol. 8, p. 162.

3 *MLL*, p. 229.

4 *MLL*, p. 230.

5 *MLL*, p. 229.

6 Algernon Percy, *A Bearskin's Crimea: Colonel Henry Percy VC & his Brother Officers* (Pen and Sword, 2007), p. 81.

7 *MLL*, p. 232.

8 Robert Lindsay, later Lord Wantage, VC.

9 Henry was mentioned in despatches twice before becoming commissioner of the British Red Cross in France in 1914. He joined the RFC and became Lt-Col. in the RAF in 1918. His children excelled in their chosen fields: Norma became a leading garden designer and David Ludovic Peter went on

to create the French ski resort of Méribel after a distinguished army career in which he received the DSO.

10 *Illustrated London News*, 8 June 1889.

11 Ibid., 30 Mar. 1878.

12 Marion Margaret Violet Manners, Marchioness of Granby, Duchess of Rutland (1856–1937).

13 Kirsty Stonell Walker, 'Violet Manners: Aristocrat and Portraitist to "The Souls"' (available online at Art UK).

14 Max Beerbohm, *Herbert Beerbohm Tree: Some Memories of Him and of his Art* (Hutchinson & Co., 1920).

15 Diana Manners' father was rumoured to be Henry Cust.

16 The 'unplaced tomb' remained in their London house until they moved to Belvoir.

17 Wilfrid Scawen Blunt, *My Diaries: Being a Personal Narrative of Events 1888–1914. Part One: 1888–1900* (New York, Knopf, 1923) p. 53.

18 These included over forty donated by her grandson, John Julius Norwich.

8 · One of the 'hot headed ones' *pages 60–63*

1 Lady Mabel Lindsay, handwritten reminiscences (1912).

2 Collinson, Patrick. 'Pollard, Albert Frederick (1869–1948), historian.' *Oxford Dictionary of National Biography*. 23 Sep. 2004; Accessed 3 Mar. 2021. https://www.oxforddnb.com/view/10.1093/ref:odnb/9780198614128.001.0001/odnb-9780198614128-e-35556.

3 *BL*, p. 109.

4 *MLL*, p. 238.

5 Colin Lindsay, *The Evidence for the Papacy: As Derived from the Holy Scriptures and from Primitive Antiquity* (Longmans, Green, and Co., 1870).

6 'Honiton Holy Family RC Church: Our History', https://www.honitoncatholicchurch.co.uk/our-history.

7 William Alexander Lindsay CVO became Clarenceux King of Arms, the senior of the two English provincial Kings of Arms.

DUNECHT pages 64–69

1 *BL*, p. 125.

2 *BL*, p. 132. Letter from Anne Lindsay (née Trotter, wife of General James Lindsay) to Lady Trotter, 9 Oct. 1849.

3 Lady Mary Meynell, *Sunshine and Shadows over a Long Life* (John Murray, 1933), p. 56.

4 *BL*, p. 133, Letter from Lord Lindsay to Gen. James and Anne 25 Aug. 1853.

5 Lady Jane Lindsay, Earliest Written Memories, begun in 1928.

6 *Aberdeen Press & Journal*, 11 Oct. 1871.

7 *BL*, p. 228, Lindsay report, epilogue, xxxi-iv.

8 George Street later became most famous for his law courts (now the Royal Courts of Justice) in the Strand in London.

9 Meynell, *Sunshine and Shadows*, p. 33.

10 *Aberdeen Press & Journal*, 6 Nov. 1872.

11 See chapter 5: Alexander, 25th Earl of Crawford.

9 · 'A decided soldier' *pages 70–75*

1 Later 26th Earl of Crawford and 8th Earl of Balcarres.

2 History of Parliament https://www.historyofparliamentonline.org/volume/1820–1832/member/lindsay-james-1791–1855.

3 Anne Barnard to James Lindsay, 16 Sept. 1811.

4 *LL* ii, pp. 386–7.

5 Micheal Clodfelter, *Warfare and Armed Conflicts: A Statistical Encyclopaedia of Casualty and Other Figures, 1492–2015* (McFarland and Co. Inc., 2017) p. 157.

6 Philip Henry Stanhope, 5th Earl of Stanhope, *Notes of conversations with the Duke of Wellington 1831–1851* (John Murray, 1889) p. 24.

7 *LL* iii, p. 154.

8 *MLL*, p. 183.

9 Lady Mary Meynell, *Sunshine and Shadows over a Long Life* (John Murray, 1933), p. 83.

10 Stephen Taylor, *Defiance: The Life and Choices of Lady Anne Barnard* (Faber & Faber, 2016), chapter 19.

11 *MLL*, p. 185.

12 Harriet S. Loyd, *Lord Wantage: A Memoir, by his wife* (1907), p. 6.

13 Ibid., p. 6.

14 http://www.historyofparliamentonline.org/volume/1820–1832/member/lindsay-james-1791–1855

15 *BL*, p. 82.

16 *MLL*, p. 198.

17 *MLL*, p. 191.

18 Robert Evans, 'Blast from the Past', *Smithsonian Magazine*, July 2002.

19 History of Parliament online.

20 Meynell, *Sunshine and Shadows*, p. 83.

21 Lady Mabel Lindsay, handwritten reminiscences.

10 · 'He keeps me in a constant state of terror' *pages 76–84*

1 By Julia Margaret Cameron at Little Holland House, May 1865.

2 Virginia Surtees, *Coutts Lindsay, 1824–1913* (Michael Russell Publishing Ltd, 1993), p. 11.

3 Ibid., p. 22.

4 Alexander, Lord Lindsay, 25th Earl of Crawford & 8th Earl of Balcarres.

5 Surtees, *Coutts Lindsay*, p. 36.

6 *BL*, p. 143.

7 Surtees, *Coutts Lindsay*, p. 70.

8 *BL*, p. 147.

9 Lady Jane Lindsay, Earliest Written Memories, begun in 1928.

10 *BL*, p. 295.

11 See Balcarres, pages 85–93.

12 *BL*, p. 134.

13 Louise Jopling, *Twenty Years of My Life* (John Lane, The Bodley Head, 1925), p. 74.

14 Natasha Tripney, *The Cult of Beauty: The Aesthetic Movement 1860–1900* (companion to V&A exhibition, 2011).

15 *BL*, p. 232.

16 Lady Jane Lindsay, Reminiscences.

17 Surtees, *Coutts Lindsay*, p. 188.

18 Harriet Kate Burfield, whom he married in 1912.

19 Surtees, *Coutts Lindsay*, p. 190.

20 *Vanity Fair*, 3 Feb. 1883, p. 63

BALCARRES *pages 85–93*

1 Revd Walter Wood, *The East Neuk of Fife Its History and Antiquities* (A. M. Elie, 1877), p. 233.
2 'Registrum Secreti Sigilli Regum Scotorum', The Register of the Privy Seal of Scotland. vol. 1, 1488–1529.
3 'Balcarres, Fifeshire', Country Homes, Gardens Old & New, *Country Life*, 9 Aug. 1902.
4 *LL*, p. 130.
5 David, 28th Earl of Crawford, to his sons in *c.* 1944 describing life at Balcarres.
6 Reduced to just two floors in the 1820s.
7 According to Lady Anne Barnard, the roof was removed by Colin, the 3rd Earl of Balcarres, towards the end of the seventeenth century 'to prevent a salary being annexed and a priest installed'.
8 Sir Herbert Maxwell, *Scottish Gardens, being a Representative Selection of Different Types, Old and New* (1908), p. 153.
9 This was brought to Balcarres from Leuchars Castle in 1873.
10 *Country Life*, vol. XII, no. 292, 9 August 1902.
11 *BL*, p. 297.
12 The Queen's Bath House at Holyrood.
13 Sir John Sinclair, *The Statistical Account of Scotland*, also known as *The Old Statistical Account* (1791).

11 · 'Balls were held of dazzling brilliancy' *pages 94–97*

1 Virginia Surtees, *Coutts Lindsay, 1824–1913* (Michael Russell Publishing Ltd, 1993), p. 66.
2 Harriet S. Loyd, *Lord Wantage: A Memoir, by his wife* (1907), p. 21.
3 *BL*, p. 145.
4 Christopher Simon Sykes, *Private Palaces: Life in the Great London Houses* (Chatto & Windus, 1985), p. 291.
5 Edwin Beresford Chancellor, *A History of the Squares and Palaces of London* (Kegan Paul, Trench, Trübner & Co., 1908).
6 Christopher Hussey, 'Dorchester House', *Country Life*, 5 May 1949, p. 652.
7 Lady Jane Lindsay, Earliest Written Memories, 1928.
8 *Spectator*, 25 Jan. 1879.

12 · For Valour *pages 98–107*

1 *MLL*, p. 246.
2 The Vale and Downland Museum Local History Series, Wantage.
3 Harriet S. Loyd, *Lord Wantage: A Memoir, by his wife* (1907), p. 13.
4 Ibid., p. 27.
5 John Grehan, *The First VCs: The Stories Behind the First Victoria Crosses in the Crimean War and the Definition of Courage* (Frontline Books, 2016), p. 34.
6 Lord Wantage's private correspondence with his family.
7 Anthony Leask, *Sword of Scotland: Jocks at War* (Pen and Sword, 2006), p. 112.
8 Lord Wantage's private correspondence with his family.
9 Harriet S. Loyd, *Lord Wantage: A Memoir, by his wife* (1907), p. 50.
10 'Robert Loyd-Lindsay' by the Staff of the Department of Leisure & Arts and John Lange, Curator of the Vale and Downland Museum.
11 *MLL*, p. 254.
12 Mike Weaver, 'Whisper of the Muse, The Overstone Album other photographs by Julia Margaret Cameron' (exhibition catalogue, 1987), p. 18.
13 *BL*, p. 148.
14 On Harriet's death the collection was divided between Robert's nephew, David, 27th Earl of Crawford, and Lady Wantage's cousin A. T. Loyd.
15 Loyd, *Lord Wantage*, p. 220.
16 Hansard, ccxxxiv. 702.
17 See chapter 10: Sir Coutts Lindsay.
18 See Electricity, pages 124–129.
19 Loyd, *Lord Wantage*, pp. 430 and 428.
20 Lockinge Estate archives.

13 · 'The most professional amateur I ever met' *pages 108–117*

1 Also KT, LLD, FRS, KGStJ, Cmdr. LH, PFAS, FSA.
2 See chapter 10: General James and Anne Lindsay.
3 See Astronomy, pages 158–163.
4 Ibid.
5 *BL*, p. 371.

14 · The Chatelaine of Balcarres, Haigh, Palmieri and Dunecht *pages 118–123*

1 *MLL*, p. 275.
2 *CP*, p. 570.
3 *BL*, p. 303.

ELECTRICITY *pages 124–129*

1 Harriet S. Loyd, *Lord Wantage: A Memoir, by his wife* (1907), p. 304.
2 135/137 New Bond Street became the Belstaff boutique in the early twenty-first century. It still has the grand Romanesque-style portico that Coutts brought back from Italy as its front entrance.
3 Norman R. Ball and John N. Vardalas, *Ferranti-Packard: Pioneers in Canadian Electrical Manufacturing* (McGill-Queen's University Press, 1994), p. 14.
4 *BL*, p. 303.
5 J. F. Wilson, *Ferranti and the British Electrical Industry, 1864–1930* (Manchester University Press, 1988) p. 21.
6 Loyd, *Lord Wantage*, p. 307.
7 Ibid., p. 309.
8 By 1912 Deptford power station was generating 83Hz and 3-phase 25Hz 10kV through AC distribution.
9 The IEE merged in 1991 with the Institution of Manufacturing Engineers to form today's Institution of Engineering and Technology (IET).
10 Grace's Guide to British Industrial History (website).
11 Ibid.

12 Donald Anderson and A. A. France, *Wigan Coal and Iron* (Smiths of Wigan, 1994), p. 163.
13 See The Yachts and their Stories, pages 187–197.
14 'Linking the Pacific', *Sydney Morning Herald*, 8 Sept. 1908. p. 4.
15 'Wireless in Polynesia' *Daily Telegraph*, Australia, 10 Sept. 1909. p. 7.

15 · 'Handsome, clever, impetuous and satirical' *pages 130–133*

1 Lady Jane Lindsay, Memories As They Come (manuscript, 1844).
2 Felicity Ashbee, *Love, Marriage, and the Arts and Crafts Movement* (Syracuse University Press, 2002).
3 The Royal East Coast Regiment, one of the first infantry regiments in the British Army.
4 George's ancestor, Sir John Houblon, was the first governor of the Bank of England. His likeness later appeared on the £50 note.
5 *The Houblon Family, Its Story and Times* (Archibald Constable and Co. Ltd, 1907).
6 *Guardian*, 22 July 1904 and *Essex County Standard*, 22 July 1899.
7 Great Hallingbury Parish Council/a/4192702–8580310
8 *The Times*, 4 Oct. 1915.
9 *The Dragon* (regimental paper of the Buffs), no. 658, Sept. 1954.

16 · Sunshine and Shadows *pages 134–139*

1 Lady Mary Meynell, *Sunshine and Shadows over a Long Life* (John Murray, 1933).
2 Ibid., p. 45.
3 Lady Jane Lindsay, Reminiscences (manuscript, 1935).
4 Ibid.
5 Frederick's father, Charles Wood, became the first Lord Viscount Halifax after serving as chancellor of the exchequer in Lord John Russell's government. He married Mary, daughter of Charles Grey, the 2nd Earl Grey.
6 Lady Jane Lindsay, Reminiscences (manuscript, 1935).
7 Meynell, *Sunshine and Shadows*, p. 216.
8 Ernestine Emma Horatia Edgcumbe, *Four Months' Cruise in a Sailing Yacht*, 1888.
9 The Hon Robert Lindsay, later Loyd-Lindsay, VC, later Lord Wantage.
10 Meynell, *Sunshine and Shadows*, p. 291.

17 · 'A writer who possesses an excellent gift of humour' *pages 140–145*

1 Lady Mary Meynell, *Sunshine and Shadows over a Long Life* (John Murray, 1933), p. 94.
2 Ibid., p. 92.
3 https://www.victorianresearch.org/atcl/show_author.php?aid=575.
4 *The Graphic*, 17 Nov. 1877, p. 475.
5 *Pall Mall Gazette*, 21 Oct. 1887, p. 3.
6 *Liverpool Mercury*, 8 May 1886.
7 Lady Mabel Lindsay, handwritten reminiscences.
8 In recent times his name became attached to the tragic incident of the Grenfell Tower fire. The tower bears the name of the road which commemorates him.

18 · 'She might have become a great engineer' *pages 146–149*

1 Lady Jane Lindsay, Second Writing of Memories (manuscript, 1935).
2 The 25th Earl and Countess of Crawford & 8th Earl of Balcarres.
3 Amy married the Hon. Frederick Meynell, son of Charles Wood, 1st Viscount Halifax of Monk Bretton and Lady Mary Grey, daughter of Charles, 2nd Earl Grey.
4 Lady Jane Lindsay, Earliest Written Memories (manuscript, 1928).
5 Lady Mabel Lindsay, handwritten reminiscences.
6 Amelia Ann Blandford Edwards, *A Thousand Miles up the Nile* (George Routledge & Sons, 1891), from chapter 17: The Second Cataract.
7 The 25th Earl of Crawford & 8th Earl of Balcarres.
8 Sandi Toksvig, 'Mothers of Invention', *Independent*, 11 Nov. 2003.
9 *The Times*, 21 Apr. 1898.
10 Patent nos: GB189713237, GB189725289 & GB189806433.
11 Anne was married to the Hon. Francis Bowes-Lyon, son of the 13th Earl of Strathmore, uncle of the future Queen Elizabeth, the wife of King George VI.
12 *Banbury Beacon*, 3 Sept. 1904.
13 *Liverpool Mercury*, 12 Oct. 1978.
14 Alexander William Crawford Lindsay, *The Creed of Japhet* (printed for private circulation, 1891).
15 Mabel M. Lindsay, *Anni Domini: A Gospel Study*, two vols. (Methuen & Co.,1890).
16 *Spectator*, 25 Sept. 1909, p. 22.
17 Lady Jane Lindsay, reminiscences.

19 · A Marriage Within Two Ancient Clan Rivals *pages 150–153*

1 Francis was the next younger brother of Claude George Bowes-Lyon, 21st Lord Glamis, later 14th Earl of Strathmore & Kinghorne, married to Nina Cecilie (Cecilia) Cavendish-Bentinck.
2 Lady Jane Lindsay, Second Writing of Memories, written at Ridely Hall (1935).
3 Lady Mary Meynell, *Sunshine and Shadows over a Long Life* (John Murray, 1933), p. 161.
4 Lady Jane Lindsay, handwritten reminiscences.

20 · The Family's Most Accomplished Artist *pages 154–157*

1 Jeanie recorded many of her thoughts in her unpublished Earliest Written Memories, 1928; Second Writing of Memories, 1935; and Memories as They Come, which she began in 1944.
2 Lady Jane Lindsay, Earliest Written Memories (1928).
3 Lady Jane Evelyn, Memories as They Come, first entry, March 1944.

4 The *Toski* had previously been used for the 1885 Khartoum expedition.
5 The 26th Earl of Crawford & 9th Earl of Balcarres.
6 Lady Jane Evelyn, Memories As They Come.
7 *Chelmsford Chronicle*, 9 Jan. 1948.

ASTRONOMY *pages 158–163*

1 One of the Lindsay mottos: 'The star is my camp, and God my light and strength.'
2 BL, p. 234.
3 Monthly Notices of the Royal Astronomical Society vol. XXXI, 13 January 1871, no. 3, p. 59.
4 John S. Reid, 'David Gill FRS (1843–1914): The Making of a Royal Astronomer', *Journal for the History of Astronomy*, vol. 49, issue 1, pp. 3–26.
5 Ibid., at p. 8.
6 Ibid.
7 Ibid.
8 M. T. Brück, 'Lord Lindsay's expedition to Mauritius 1874', *Proceedings of the International Astronomical Union* (2004), pp. 138–45.
9 Ibid., p. 143.
10 MLL, p. 269.
11 Quoted in John Westfall and William Sheehan, *Celestial Shadows: Eclipses, Transits, and Occultations* (Springer-Verlag, 2015).
12 Reid, 'David Gill FRS', p. 8.
13 BL, p. 246.
14 www.roe.ac.uk/roe/library/crawford/.
15 Memories, begun in 1928.
16 H. A. Brück, *The Story of Astronomy in Edinburgh* (The Royal Scottish Observatory, Edinburgh, 1983), p. 45.
17 Ibid., p. 53.

21 · A Marriage of Mining Families *pages 164–167*

1 Evelyn Bootle-Wilbraham married Sir John Kennedy, whose daughter Kathleen (Yone) married her first cousin, Evelyn Mason's brother Lionel Lindsay.
2 James Pope-Hennessy, *Queen Mary, 1867–1953* (George Allen and Unwin Ltd, 1959), p. 32.
3 M. J. Ramos, 'San Domingos Mine's English and Cornish Connections', paper given at the 8th International Mining Congress held at Redruth, Cornwall, under the auspices of the University of Exeter, 12–15 June 2009.
4 James Mason, 'Field Experiments on the Fixation of Free Nitrogen', *JRASE* 3rd ser., 3 (1892), pp. 651–67; A. D. Hall, 'The Agricultural Experiments of the Late Mr. James Mason', *JRASE* 65 (1904), pp. 106–24.
5 https://discovery.nationalarchives.gov.uk/details/r/bfd8dcd2-a3f6-4a25-94e3-d2f5638acece
6 *The Victoria County History of Oxfordshire*, vol. 12, pp. 98–115 (Eynsham); 213–19 (North Leigh); 238–41 (South Leigh).
7 Ranulph Fiennes, *Killer Elite* (originally published as *The Feather Men*, Bloomsbury, 1991), chapter 4.
8 Lady Alice, née Villiers, daughter of the 4th Earl of Clarendon, was the wife of the 1st Earl of Lathom, Lord Chamberlain 1895–92.
9 *Banbury Guardian*, 25 Nov. 1897 and *Lloyd's Weekly*, 28 Nov. 1897.
10 Lady Evelyn and Jim Mason had further properties in Curzon Street and Grosvenor Square.
11 Jerry White, *Zeppelin Nights: London in the First World War* (Bodley Head, 2014), p. 141.
12 *Windsor and Eton Express*, 20 Jan. 1906.
13 Letter to *The Times*, 28 Nov. 1935 on the merits of a .22 calibre rifle for Peter Fleming.
14 Fiennes, *Killer Elite*, chapter 4.

22 · Endure Fort *pages 168–177*

1 Honours: KT, PC, DL, FRS and FSA.
2 Arthur L. Humphreys, *John O' London Weekly*, 10/05/1924, p. 187.
3 MLL, p. 282.
4 CP, 28 Jan. 1895.
5 HRH Princess Mary, Duchess of Teck; daughter of the first Duke of Cambridge, son of George III; mother of Queen Mary.
6 G. J. Goschen, the 1st Viscount Goschen (1831–1907) Liberal chancellor of the exchequer, 1886–92; First Lord of the Admiralty, 1886–92. Diary entry, 4 Feb. 1907, and CP, 29 Aug. 1895.
7 In 1996 Sir Lindsay Hoyle was first elected to the same Chorley seat for the Labour Party and was made speaker of the House of Commons in 2019. His Christian name is a coincidence: he was named after the Australian cricketer Lindsay Hassett.
8 CP, 17 Nov. 1897.
9 CP, 4 Mar. 1911.
10 This was by virtue of his junior title of Baron Wigan, which was in the peerage of the United Kingdom.
11 CP, 31 Dec. 1913.
12 Approximately £58 million today. CP, 30 Apr. 1913, p. 313.
13 Ibid., 27 July 1914, from Bayreuth.
14 Christopher Arnander ed., *Private Lord Crawford's Great War Diaries: From Medical Orderly to Cabinet Minister* (Pen & Sword Books Ltd, 2013), p. 68.
15 David, 28th Earl of Crawford & 11th Earl of Balcarres, reminiscences (manuscript).
16 Arnander ed., *Private Lord Crawford's Great War Diaries*, p. 196.
17 CP, 21 Apr. 1926, p. 512.
18 CP, 19 Sept. 1892, p. 18.
19 *Sheffield Daily Telegraph*, 21 Mar. 1931.
20 Charles Molesworth, *The Capitalist and the Critic: J. P. Morgan, Roger Fry and the Metropolitan Museum of Art* (University of Texas Press, 2016), p. 84.
21 *Bulletin of the John Rylands Library Manchester*, Apr. 1940, vol. 24, no. 1.
22 CP, 22 June 1900.
23 Ibid.,10 Nov. 1938, p. 591.
24 Ibid., 3 Aug. 1939, p. 610.
25 *Donatello* (Duckworth, 1903).
26 CP, 4 Mar. 1936, p. 568.
27 David, 28th Earl of Crawford, Reminiscences to his sons (manuscript, 1940).

28 *MLL*, p. 300.
29 *MLL*, p. 285.

23 · 'Definitely not of common clay' *pages 178–181*

1 *Morning Post*, 8 June 1877.
2 1818–1914.
3 *CP*, p. 61.
4 *CP*, p. 58.
5 *CP*, p. 142.
6 Christopher Arnander ed., *Private Lord Crawford's Great War Diaries: From Medical Orderly to Cabinet Minister* (Pen & Sword Books Ltd, 2013), p. 155.
7 James Lindsay, *A Lindsay Family Story* (private publication, 1989), p. 348.
8 *Dundee Courier*, 10 Jan. 1947.

24 · 'The Sensible Captain Lindsay' *pages 182–186*

1 M. Holroyd Smith was best known for his work on developing the electric tramway in Blackpool.
2 *Grace's Guide* notes that Walter worked with Philaerion Ltd on gyropter blades. It is not known if this company had anything to do with the Davdison Flying Machine Co., but the timing of events makes it appear possible.
3 See chapter 10: Sir Coutts Lindsay.
4 *BL*: Ludovic, Earl of Crawford, letter to J. P. Edmond, head librarian of Haigh Hall, 26 Feb. 1899.
5 *New York Tribune*, 27 Dec. 1902.
6 Mosley, Charles, *Burke's Peerage, Baronetage & Knightage*, 107th edition.
7 See The Yachts, pages 187–197.
8 M. J. Nicoll, *Three Voyages of a Naturalist: Being an Account of Many Little-Known Islands in Three Oceans Visited by the* Valhalla (1908), p. xxi.
9 Ibid.
10 Brooklands Museum Archives. 3 p.m. Race Results, 4 July 1908.
11 Christopher Arnander ed., *Private Lord Crawford's Great War Diaries: From Medical Orderly to Cabinet Minister* (Pen & Sword Books Ltd, 2013), p. 173.
12 Obituary, *The Times*, 7 July 1936.
13 Obituary, *The Die-Hards, Journal of the Middlesex Regiment* (Duke of Cambridge's Own), Aug. 1936.
14 Obituary, *The Times*, 7 July 1936.

THE YACHTS & THEIR STORIES pages 187–197

1 James Ludovic Lindsay, later the 26th Earl of Crawford and 9th Earl of Balcarres.
2 *BL*, p. 263.
3 'On the Sea-birds Obtained During the Voyage of Lord Lindsay's Yacht *Venus* from Plymouth to Mauritius in 1874', *Proceedings of the Scientific Meetings of the Zoological Society of London for the year 1880.*
4 Gavine, David. 'Copeland, Ralph (1837–1905), astronomer.' *Oxford Dictionary of National Biography.* 23 Sep. 2004; Accessed 15 Mar. 2021.
5 There has been some confusion as to whether there was one yacht, or two of the same name. The first, occasionally referred to by the Hon. Edward Lindsay in the photograph albums as *Consuelo*, was a 546-ton vessel with engines and funnel towards the rear with steeply angled masts, while the later and larger 708-ton *Consuelo II* was somewhat less elegant, with its engines and funnel in the forward third of the yacht along with perpendicular masts.
6 A. B. Demaus, *RYS* Wanderer*: From Aristocrat to Tramp* (Tempus, 2001), p. 16.
7 https://www.navyhistory.org.au/history-of-the-consuela-figurehead-at-garden-island/3/
8 Demaus, *RYS* Wanderer, p. 157.
9 Edward Keble Chatterton, *Sailing Ships: The Story of their Development from the Earliest Times to the Present Day* (Sidgwick & Jackson Ltd, 1909), p. 328.
10 The two brass signalling cannons by Holland & Holland can be seen in the showroom window in Bruton Street, London.
11 The Esoteric Curiosa (website). 16 Dec. 2012.
12 *Chikasha Daily Express*, 13 Feb. 1905.
13 A sighting scope.
14 A device that measures the speed of a vessel over a specific distance.
15 *New York Tribune*, 5 May 1905, p. 12.
16 M. J. Nicoll, *Three Voyages of a Naturalist: Being an Account of Many Little-Known Islands in Three Oceans Visited by the* Valhalla (1908), p. xx.
17 *New York Times*, 14 May 1905.
18 *BL*, p. 354.
19 Nicoll, *Three Voyages*, p. xii.
20 Ibid., p. xxv.
21 Scott Cookman, *Atlantic: The Last Great Race of Princes* (John Wiley & Sons, Inc., 2002), p. 1.
22 *New York Tribune*, 14 May 1905, p. 2.
23 Cookman, *Atlantic*, p. 221.
24 https://www.nytimes.com/1905/05/30/archives/atlantic-wins-the-kaisers-cup-breaks-record-across-the-atlantic-to.html
25 Nicoll, *Three Voyages*, Preface, p. 23.
26 *BL*, p. 363; letter from Ludovic to Min, 14 May 1906.
27 *East Fife Record*, 21 Dec. 1906.
28 *Narcissus* was built by Fairfield Shipbuilding & Engineering Co. Ltd, Govan.
29 G. Meade-Waldo, 'Description of a new toad from Sumatra', *Proceedings of the Zoological Society of London*. 1908: 786–788.
30 D. Iskandar, *The IUCN Red List of Threatened Species*. The toad is endemic to Weh Island, off Sumatra, but now has no forest habitat and may be extinct.
31 F. J. Dittmar and J. J. Colledge, *British Warships 1914–1919* (Ian Allan 1972).
32 The Caledonian Maritime Research Trust recorded her as: '1911 Re-Registered Cowes By 1915 George J. Marvin. Cowes. Isle of Wight. WWI War Service RN. (*Valhalla II*) By 1918 B.H. Clerc. Reg. Cowes. 1919 Register closed. Sold to France – Alexandre & André Soc Merrienne. F. Baudoin. Le Havre. France.'
33 https://www.wrecksite.eu/wreck.aspx?270623

25 · Aide to the Tsar and Curzon *pages 198–205*

1 *Surrey Advertiser*, 18 Feb. 1893.

2 *Dublin Evening Mail*, 5 Oct. 1896.

3 *Scotsman*, 17 Apr. 1899.

4 *New Zealand Times*, 14 July 1899.

5 *Wigan Observer and District Advertiser*, 26 Nov. 1899.

6 *Argus*, 16 July 1900.

7 *Wigan Observer and District Advertiser*, 8 July 1903.

8 'Clarke, Sir William John (1831–97)', *Australian Dictionary of Biography* (National Centre of Biography, Australian National University, 1969).

9 In 2004 the seven-acre Royal Exhibition Building became Australia's first building to be designated a World Heritage Site.

10 *Wigan Observer and District Advertiser*, 8 July 1903.

11 *Sporting Times*, 29 Aug. 1882.

12 'The Ashes started out in Sudbury as part of a love story', *Herald Sun*, 25 Dec. 2013.

13 Obituary, *Publications of the Clan Lindsay Society*, by John Lindsay.

14 *St Andrews Citizen*, 16 Dec. 1911.

15 Obituary, *Publications of the Clan Lindsay Society*, by John Lindsay.

16 Martin Lindsay was the 22nd in descent from Sir William Lindsay, 1st of Dowhill, younger son of the 1st Earl of Crawford.

17 Martin Lindsay, *So Few Got Through: Gordon Highlanders with the 51st Division From Normandy to the Baltic* (Pen & Sword Books Ltd, 2000, reissued 2008).

26 · Serving God and Country *pages 206–209*

1 *BL*, p. 338.

2 *Wigan Observer and District Advertiser*, 24 Nov. 1900.

3 *Charterhouse Register*, 1903.

4 Cosmo Lang became Archbishop of Canterbury in 1928.

5 *Furrows in Time: A History of Balcarres and District* (Balcarres History Book Committee, 1987).

6 *The Plaindealer*, Alberta, 7 May 1914.

7 Old Carthusian Notes, *The Carthusian*, June 1917.

8 In 1924 the Royal Garrison Artillery (RGA) merged with the Royal Field Artillery (RFA) to form the Royal Artillery.

9 Regimental Number 163884.

10 The Military Medal was discontinued in 1993 and replaced by its equivalent, the Military Cross, which could be awarded to personnel of all ranks.

11 *Catholic Herald*, 22 June 1951.

12 *Lichfield Mercury*, 21 Jan. 1938.

27 · 'An immensely dignified diplomat' *pages 210–219*

1 'The Cabinet: New Deal: World Phase', *Time*, 17 Apr. 1933.

2 The Hon. Sir Ronald Lindsay, 'Sic Fatur Nuntius', unpublished memoirs, May 1941.

3 Keith Neilson and T. G. Otte, *The Permanent Under-Secretary for Foreign Affairs, 1854–1946* (Routledge, 2009) p. 189.

4 Lindsay, 'Sic Fatur Nuntius'.

5 Ibid.

6 Member of the Royal Victorian Order.

7 Michael L. Dockrill, Brian J. C. McKercher eds., *Diplomacy and World Power: Studies in British Foreign Policy, 1890–1951* (Cambridge University Press, 1996).

8 Neilson and Otte, *The Permanent Under-Secretary*, p. 202.

9 Henry Adams was grandson of John Quincy Adams and great-grandson of John Adams, the sixth and second presidents of the United States respectively.

10 Henry Adams, *The Letters of Henry Adams* (Harvard University Press, 1988), p. 663.

11 Ernest Samuels, *Bernard Berenson: The Making of a Legend* (Harvard University Press, 1987), p. 187.

12 John Newman and Nikolaus Pevsner, *Dorset* (Pevsner Buildings of England), (Yale University Press, 1972), p. 241.

13 Neilson and Otte, *The Permanent Under-Secretary*, p. 203.

14 Ibid., p. 190.

15 Gaynor Johnson ed., *Our Man in Berlin: The Diary of Sir Eric Phipps, 1933–1937* (Palgrave Macmillan, 2008), p. 8.

16 *Spectator*, 16 Nov. 1929.

17 Neilson and Otte, *The Permanent Under-Secretary*, p. 206.

18 See chapter 33: Lady Elizabeth Lindsay.

19 Barry Singer, *Churchill Style: The Art of Being Winston Churchill* (Abrams, 2012), p. 139.

20 Charles Higham, *Wallis: Secret Lives of the Duchess of Windsor* (Sidgwick and Jackson, 1988), p. 213.

21 Alistair Cooke, *Letter from America*, BBC broadcast, 11 Jan. 1976.

22 Congressional Record, US Government Printing Office, Washington, DC, 12 June 1945.

23 From *Guardian* review of Anthony Seldon and Daniel Collings, *The Architecture of Diplomacy: The British Ambassador's Residence in Washington* (Flammarion, 2014).

24 George Caspar Homans, *Coming to My Senses: The Autobiography of a Sociologist* (Transaction Publishers, 1983, reissued Routledge, 2017), p. 174.

28 · 'An example of determination and heroism' *pages 220–225*

1 Monthly Army Lists 1914–1918, National Library of Scotland.

2 The Hon. Sir Ronald Lindsay, 'Sic Fatur Nuntius', unpublished memoirs, May 1941.

3 *BL*, p. 333.

4 Lionel eventually became a lifelong member of the Malacological Society of London, dedicated to the advancement of research and education on molluscs. He was also a member of the Marine Biology Society of the UK.

5 See chapter 26: The Revd Hon. Edward Lindsay.

6 Lindsay, 'Sic Fatur Nuntius'.

7 Captain E. D. Miller, *Modern Polo* (Hurst and Blackett Ltd, 1902), p. 457.

8 Gelasio Caetani's father was Onorato, 14th Duke of Sermoneta, 4th Prince of Teano. He was married to Ada Bootle-Wilbraham, Lionel's mother's younger sister. Gelasio fought with distinction in the First World War, using his mining engineering skills in tunnelling attacks. He served as mayor of Rome before Mussolini made him Italian ambassador to the United States, 1922–5 – just five years before Lionel's brother, Ronald, took up the ambassadorial post on behalf of Great Britain. He rebuilt the Gardens of Ninfa and died in 1934.

9 *Mining & Scientific Press*, January–June 1917.

10 'Colorado Ghost Town Photography – Tomboy, Colorado', *Colorado Post*, 14 March 2016.

11 Harriet Fish Backus, *Tomboy bride: A Woman's Personal Account of Life in Mining Camps of the West* (Pruett Publishing, 1969), chapter 14.

12 'The Long, Long Trail, researching soldiers of the British Army in the Great War' (website).

13 See chapter 17: Margaret Majendie.

14 *London Gazette*, 1914, Issue 28,986, p. 9,974 and 1915 Issue 29,096, p. 2,484.

15 *KRRC Chronicle*, 1916, p. 254.

16 *London Gazette*, 1917, Issue 29,898 p. 459.

17 *The Times*, 25 Oct. 1920.

18 1880–1970.

19 *London Gazette*, 10 September 1897, p. 5,059.

20 See chapter 15: Emily, Countess of Crawford.

THE HAIGH COLLIERY & FOUNDRY AND THE WIGAN COAL & IRON COMPANY *pages 226–235*

1 See chapter 1: General Alexander, 6th Earl of Balcarres.

2 'Haigh Cannel', an address by the 27th Earl of Crawford to the Manchester Statistical Society, 15 Nov. 1933.

3 Donald Anderson and A. A. France, *Wigan Coal and Iron* (Smiths of Wigan, 1994), p. 16.

4 See note 2 above.

5 John Hannavy and Chris Ryan, *Living and Working in Wigan* (Smiths Books, 1986), p. 37.

6 Anderson and France, *Wigan Coal and Iron*, p. 63.

7 The Northern Mine Research Society.

8 *MLL*, p. 166.

9 *MLL*, p. 69.

10 Collieries included: Alexandra, Aspull, Bawkhouse, Blackrod, Bridge, Crawford, Eatock, Haigh, Hewlett, Kirkless, King Coal, Ladies Lane, Lindsay, Meadow, Morr, Parsonage, St Helens, four at Standish, Snapes, Sovereign, Westhoughton, Westleigh and Woodshaw.

11 *CP*, 13 Nov. 1935, p. 565.

12 Anderson and France, *Wigan Coal and Iron*, p. 23.

13 Derek Winstanley, 'The Walking Horse and Clarke's Railway', paper published for 2014 International Early Railway Conference, Caernarfon.

14 Grace's Guide to British Industrial History website, www.gracesguide.com.

15 Alan Birch, *The Haigh Ironworks* (John Rylands Library, 1953), p. 332.

16 E. W. Binney FRS speaking at the Manchester Geological Society, 1871.

17 Anderson and France, *Wigan Coal and Iron*, p. 111.

18 Ibid., p. 100.

19 Ibid., p. 89.

20 Grace's Guide to the Industrial Revolution, www.Gracesguide.com.

21 Anderson and France, *Wigan Coal and Iron*, p. 117.

29 · The Art Historian's Art Historian *pages 236–242*

1 Honours include: KT, GBE, DL, FRSE.

2 Taken from a bound, typed letter from David, 28th Earl of Crawford to his sons from *c.* 1944 describing life at Balcarres.

3 Ibid.

4 *BL*, p. 371.

5 Ibid., p. 372.

6 As note 2 above.

7 Anthony Blunt, 'Mr. A. S. F. Gow', *The Times*, 11 Feb. 1978.

8 http://eodg.atm.ox.ac.uk/user/dudhia/rowing/bumps/t1919/

9 D. R. Thorpe, Eden: *The Life and Times of Anthony Eden First Earl of Avon, 1897–1977* (Chatto & Windus, 2003), p. 51.

10 'A Government of Cousins', Time, 7 Aug. 1939.

11 *CP*, 31 Dec. 1935, p. 565.

12 Andrea Geddes Poole, 'Stewards of the Nation's Art: Contested Cultural Authority, 1890–1939', *Twentieth Century British History*, vol. 21, Issue 3, Sept. 2010, pp. 419–21.

13 As note 2 above.

30 · The Countess Rode a Donkey *pages 243–247*

1 David Lindsay, Lord Balniel, became the 28th Earl of Crawford in 1940 on the death of his father.

2 Adrian Tinniswood, *The Long Weekend: Life in the English Country House Between the Wars* (Jonathan Cape, 2016), p. 41.

3 Hugh Cavendish, *A Time to Plant: Life and Gardening at Holker* (Frances Lincoln, 2012), p. 56.

4 Ibid., p. 50.

5 Ibid., p. 74.

6 Photographed riding beside a distant kinswoman, Lady Lindsay from Kilconquhar House.

31 · 'Supreme self-possession that was disconcerting at first' *pages 248–251*

1 *Dundee Courier*, 31 July 1929.

2 Evelyn Bevan, 'Unlucky Vieve Goes Visiting', *Morning Leaders Torchbearers' Carry On Magazine*, Regina, Saskatchewan, 30 April 1927.

3 George Henry Iles, War Diary, aboard HMAS *Melbourne*, 1914–19.

4 *Winnipeg Tribune*, 24 May 1924.

5 *Dundee Evening Telegraph*, 29 Oct. 1928.

6 *St Andrews Citizen*, 27 Oct. 1928.

7 See chapter 26: The Revd Hon. Edward Lindsay.

8 See note 2 above.

9 1896–1979.

10 *Reading Mercury*, 10 Mar. 1917.

11 *London Gazette*, 2 May 1916.

12 *Leeds Mercury*, 7 Mar. 1917.

13 *Sheffield Daily Telegraph*, 13 Dec. 1918.

14 Wydale Hall, near Scarborough, had been bought by the Illingworths in the early 1900s. Sir George Cayley, the inventor and aeronautical pioneer, had lived there; he designed the first successful glider that flew from close by in 1853 and was the basis for what became the first aeroplane.

15 Francesca Wall (née Fummi), Reminiscences for Camilla and Dominic, My Life Story!, 2020.

16 *London Gazette*, 26 Feb. 1932.

17 Ibid., 31 May 1935.

18 Ibid., 14 Jan. 1944.

32 · At Home But a Refugee *pages 252–256*

1 *Leven Advertiser and Wemyss Gazette*, 20 May 1930.

2 *St Andrews Citizen*, 25 Apr. 1925.

3 Earl of Elgin and Kincardine.

4 *Winnipeg Tribune*, 2 Dec. 1931.

5 *Dundee Courier*, 1 Mar. 1933.

6 Asa Rausing-Roos, 'Who They Were', *Friends of the Non-Catholic Cemetery in Rome Newsletter*, Spring 2016.

7 Francesca Wall (née Fummi), Reminiscences, 2020.

8 *Guardian*, 3 Apr. 1934.

9 Now the Canadian ambassador's residence.

10 Francesca Wall, Reminiscences, 2020.

11 Ibid.

12 Text of the Lateran treaty of 1929, https://archive.org/stream/TheLateranTreaty11thFebruary1929/The%20Lateran%20Treaty%2011th%20February%2C%201929_djvu.txt.

13 Ron Chernow, *The House of Morgan An American Banking Dynasty and the Rise of Modern Finance* (Atlantic Monthly Press, 1990), p. 279.

14 Ibid., p. 457.

15 Now the Malvern Hills Hotel.

16 George M. Taber, *Chasing Gold: The Incredible Story of How the Nazis Stole Europe's Bullion* (Pegasus Books, 2014).

33 · The Most Creative Lindsay of His Generation *pages 257–369*

1 David, 27th Earl of Crawford & 10th Earl of Balcarres.

2 *London Gazette*, 19 Feb. 1935.

3 The Yeomanry Regiment of the Territorial Army.

4 *CP*, 24 Oct. 1939, p. 607.

5 *Western Morning News*, 27 Apr. 1933.

6 The eldest, Hugh (b. 1934), joined the Black Watch before becoming a chartered accountant and marrying Constance Buchanon. Alexander (b. 1936) left Oxford University with an MA in Engineering Science and became colonel of the 17th/21st Lancers and married Jessie Barstow. Like his father he became a master craftsman, creating inlaid veneered pieces, many relating to the Society of Heraldic Arts. Stephen (b. 1940) rose to Lt-Col. of the Black Watch. In 1966 he married Margaret Powell. Julia Margaret (b. 1941) married banker Peter Barton, who became high sheriff of Greater London.

7 Brigadier-General Sir Joseph 'Joe' Laycock, who had commissioned James's grandfather's yacht, the *Valhalla*, also competed.

8 Lord Howard de Walden, *Earls Have Peacocks: The Memoirs of Lord Howard de Walden* (Haggerston Press, 1992) p. 36.

9 William Alexander, 25th Earl of Crawford & 8th Earl of Balcarres.

10 The Hon. James Lindsay, *More Lives of the Lindsays* (privately published, 1970). This, in turn, was edited by his nephew Christopher Folke Arnander into *A Lindsay Family Story* (ALFS Books, 2019).

34 · Such Potential Cut Short *pages 262–262*

1 Evelyn (née Petty-Fitzmaurice), Duchess of Devonshire, married to Victor, 9th Duke of Devonshire.

2 *Dundee Courier*, 26 May 1927.

3 Ibid., 30 July 1931.

4 *Scotsman*, 5 Feb. 1937.

5 See chapter 32: Lady Cynthia Anne Lindsay.

35 · A Remedy for a Bullying Manner *pages 263–265*

1 'Viscountess Dilhorne' (obituary), *Daily Telegraph*, 1 Apr. 2004.

2 1905–80.

3 *Northern Daily Mail*, 25 Nov. 1930.

4 See chapter 22: David, 27th Earl of Crawford & 10th Earl of Balcarres.

5 *Portsmouth Evening News*, 19 Dec. 1930.

6 John, 2nd Viscount Dilhorne (b. 1932) served in the Coldstream Guards, became a barrister and latterly a member of the EC Select Committee (Law & Institutions); the Hon. Marion (1934–2013) became chatelaine of her husband Edmund Brudenell's Deene Park; the Hon. Eliza (b. 1948) was made director general of the Security Service (head of MI5) in 1997 and appointed Dame (DCB) in 2008 and Lady Companion, Order of the Garter (LG) in 2014; the Hon. Anne (b. 1951) married Sir John Parsons, who became deputy treasurer to the Queen.

7 Bernard Levin gave him this nickname in the 1950s in a parliamentary sketch and renamed him Lord Stillborn when he was elevated to the peerage.

8 *Bystander*, 27 Apr. 1938.

36 · The Daughter, Wife, Sister and Mother to Four MPs *pages 266–268*

1 *Leven Advertiser and Wemyss Gazette*, 27 Aug. 1935.

2 *Dundee Evening Telegraph*, 30 June 1936.

3 J&W Nicholson & Co. (who supplied the Duke of Wellington and Sarah Bernhardt).

4 Sir Godfrey Nicholson, 1st Baronet (1901–91).

5 Godfrey sponsored the Workmen's Compensation (Coal Mines) Act of 1934.

6 Emma Nicholson's interview for the History of Parliament oral history project, recorded 5 Aug. 2013.

7 John Parker, *Commandos: The Inside Story of Britain's Most Elite Fighting Force* (Headline, 2013), chapter 2.

8 Rose (b. 1937) married Richard Luce, an MP and government minister before becoming governor of Gibraltar, then lord chamberlain to the Queen, appointed Knight of the Garter and eventually created Baron Luce. Laura (b. 1939), married Sir John Montgomery Cuninghame, an investment banker and venture capitalist. Emma (b. 1941) entered the Royal Academy of Music even though 90 per cent deaf. She was later made baroness her achievements in the nascent computer industry, Save the Children, and as a MP. She was married to Sir Michael Harris Caine, chairman of Booker plc, who was knighted for his philanthropic work in Africa. Harriet Mary (b. 1946) married Charles Flower.

9 See note 6 above.

37 · Lady Omega *pages 269–270*

1 Christopher Arnander ed., *Private Lord Crawford's Great War Diaries: From Medical Orderly to Cabinet Minister* (Pen & Sword Books Ltd, 2013), p. 102.

2 *St Andrews Citizen*, 16 Apr. 1932.

3 See chapter 32: Lady Cynthia Anne Arnander, then Fummi, (née Lindsay).

4 See chapter 34: Lady Elizabeth Lindsay.

5 *Tatler*, 25 Jan. 1939.

6 *Dundee Evening Telegraph*, 13 Apr. 1939.

7 'Rusper: Manors and other Estates', British History Online (website). Originally published in *A History of the County of Sussex* (Victoria County History, 1987).

8 Elizabeth, (b. 1940) married Angus Gilroy, commissioned in the Black Watch before becoming an accountant; Cecilia (b. 1944) married (later Lord) Alastair Goodlad MP, chief whip of the House of Commons and British high commissioner to Australia; Robert (b. 1945) ran the Rusper Nunnery Farm with his wife Christina (née Edwards) and finally Katharine (b. 1948) married first Donald Corbett, with whom she had two children and four years after she was widowed in 1987, she married Peter Noel Gibbs.

38 · Three Sons of Balcarres *pages 271–276*

1 National Library of Scotland: https://digital.nls.uk/catalogues/snpc/collection/?id=31

2 The Malayan National Liberation Army referred to it as the Anti-British National Liberation War.

3 Now lived in by his youngest son, Valentine Lindsay, and family.

4 Twenty-six of the pages were contemporaries of Tom at Eton.

5 See chapter 17: Lady Margaret & Lewis Majendie (née Lindsay).

6 Hedingham Castle was given to Tom's son, Jason Lindsay, who lives there with his wife, Demetra (née Ryder Runton) and family.

328 Balcarres from the park. The palest stonework marks the sixteenth-century house onto which William Burn's 1840s wings were added to the east and west, and David Bryce's baronial extension to the north, in 1865.

Index

Note: page references in *italics* refer to photographs or illustrations

I

J

K

L